3/12

D1173889

Mexico, Nation in Transit

Contemporary Representations of Mexican Migration to the United States

CHRISTINA L. SISK

The University of Arizona Press • *Tucson*

The University of Arizona Press
© 2011 The Arizona Board of Regents

www.uapress.arizona.edu

Library of Congress Cataloging-in-Publication Data

Sisk, Christina L., 1974–
    Mexico, nation in transit : contemporary representations of Mexican migration
to the United States / Christina L. Sisk.
        p. cm.
    Summary: "This book argues for a deterritorialized notion of Mexican national,
regional, and local identities by analyzing the representations of migration within
Mexican and Mexican American literature, film, and music from the last twenty
years"—Provided by publisher.
    Includes bibliographical references and index.
    ISBN 978-0-8165-2955-1 (hardback)
    1. American literature—Hispanic American authors—History and criticism.
2. American literature—20th century—History and criticism. 3. American
literature—21st century—History and criticism. 4. Mexican literature—20th
century—History and criticism. 5. Mexican literature—21st century—History and
criticism. 6. Emigration and immigration in art. 7. Displacement (Psychology)
in art. 8. National characteristics, Mexico, in literature. 9. National characteristics,
American, in literature. I. Title.
    PS153.H56S57 2011
    810.9'35296872—dc23   2011026606

Publication of this book is made possible in part by a grant from the Small Grant
Program of the University of Houston's Division of Research.

Manufactured in the United States of America on acid-free, archival-quality paper
containing a minimum of 30 percent post-consumer waste and processed chlorine
free.

16 15 14 13 12 11   6 5 4 3 2 1

Contents

Acknowledgments

IN THE YEARS THAT I was writing this book, my studies and my work took me from New Orleans to Philadelphia and then to Houston. I am indebted to those who influenced my thought and those who supported me throughout the various stages of the writing process, and to the institutions that made this research possible.

In this book, you will find ideas that first appeared in my dissertation but that later evolved into a much larger project. I will always appreciate my academic family in the Department of Spanish and Portuguese at Tulane University, especially my mentors: Ana López, Robert McKee Irwin, Idelber Avelar, and Maureen Shea. Ana and Robert were great co-directors, who helped me shape my arguments and who introduced me to the larger academic community. Ana taught me to love cinema, to see the big picture, and to develop a tough skin. From Robert I learned to love the editing process and to pay attention to the details to strengthen my arguments and to improve my writing. Apart from all of the helpful comments on my dissertation, Idelber's advice was crucial in the latter stages of editing the introduction to this book. Maureen first became my mentor when I was an undergraduate student. Her influence is most visible in the parts of the book that discuss indigenous cultures.

The University of Houston was an ideal place to complete this project. I received a New Faculty Grant and a Small Grant from the Division of Research, and additional funding from the Center for Mexican American Studies. Now retired, Marc Zimmerman was a great mentor and interlocutor on transnationalism. María Elena

Soliño, Guillermo De Los Reyes, and Anadeli Bencomo mark my daily life at Agnes Arnold Hall, travel with me to conferences, and encourage me even through my darkest days. I also appreciate the support I have received from colleagues in other departments: Tatcho Mindiola, Raúl Ramos, and Mónica Perales.

Many individuals supplemented my research and helped me to add some pieces of information to the puzzle. I am grateful to Nicolás Kanellos, my colleague at UH, for giving me a copy of the original typewritten version of *Diario de un mojado* and for putting me in touch with Dick J. Reavis and Ramón "Tianguis" Pérez. Both Reavis and Pérez supplied much-needed background information that allowed me to complete chapter 4. A previous version of this chapter first appeared in *Aztlán*, which has granted permission for the reprint. Rubén Martínez was open and honest in answering my questions about the discussion in chapter 6. I appreciate the dialogue that he and I started when I was a graduate student. I thank José Manuel Valenzuela Arce for his generosity and kindness during my first trip to Tijuana.

To the anonymous readers, your comments were invaluable in transforming the manuscript and strengthening my arguments. Elizabeth Smith, the copy editor, was so easy to work with that she made the process of editing painless. It was also great to work with Kristen Buckles, Alan Schroder, and the rest of the staff at the University of Arizona Press. Thank you for all of your support throughout the publishing process.

My students at the University of Houston are an inspiration to me. Many of them came to my office to recount their difficulties in being undocumented immigrants. I thank them for their trust. Their stories undoubtedly influenced my work. Several of my students were involved at various stages of this project. Brenda Swart and Marisol Mancera were excellent research assistants. Bradly Drew translated the majority of the quotes in Spanish into English and edited several sections of the manuscript. Jorge Iglesias combed through the entire book for accuracy.

Uriel Quesada, Ana Yolanda Contreras, Michelle Nasser, Roberto Carlos Ortiz, Fernanda Zullo, and James Buckwalter-Arias are my peers from graduate school who lent their ears to my ideas. Uriel and Michelle also lent their eyes to my writing and commented on several portions of the book. I must also thank many colleagues at various institutions: Carla Giaudrone, Manuel Gómez, Vicky Mayer, Carlos Alonso, Maarten Van Delden, Yolanda Padilla, and Laura Isabel Serna.

Additionally, I could not have survived without the support of my friends outside of academia. Mai Lacombe and her family opened their home to me on more than one occasion, fed me, and made me feel at home in Houston. I thank Melanie Curiel for always listening to my stories and being by my side through thick and thin. I am fortunate to have many friends who have supported me over the years. I thank each and every one of them.

This book would not exist without my family in El Paso, Ciudad Juárez, and Guadalajara. A Dante Nava y a su esposa Rocío, les agradezco su generosidad cada vez que llego a Guadalajara. Esos viajes han sido fundamentales para mi investigación. I am saddened that I did not get to show my abuelito, Gilberto Nava Hernández, a published copy of this book before his death. Lo extraño mucho. I thank the migrants in my life, my mother and my tía Costa. I admire their hard work and their dedication to our family on both sides of the border. I am indebted to my mother for all that she has done for me throughout the years. No hay suficientes palabras para agradecerle a mi madre.

Mexico, Nation in Transit

Introduction

Migrating Nation, Transnational Web of Communities

THIS BOOK EXPLORES how migrants are represented as intermediaries that connect Mexico to the United States by navigating between both national systems as a form of survival and, at times, as a cultural tradition or rite of passage. Through the analysis of film, literature, and music, I delve into the ways that migrants fit into the imaginaries of their communities at the local and (trans)national levels. I draw on the social sciences as a tool to read and analyze the various types of cultural production included here. Much like in this introduction, in each of the chapters I use many anthropological and sociological studies to provide a backdrop for how migration is represented. The different modes of artistic representation that I analyze have their specific histories and social contexts, and I read them as part of the imagination of the Mexican people. I study various types of cultural production generated from the early 1990s and into the new millennium by those who are left behind in Mexico, the migrants who have ventured to leave their communities, and the immigrants' children who travel south from the United States to Mexico.

Although I may refer to the Mexican national imaginary in the singular, it is more correct to refer to the imaginaries, plural. As Néstor García Canclini contends, "Those works with the imaginary, the metaphors and narratives, are producers of knowledge that attempt to capture what becomes fugitive in the global disorder, that which does not allow itself to be surrounded by the borders but rather crosses them, or believes to cross them and sees them reappear up ahead, within the barriers of discrimination. The metaphors tend to figure, to make visible that which moves, combines, or is blended. The narrations seek to trace an order in the profusion of voyages and communications, in the diversity of 'others'" (58). Arjun Appadurai similarly argues that the imagination can be viewed as social practice: "The imagination is now central to all forms of agency, is itself a social fact, and is the key component of the new global order" (31). Both García Canclini and Appadurai see the imaginary giving meaning to the complex processes involved in globalization. For me, the imaginary is produced by its social and historical context and is a social practice in itself. As an anthropologist, Appadurai explains that "many lives are now inextricably linked with representations, and thus we need to incorporate the complexities of expressive representation (film, novels, travel accounts) into our ethnographies, not only as technical adjuncts but as primary material with which to construct and interrogate our own representations" (63–64). As a specialist in the humanities, I outline in this introduction the objective processes that provide the background against which to read the representations presented in the following chapters.

A Nation in Transit

The Mexican population is often described as spilling out from Mexico's borders, but the regional map that I propose is much more complex. I argue that representations of migration must be placed within the specific regional contexts in which they are produced—whether by the sending area, the points along the U.S.–Mexico border where the migrants cross the national boundaries, or the receiving areas in the United States. As I contend, these regions become intertwined because of the movement of people, information, and capital across national borders. Jorge Bustamante and his collaborators argue that "although migrants originate from throughout Mexico, the west-central region (Michoacán, Guanajuato and Jalisco) traditionally has had the highest levels of out migration" (116). They mention that Zacatecas, Durango, Mexico City, Chihuahua, Tamaulipas, Guerrero, and the state of Mexico should be included in the list of sending cities and states within Mexico. As Alex Rivera visually demonstrates in his documentary *The Sixth Section* (2001), the transnational migrant circuits force us to reimagine a cartography that links the migrants' hometowns to their destinations in the United States. Using a map that includes Mexico and the United States, Rivera draws lines connecting the various areas in Mexico to the receiving areas in the United States. Although he focuses on one such connected community between Puebla and New York, his map suggests that this is a wider trend occurring across the two countries. The web of social relations functions variously through migrant networks, Mexican consulates in specific cities such as Houston and Los Angeles, and Western Union locations across the United States and Mexico, and in a number of other ways.[1] I analyze the different texts as representations of some of the different nodes within this web, and each of the chapters provides a specific context for how these nodes are imagined.

I use the term "transnational communities" to refer to the contact that migrants living in the United States have with their hometowns and their country of origin, Mexico. For me, this term captures the various ways that migrants can be involved in national and local institutions and organizations in Mexico and in the United States, but it also includes the assorted familial and noninstitutional modes of contact between migrants living in the United States and Mexicans still residing in Mexico. Roger Rouse explains that the "transnational migrant circuit" allows for "a single community spread across a variety of sites" (254). Those left behind—individuals, families, and institutions—must also grapple with migration.[2] Robert Courtney Smith defines "transnational life" more broadly to include those who stay in the hometowns: "Transnational life usually involves travel between the home and host destination, but it can also include the experience of stay-at-homes in close relationships with travelers" (6–7). Transnational life can include contact with family, but also with political and religious institutions achieved through hometown associations and other migrant networks. Smith notes that transnational life can change over the course of a migrant's life, coming to include his children and grandchildren.[3]

Rather than dismiss national identity altogether, I have found it useful to place these narratives into context and analyze how they are constructed. Although these archetypes are used by the dominant classes, they are also reimagined from below. These master narratives get reinvented in the popular imagination. In his book *Imágenes de la tradición viva*, Carlos Monsiváis is a proponent of these "images of the live tradition," as his book is titled. Monsiváis borrows from Eric Hobsbawm's notion of invented tradition, which takes into account both the institutional uses of tradition and those that generate a sense of group cohesion. Monsiváis criticizes the institutionalization of these traditions within the educational system, but he also argues that historical tradition and its system of references, once secularized, are able to generate group cohesion (208). I criticize the use of these archetypes when migrants, Mexican Americans, and the indigenous are left at the margins of national identity. I admit that my perspective in this regard may seem rather narrow, but I find it hard to escape my convictions about migration given that my mother is a Mexican immigrant. I also understand that these archetypes have a life of their own, that they are reinvented in ways that are outside of institutional reach. As I demonstrate in chapters 5 and 6, the ethnic-Mexican community in the United States uses many of these same tropes to articulate its difference from the mainstream notions of U.S. national identity.

This present study analyzes the intersection of migration and Mexican national identity, but its approach varies depending on the cultural production, the subject position, and the type of representation of migration. In "México en su sitio: México en Chicago, Tucson, Los Angeles, Dallas, San Antonio, Nueva York, y la lista se amplía," Monsiváis explores how Mexico is defined by its institutions and intellectual sectors and their neoliberal policies, which results in unequal development, the contradictory and complementary system of mythology, the country's inability to stop the out-migration of its citizens, and the list continues. The effect, as Monsiváis argues, is that Mexican national identity is losing its force from within Mexico, because the people have lost faith in their country's institutions. Meanwhile, those in the United States revive national identity and remain loyal to Mexico through nostalgia. As he contends, "The nationalism of the Mexicans in Mexico ends up coming into conflict with the desire for universality; that of the Mexicans in the United States, notwithstanding some evocative deliriums, comes from the desire to contribute to diversity" ("México" 341). My observations differ somewhat from Monsiváis's. From within Mexican territory, I argue that the boundaries between Mexican and U.S. national identities have been drawn even as economic pacts, such as the North American Free Trade Agreement (NAFTA), further link the economies of these two countries. While the emigrant community is absorbed into the Mexican imaginary, those in Mexico still draw lines between Mexicans and white Americans. In much of the cultural production made in Mexico, I notice a representational trend of the migrant as an archetypal figure that is absorbed into the Mexican national imaginary. With the migrant as part of the imaginary, the nation spills out into the United States.

Although I study the intersection of migration and national identity, I also demonstrate that some of the constituents' preferences for local and/or indigenous identities point to the inequalities of the nation-state. Toward the latter half of the study, I switch my focus from the archetypal figure of the migrant to various perspectives that migrants produce. National identity is by its nature exclusive. One of the prime examples is the exclusion of indigenous peoples from representation within the nation-state, a topic that I discuss in chapter 4. Despite such exclusions, the persistence of national identity in the context of globalization reminds us that the world is still quite diverse and that people have different ways of defining their identities.

I find that, despite the effects of transculturation, people can still maintain a sense of national identity. For example, although *fronterizos* are often criticized as being Americanized, they still imagine themselves as Mexicans. As Pablo Vila asserts in *Crossing Borders, Reinforcing Borders*, the people of the El Paso–Cd. Juárez region have various ways of constructing borders. They assert their Mexicanness because in their reasoning they are sure of what they are not, that they are not Americans. Within the United States, migrants are transformed by contact with the new society. As Tamar Jacoby explains, the migrants and their children gradually change what are usually considered core Hispanic values like a focus on the family. Migrants want "to become Americans and hold on to their old cultures, too" (27). The cultural changes that both migrants and fronterizos undergo because of their contact with the United States are typical, but both groups tend to imagine themselves as Mexicans. On a larger scale, the flow of information through the Internet and other forms of media reaches practically every part of the globe. Such global connections reconstruct national identity in a new context even for those who never leave their countries. National identities seem timeless and unchanging, yet they are more malleable than they appear on the surface. They allow for difference even though they function through a sense of commonality and sameness.

I contend that there is a rupture between national identity and the nation-state that is seen at the level of citizenship. The state may define legal citizenship, but the cultural ties between people help to define the nation on different terms. We see this point most clearly in the representations of migration by the second and third generation of immigrants. They share a concept of Mexicanness despite their U.S. citizenship, and many participate in migrant networks traveling to and from Mexico. A Mexican migrant who is not a citizen of the United States may still feel that he or she is part of its society. The legal concept of citizenship has yet to evolve sufficiently to include people's overlapping national identities.

Assimilation and U.S. National Identity

Whereas those in Mexico draw the lines of the nation between Mexicans and white Americans, in the United States, national boundaries are constructed through citizenship and the policing of national borders. Migration figured in the negotiations of NAFTA, but it did not come to be officially part of the agreement. To date, there is no bilateral agreement between Mexico and the United States that deals with the issue of migration. Its exclusion allows for the militarization of the border to continue, even as economic markets open. Peter Andreas explains, "Even while border controls may fail as a serious deterrent, they reinforce territorial identities, symbolize and project an image of state authority, and relegitimize the boundaries of the 'imagined community'" (615). The state's enforcement of territorial boundaries manifests in very tangible ways: fences, the picket lines of patrol cars of Operation Hold the Line, as well as other types of vigilance and security measures that go so far as to include night-vision goggles used to spot migrants and narco-traffickers crossing the border. Such measures influence how migrants imagine their identities, often in ways that challenge the nation-state.

In spring 2006, because of their desire to legalize their status, millions of undocumented immigrants walked off the job to protest the Border Protection, Antiterrorism, and Illegal Immigration Control Act of 2005 (H.R. 4437), legislation that included a provision to punish those who helped the undocumented. One of the biggest criticisms leveled at the migrant protesters was the presence during the protests of the Mexican flag, which was understood as a challenge to U.S. sovereignty. Raul Ramos, a history professor at the University of Houston, explained to the *Washington Times*, "Flying the flag is a ceremonial practice. In this case, the Mexican flag has nothing to do with citizenship or politics; it has to do with ethnic pride" (quoted in "Principal"). Although this is true for Mexican Americans born in the United States, the use of the Mexican flag, from my point of view, was symbolic of the Mexican citizenship of many of these undocumented protesters. When word circulated that they needed to show their support for and loyalty to the United States, the protesters quickly began waving U.S. flags to show their allegiance to the United States but also to demand inclusion within the American system. As I contend, these displays of national identity demonstrate that the immigrant protesters are able to show their allegiance to both the United States and Mexico as coexisting national identities.

Despite the breaks and discontinuities prevalent in the Mexican imaginary, I argue that the United States is represented in more volatile ways. For migrants, entering the United States can be an alienating experience, especially when the receiving country is hostile toward them. Immigrants' responses to U.S. national identity are often tied to legal status. Most migrants manage to incorporate themselves into U.S. society to some degree, but those who feel that they have been discriminated against in the United States find it harder to take on the U.S. national identity and to feel as though they are Americans. Yet there are those migrants who eventually identify as American to some degree and who plan their futures within the United States. As I demonstrate in chapter 4, even those migrants who never come to identify with the United States find ways of incorporating themselves into the system by finding jobs and managing their daily lives. As García Canclini reminds us, "All migrants, even those ripped from local Edenic 'harmony' by globalization, are subjects that are both offered and condemned to speak from more than one place" (123). For migrants to be able "to speak from more than one place," the concept of sovereignty in the United States would have to loosen enough to allow dual citizenship, but it is unlikely to happen anytime soon.

The resilience of Mexican national identity and transnational hometown identities within the United States is often seen as a threat to a U.S. identity by seemingly running counter to normative expectations of assimilation. Samuel Huntington argues that recent immigrants are not assimilating into U.S. society, so they are less willing to acculturate and become "loyal" Americans. Patriotic loyalty, as Huntington understands it, should not be split between two countries. The first problem with Huntington's assessment of immigrant identity is his perception of the past. Immigrants from a century ago did not acculturate so easily. The residual of those national identities is still seen in American culture today in the form of Italian, German, and Irish cultural traits.[5] Second, by what standard does Huntington measure the level of patriotic loyalty? The supposed driving force of assimilation was to move away from one national identity to another. The migrant could only participate within one nation-state, although the migrant identity could have vestigial characteristics from the sending country. In response to Huntington, I argue that it is necessary to move beyond the concept of acculturation, the idea that immigrants must lose their national identity from their countries of origin, as a prerequisite to assimilation. Huntington insists that recent immigrants, particularly those of Mexican origin, are less likely to be loyal Americans, but the research demonstrates otherwise. Roger Waldinger argues that naturalized citizens are more likely to identify as American. In a Pew Hispanic Center survey in 2006, he reports, only 22 percent of noncitizen immigrants described themselves as American, whereas 52 percent of naturalized immigrants did so (12). From these results, we can conclude that immigrants would be more willing to pledge their loyalty to the United States if they were allowed to become citizens.

Both Here and There

Despite critics such as Huntington, the question of overlapping identities is becoming increasingly accepted within the United States. Renato Rosaldo argues for a widening of the concept of cultural citizenship to allow for difference: "From a Chicano perspective, one cannot help to notice that the doctrine of sameness fails to consider the possibility of polyglot citizens" (403). Although Rosaldo is mainly concerned with the issue of language and U.S. national identity, his concept of the polyglot citizen paves the way for those who have overlapping national identities. The next step would be to allow a space for polynational identities. As I argue in chapter 6, this is most evident in the second and third immigrant generations who were born in the United States but who have active transnational lives.

As the daughter of a Mexican migrant woman and a white American man, I have a hybrid identity, but I resist how this term is used in a negative sense. It has the implication of destabilizing categories or not fully fitting within any classification, but those same categories and classifications are elusive and constantly changing. There is nothing fixed about them, except for perhaps a general consensus by the people that use them; they are social constructions that evolve over time. I admit that I play a balancing act between these two identities, but I can also say that I function well within both. In Rosaldo's terms, I am a polyglot citizen. Others are not so quick to accept this combination of identities as positive. Many people discriminate against those of us with multiple cultural identities for being different, but ethnic and national categories were never homogeneous. These biases are still present within many representations of migration. As I discuss in chapter 1, María Novaro's film *El jardín del Edén* (1994) features a Chicana character, Liz, who has a terrible complex because she is caught between two cultures. She sits and cries as she watches Guillermo Gómez-Peña in *Border Brujo* (Isaac Artenstein, 1989), who speaks of a fragmented paradise. Liz's weaknesses are attributed to her inability to function between two cultures. The problem with this representation of the Chicana is that it paints her as a *pocha*, a half-breed who is unable to function precisely because of her hybrid identity.

If Mexican Americans feel that they do not fully fit within either national system, it is not because their hybridity does not allow them to, but because neither system has given them the tools to do so. As I show in chapter 4, one of the reasons Ramón "Tianguis" Pérez rejects Mexican and American national identities is that he and his community were discriminated against by the Mexican state and pushed out of their land by the agricultural companies. In a similar way, many Mexican Americans can feel that neither system represents them. Despite this feeling of discrimination, people find ways of surviving in the United States, often contesting the nation-state. Inversely, it is less likely that Mexican Americans will know how to navigate within Mexico if they have never had any contact with the country.

The entire ethnic-Mexican community shares cultural traits, but many divisions exist, especially since this group includes people from different backgrounds: descendants of those who already inhabited the Southwest, migrants who arrived more recently, and the generations of people descended from *braceros* (laborers) and other types of migrants. For me, Mexican Americans represent both diasporas and webs of transnational communities. This study delves into the latter of these; however, it is impossible to completely separate them. Diasporas tend to continue to evoke cultural traits and identifiers of the country of origin for generations after contact ceases. Transnational communities work across national boundaries, but these connections have their limits. One can say that transnational communities are in transition to becoming diasporas. Many migrants lose contact with Mexico on arrival in the United States, yet others have families that maintain contact for more than one generation. This study does not aim to represent all types of migration, but instead it pays special attention to transnationalism's effects on the ways that national identity is imagined. While transnational communities are not new, advances in technology give us an immediacy of contact that was unheard of a hundred years ago; thus, we are in the middle of changes leading to the prevalence of transnational processes.

The Work of the Imagination

Various theorists in both Mexican and Mexican American studies have informed this present study, including Norma Iglesias Prieto,

José Limón, María Socorro Tabuenca Córdoba, Debra Castillo, Josh Kun, and Eric Zolov. Most of these studies analyze various types of cultural production through transnational theoretical frameworks. Several readers and collections of articles—such as David Maciel and María Herrera-Sobek's *Culture Across Borders*, Sonia Baez Hernández, Anadeli Bencomo, and Marc Zimmerman's *Ir y venir: Procesos transnacionales entre América Latina y el norte*; Gail Mummert's *Fronteras fragmentadas*, and Denise A. Segura and Patricia Zavella's *Women and Migration*—have been the most effective at bringing interdisciplinary approaches together with cross-border perspectives to study migration. This book goes a step further by offering dialogues specific to each of the forms discussed (literature, film, and music) while also presenting a comprehensive study of migration from the humanities by borrowing from current debates in the social sciences.

The first half of this study shifts between the different regional points of view within and outside of Mexico. As I argued in "*Revista Generación*: Mexican Regionalism and Migration in Tijuana and Chicago," Mexican migration to the United States complicates the regional tensions that have existed between northern Mexico, Mexico City, and other regions within Mexico. With this in mind, I have laid out the first half of this study as a regional map. In Mexico City's film production, migration is represented as key to the construction of national identity at the U.S.–Mexico border. Chapter 1 analyzes the representations of migration within Mexican border film. Despite its name, this film genre imagines the border from outside the Mexican borderlands because most of the films are produced in Mexico City. I argue that beginning in the 1990s, representations of migration incorporated migrant networks into the imaginary of the nation. The chapter focuses on *El jardín del Edén*, *Santitos* (Alejandro Springall, 1998), and *De ida y vuelta* (Salvador Aguirre, 2000), three films that offer various alternatives for Mexican national identity following the implementation of NAFTA.

Chapter 2 shifts the perspective presented in chapter 1 by concentrating on Mexican border literature (*la literatura de la frontera*), which demonstrates that crossing national borders does not entail a questioning of national identity. In this chapter, I analyze the representations of migration within the short stories of Rosario Sanmiguel, Eduardo Antonio Parra, and Luis Humberto Crosthwaite.

I also examine Crosthwaite's *Lo que estará en mi corazón* (1994), a testimonial by a Mixtec/Oaxacan migrant named Fidencio Vázquez, and show that the migrant characters are not experiencing a crisis of identity, although the social problems depicted demonstrate that migration is symptomatic of the living conditions in Mexico. These authors portray people affected by the absence of a family member as well as by the very difficulties that compelled them to leave their communities.

Whereas chapters 1 and 2 set up a regional dichotomy between Mexico City and the U.S.–Mexico border, chapter 3 demonstrates that various regional identities can overlap with Mexican national identity. Migration figures prominently in the imagination as presented in rock music. The bands studied in this chapter are from Tijuana, Mexico City, Guadalajara, and Monterrey, Nuevo León: Tijuana No, El Tri, Maldita Vecindad y los Hijos del Quinto Patio, Maná, Control Machete, and El Gran Silencio. Despite their different regional backgrounds, these bands express common themes and voice similar concerns about how migrants are treated and the hardships they face. While the music demonstrates that global processes have produced a musical influence, the lyrics of these bands' songs demonstrate a local interest centered within the context of each city.

The ensuing two chapters give voice to two different types of migrants, therefore the representations of migration reflect these differences. The centerpiece of chapter 4 is my in-depth analysis of Ramón "Tianguis" Pérez's *Diario de un mojado* (English translation 1991, Spanish original 2003), which describes how a transnational migrant community functions. The diary connects San Pablo de Macuiltianguis, Pérez's hometown, to various points of destination within the United States. This is a key chapter in this study. In it, I enter into a theoretical discussion of how postnationalism is defined and contend that we cannot declare the end of the nation-state. It might seem initially that this chapter is in opposition to what I have proposed in this introduction, because Pérez does not identify as a Mexican per se; he explains why neither a Mexican nor a U.S. national identity represents his community. However, in accord with this introduction, his local and indigenous identities can be understood only within the context of the existing nation-states, both Mexico and the United States.

Chapter 5 explores the artistic migrations undertaken by directors Alejandro González Iñárritu and Alfonso Cuarón. These directors also depict migration in their films *Babel* and *Children of Men*, respectively, both released in 2006. These films must also be seen in relation to the filmmakers' incorporation into the U.S. film industry. I place the films and their filmmakers within the historical context of artistic migrations that dates back to Emilio "el Indio" Fernández. Although I do not seek to portray economic migration as irrelevant, I argue that artistic migration can be understood as a filmmaking strategy, especially in the context of waning funding for cinema in Mexico. Whereas *Babel* represents Mexican national identity as part of a global network of people, *Children of Men* constructs a fictive world on the brink of human extinction, a future in which a third-world or Global South identity is seen as the alternative for the existence of the human race.

Within the humanities, the second and third generations of Mexican Americans born in the United States have yet to be considered as part of transnational communities. Chapter 6 addresses this issue by analyzing Rubén Martínez's *Crossing Over: A Mexican Family on the Migrant Trail* (2001), a nonfictional account of a transnational community, and Sandra Cisneros's *Caramelo* (2002), a fictional novel of a family's history of migration. Despite belonging to different literary genres, both books describe the ways in which migration affects Mexican regional identities from the perspective of Mexican American authors born in the United States: Martínez, a third-generation immigrant, and Cisneros, a second-generation immigrant. Both writers offer reflections about how the children and grandchildren of immigrants think of themselves as part of Mexico.

In this last chapter, I finally write about my transnational family and how it affects how I view my identity. I use the social sciences as a means to move beyond my complex identity, that of a mixed ethnicity Mexican American, yet I cannot separate myself completely. My family members' stories are weaved in between the lines of these chapters even when I omit their names. The beginning of the study takes on a distanced tone, but by the last chapter I am unable to keep my first-person point of view out of my analysis. When I first started the research for this project, I quietly thought of my mother, but in the process of writing, I found out that I was also writing about myself.

I

Romancing the Nation

Migration Imagined from Mexico City

MEXICAN BORDER FILMS of the 1990s demonstrate an increasing acceptance of migrant networks. Whereas in the 1950s, Mexican migrants and Mexican Americans were thought to be *agringados* and traitors to Mexico, the homeland, migrants were by the 1990s becoming increasingly accepted within the Mexican imaginary of the nation. *El jardín del Edén* (María Novaro, 1994), *Santitos* (Alejandro Springall, 1998), and *De ida y vuelta* (Salvador Aguirre, 2000) present romances affected by migration. While the role of the romance in nineteenth-century Latin American literature was to consolidate the nation, romances since the late 1990s offer different responses to how migration affects national identity. Articulating stereotypes that are characteristic of the mythology of mexicanidad, *El jardín del Edén* questions national borders but ends up imposing national identity. In this film, the relationships between Mexicans and white Americans are erotic, but they do not lead to romance. Esperanza, the main protagonist in *Santitos*, has three relationships that represent both the disintegration of national borders and the unification of a Mexican transnational community. Finally, *De ida y vuelta* completely questions national identity. As a group, the three films demonstrate different alternatives for national identity at the turn of the millennium.

Produced from resources and by directors from the center of the country, as Norma Iglesias Prieto argues in "El desarrollo del cine fronterizo," Mexican border cinema has propagated a variety of myths and stereotypes of the border: the violent and fantastic space of Indians, miners, saloons, and gunfighters; the place of perdition, brothels, and prostitution; and the passageway for drug trafficking. Another common theme in Mexican border film is the marginalization of Mexican migrants and Mexican Americans within the United States. According to Iglesias Prieto, these stereotypes and myths are part of how identity is constructed within these films: "The border has been associated with identity crisis, with the search for Mexicanness, with conflict and the feeling of being threatened with the loss of what is one's own. These images have played a fundamental role in the creation of myths and stereotypes about the border; they have created a cinematic border style that does not reflect the truth" (505). Iglesias Prieto is clearly focused on a particular form of cinema that is commercial and official. The theme of migration first appears in Mexican films before the golden age of Mexican cinema, although Mexican border films, as Iglesias Prieto classifies the genre, did not appear until the 1970s.[1] Mexican border cinema as a genre is low budget, commercial, and for export to the United States to target Mexican American audiences; however, many noncommercial films with themes of migration have come out since the early 1990s, demonstrating the need to expand the definition of the genre. Iglesias Prieto's analysis does not consider independent production, documentaries, or non-Mexican films such as those that I analyze in this chapter. There are few studies that follow how the genre evolved after the early 1990s.

Iglesias Prieto's study responds to the Mexican film industry's centralization within Mexico City, undoubtedly the nucleus for Mexican film. According to Iglesias Prieto, the production of these films has always been external to the area of the border itself: "The definition of the border reality has depended on the property and the control over the means of cinematic production that has never been in the hands of the border population" (522). In my view, this is quite evident in the institutions that are located in that city: the Cineteca Nacional, the film school at the Universidad Nacional Autónoma de México (UNAM), the Filmoteca of the UNAM, and all the major films studios (past and present), such as the Estudios Churubusco. Guadalajara is the only other city with such a significant film culture. The Universidad de Guadalajara has a renowned film school, and the Guadalajara International Film Festival has existed for more than two decades. Iglesias Prieto, however, is reacting to the limitations imposed by this model. She does not consider that several fronterizo directors participated in making films of that genre. For example, Raúl Fernández from Piedras Negras, Coahuila, directed one of the most famous border films, *Lola la trailera* (1983). I would not completely discount Iglesias Prieto's argument, however: stereotypes of the border and of migrants abound within this genre, and the number of directors from Mexico City is undeniable. The unfortunate result of centralization is that perspectives from Mexico City outnumber those from other areas. With such a costly art to produce, other regions are unable to compete even mildly with the capital. Despite these limitations, however, we cannot assume that these directors are all going to give stereotypical depictions of migration. As I argue later, it is possible for these directors to be self-reflexive and autocritical of Mexico's centralist culture.

Films about the border and about migration overlap thematically, but they also diverge. It is impossible to discuss migration without acknowledging that migrants cross national boundary lines in one way or another. The culture and way of life of the U.S.–Mexico border, however, should not be conflated with migration. Many people live on the border without ever expecting to reside on the other side. I delve into this issue more closely in chapter 2, but I mention it here because I do not want to completely equate migration with the border. Living on the U.S.–Mexico border and migrating to the United States involve similar processes and difficulties with the demarcation of national boundary lines, but they also offer possibilities for different types of life experiences between migrants and border dwellers, particularly Mexican fronterizos. These topics converge within Mexican border cinema. The focus of films about migration has also shifted from the U.S.–Mexico border to include other areas of Mexico, such as Veracruz, Michoacán, and even Mexico City.

As I mentioned, little has been written about how the Mexican border genre has evolved since the 1990s; most of the studies published about the genre were written in the late 1980s and early

1990s. David R. Maciel and María Rosa García-Acevedo in their study "The Celluloid Immigrant" include only *El jardín del Edén* and *Mujeres insumisas* (Alberto Isaac, 1995) as Mexican films about migration that were made during the 1990s. They argue that the "1990s brought about two distinct trends in Mexican cinema. First, the private sector film industry reached crisis proportion. Given the repetitiveness, dullness, and cheap format of their productions, their audiences disappeared, ending the demand for their films, including immigration genre ones. The other distinct direction is that prominent, established art-film directors for the first time incorporated Mexican immigration as a central theme in their narrative. Maria Novaro and Alberto Isaac, known for innovative and artistic cinema, filmed the sensitive and well-crafted immigration features *El jardín del Edén* and *Mujeres insumisas*" (184). Maciel and García-Acevedo also observe the increased development of an auteur cinema in Mexico during the 1990s.[2] While they recognize the overall shift in the Mexican border genre, their inclusion of only two films from the 1990s excludes the majority of Mexican films that have included border and migration themes and story lines. The extension of the Mexican border genre occurs alongside the more recent success of auteur cinema in Mexico.[3] We must recognize that the films of the 1990s mark a new trend. Lewis Beale describes the conditions that made the advent possible as follows: "The Mexican government, which had always been heavily involved in the industry, upgraded the nation's major film schools, encouraged new talent (particularly new women) and worked to improve ways in which producers and directors could receive seed money for their projects."

The increased number of Mexican auteur films includes many featuring story lines about migration. Unlike the films of the 1970s and '80s, which focused on migration as part of the main plot, in some of the films of the 1990s the treatment of migration is more subtle or indirect. *Hasta morir* (Fernando Sariñana, 1994) deals with the differences between youth cultures in Mexico City and Tijuana. For the two young protagonists, the prospect of migration is central to their antagonisms. In *El callejón de los milagros* (Jorge Fons, 1994), Abel and Chava travel to the United States to find work. Abel's love affair with Alma is interrupted by Abel's temporary migration to the United States to raise money to open his own barbershop in Mexico City.

Amores perros (Alejandro González Iñárritu, 2000) received international acclaim for its rough depictions of life in Mexico City. Migration, in this case, is only implied. Octavio (Gael García Bernal), one of several key characters, plans to start a new life by leaving Mexico City with his brother's wife to go to Cd. Juárez and perhaps cross the border. In González Iñárritu's third film, *Babel* (2006), Amelia (Adriana Barraza), one of the principal characters, is a Mexican nanny living in the United States who decides to take the children that she cares for to Mexico so that she can attend her son's wedding. I analyze this film in more depth in chapter 5, where I place this film within the context of González Iñárritu's incorporation into the U.S. film industry. These more nuanced representations are not completely divorced from the typical border films of the 1970s and '80s. Although the early films had low production values, their directors would later come to the forefront of Mexican cinema. Alfonso Arau and Arturo Ripstein each directed a Mexican border film earlier in their careers. Alfonso Arau directed, produced, and acted in *Mojado Power* (1986) before his commercially successful and artistically acclaimed *Como agua para chocolate* (1992). *Mojado Power*, as David Maciel notes, attempts to use Hollywood-type heroes and employs humor at the expense of the Chicano characters (*El Norte* 36–37). Arturo Ripstein, director of *La mujer del puerto* (1991) and *Profundo carmesí* (1996), directed *La ilegal* in 1979. This film starred Pedro Armendáriz Jr., Fernando Allende, and Lucía Méndez. Maciel and García-Acevedo consider it to be a B movie since it "is nothing more than a familiar soap opera" (180).

As a coproduction of Macondo Cine Video, the Instituto Mexicano de Cinematografía (IMCINE), and Verseau International, *El jardín del Edén* is a product of the type of international cooperation represented by NAFTA, except that this coproduction includes only Mexico and Canada. The film was released in 1994, the same year that NAFTA came into effect. Although the border joins Mexico and the United States, the relationship between the two countries is ambiguous and, at times, undefined. Through such agreements as NAFTA, the two countries negotiate economic integration, but they have never implemented such strategies that would solve the migration dilemma. Despite the integration that both NAFTA and the film's funding represent, *El jardín del Edén* presents a variety of stereotypes and myths that are associated with mexicanidad, therefore reinforcing national identity. *El jardín del Edén* serves as an example that economic integration does not necessarily signal the disintegration of the Mexican nation, but in fact may serve to reinforce it. As Claire Fox argues, "A strong national culture is not anathema to economic neoliberalism. In fact, a certain amount of nationalist pride may even be welcomed as a positive by-product of free trade" (38). The nationalist pride, however, is somewhat different in *El jardín del Edén* than in previous films, such as *Espaldas mojadas* (Alejandro Galindo, 1953), in that Mexico is portrayed as fragmented rather than sameness.

Like *El jardín del Edén*, *Santitos* was funded by sources from Mexico, the United States, Canada, and France. Released in 1998, the film is a post-NAFTA production that represents the type of integration that is associated with globalization. María Amparo de Escandón wrote the screenplay for the film before writing the novel of the same name, and John Sayles produced the film. Although it can be considered a transnational film because of its international sources of funding, the film won the Sundance Award for best Latin American film in 1999. Because María Novaro and Alejandro Springall are Mexico City natives, one could argue that this newly recognized border genre still excludes a fronterizo perspective. In fact, *Santitos* refers to el Santo's films of the 1970s and '80s by including scenes and characters associated with *la lucha libre*, the Mexican form of wrestling. El Santo was the masked hero of these low budget films. The melodramatic style of the film is characteristic of classic Mexican cinema of the 1940s. Like *El jardín del Edén*, *Santitos* inherits many of the stereotypes associated with mexicanidad, but the film also reflects the growing acceptance of the Mexican population that lives in the United States.

Unlike most of the films of the Mexican border genre, *De ida y vuelta* does not take place on the U.S.–Mexico border, but it should be included in the genre since its story line is based on the premise of the protagonist's migration between Mexico and the United States. Most of the film was shot on location in Michoacán, one of the states that traditionally have a large migrant population.[4] Although Salvador Aguirre, the director, is from Mexico City, *De ida y vuelta* criticizes the country's centralism. It is the only one of these three films funded completely by Mexican national sources: the Consejo Nacional para la Cultura y las Artes (CONACULTA), IMCINE, Fondo para la Producción Cinematográfica de Calidad, Estudios Churubusco Azteca, and the Centro de Capacitación Cinematográfica.

The Mexican border film may have once been synonymous with the low-budget films of the 1970s and '80s, but the films of the 1990s and in 2000 have forced a redefinition of the genre. A broader definition of the Mexican border genre allows for a larger variety of perspectives. An open definition would allow for the inclusion of *El jardín del Edén*, *Santitos*, and *De ida y vuelta*, despite the different perspectives presented in the films. Although *De ida y vuelta* is not set on the border, the similarity between this film and *El jardín del Edén* and *Santitos* is that it presents migration as central to how national identity is constructed. Migrant networks are increasingly incorporated into the imaginary of the nation; no longer are migrants portrayed as traitors as they had been in the earlier films.

The Romance and the Nation

In nineteenth-century Latin American fiction, romance was a means to express the consolidation of a national consciousness. Doris Sommer describes "the allegory in Latin America's national novels as an interlocking, not parallel, relationship between erotics and politics" (43). She explains the role of the romance for the nation: "The only problems here seem external to the couple. That they can thwart the romance, fuels our desire itself on public and private levels here; it is also the public obstacle that deters (and goads) the erotic and national projects. Once the couple confronts the obstacle, desire is reinforced along with the need to overcome the obstacle and to consolidate the nation. That promise of consolidation constitutes another level of desire and underscores the erotic goal, which is also a microcosmic expression of nationhood" (49). In the nineteenth century, literary representations of romance served to consolidate the nation by bringing together or even allegorically marrying different regions or different political factions of the country. National identity has changed over the years, and the romance is no longer just an expression of the consolidation of the nation.[5]

In *Border Matters*, José David Saldívar analyzes María Amparo Ruiz de Burton's *The Squatter and the Don*. Written in the nineteenth century, this novel takes place during the same time period as Sommer's foundational fictions. Saldívar compares Ruiz de Burton's romantic life to the one that she invents in her novel. Ruiz de Burton, born in Baja California, came to the United States to join Henry Burton, whom she would later marry. The couple represented a union between different ethnic backgrounds and different religions: she was Catholic and he was Protestant. Saldívar argues that "Ruiz de Burton uses her own authorial time (1846–1884) to ground her readers in the rhetoric of U.S. imperial temporality" (177). The marriage of Mercedes to Clarence in the novel, according to Saldívar, creates a "new national symbolism." Saldívar's analysis demonstrates that the interethnic romance incorporated Mexicans into the U.S. imaginary during the nineteenth century (175). José Limón's *American Encounters* similarly looks at the incorporation of Mexicans into the United States as a progression represented through erotic relationships in a variety of cultural productions. Saldívar's and Limón's studies are similar since both analyze the role of the romance in a U.S. context, but the intersection of romance and migration has been virtually untapped in reference to Mexico as a nation. United States representations of romance evolved to incorporate Mexican Americans into the U.S. imaginary, but Mexican films have offered varied representations of the romance and how it has evolved in the Mexican imaginary.

Limón traces the representations of sexuality and the relationship between Mexico and the United States in western novels, films, and music from the early twentieth century to the 1990s. Through analyses of different cultural productions, Limón demonstrates how Mexican culture has slowly been absorbed into the U.S. mainstream. Interracial marriages between Mexican women and white men that had once been prohibited have become accepted, although relationships between Mexican men and white women have taken more time to develop. Limón refers to a transnational definition of Mexico and what it implies to its relationship to the United States: "what I will be calling 'Greater Mexico,' referring to all Mexicans, beyond Laredo and from either side, with all their commonalities and differences.

But I stress that I am equally concerned with the United States as an Anglo-dominant entity whose representatives have come into contact with and sometimes internalized Greater Mexico and vice versa" (3). Although Limón's conclusions are excellent in demonstrating how the borders of ethnicity have slowly changed in the United States, his perspective on transnationalism is limited. The phenomena he analyzes—Tejano music star Selena and the films *Giant* and *Lone Star*, for example—mostly refer to Texas. The title, *American Encounters: Greater Mexico, the United States, and the Erotics of Culture*, and certain sections of the book suggest a broader relationship between Mexico and the United States. His analyses are centered on Texas and a history of the southern United States in relation to Texas and Mexico. The limitation may result from using the western as the main point of reference for the texts.

Mexico is also affected by having such a large percentage of its population in the United States. In the United States, migration affects ethnic/racial politics, which is not necessarily the case in Mexico. Since such a large percentage of the Mexican population lives outside the country, migration in the Mexican imaginary is constantly being negotiated, both positively and negatively. Questions dealing with race and ethnicity in Mexico are central, especially with the growing number of Mixtecs and other indigenous groups migrating to the United States. In Mexico, there is also a major concern about the political implications of having the United States as a neighbor. Mexican national identity also functions in relation to the United States, and migration complicates the love/hate relationship between the two countries.

Mexican Romance

Espaldas mojadas was a precursor to the Mexican films of migration of the 1990s and 2000 because it also features a love story that allegorically links Mexicans and Mexican Americans. This film can be seen as a direct response to Operation Wetback, which was implemented in the United States during the 1950s to police the borders and keep illegal migrants out of the country. Claire Fox describes the film as follows: "Produced at the end of the 'Golden Age,' the movie's nostalgia is self-reflexive, populist, and anti-imperialist, but, conveniently, its brand of nationalism was mainstream enough to fit with the dominant political current of the time" (118). Fox argues that this results in a contradictory representation of the *bracero* since he is a traitor, a victim of the United States, and a hero all at once. The film blames the migrants for their lack of legal documentation, which leads to their mistreatment. *Espaldas mojadas* weaves a documentary-style approach with a fictional story line, resulting in a narrative that is lineal and seems unproblematic. The film barely acknowledges the economic hardship that pushes such a large population to migrate; this leads into a discourse in which a return to Mexican territory is necessary to maintain a Mexican identity. The development of the romance in *Espaldas mojadas* reflects this need to tie the Mexican national identity to its territory.

In the film, the only type of relationship that a migrant can have in the United States is with a prostitute. The hero, Rafael Améndola Campuzano, is shown lying under a boxcar while the other men form a long line to see the prostitutes. In contrast to the other men, Rafael falls in love with María del Consuelo, a waitress in a diner. As a Mexican American, María del Consuelo's role in the film is limited to showing the opposing nationalisms of the United States and Mexico. Rafael decides to return to Mexico, but he must first escape from the authorities. As he is fleeing, he enters the diner where María del Consuelo works. María del Consuelo explains, "I am not Mexican. I was born here. I am a *pocha*." She argues that Mexican Americans could never feel at home in the United States because they long to be in Mexico, their homeland. She adds that they are also set apart from Mexicans, being called *pochos(as)*, or half-breeds. Although the distinction may be true, María del Consuelo's description accepts her position as a *pocha* in negative terms. She is unable to identify with other Mexican Americans, unlike African Americans who have a community identity. The situation of discrimination against Mexican Americans, as explained in this portion of the film, is due to Mexican Americans' lack of an identity, so the only way to resolve their identity issues is to return to Mexico. In reality, Mexican Americans may not feel that Mexico is their homeland, especially if they were born in the United States and have no direct contact with Mexico.

Claire Fox correctly argues that the film does not allow space for Mexican Americans to have an identity, and much less for females: "María finds her place then, under the sign of the three M's: man, Mexico, and monolingualism" (112). Rafael's only solution to discrimination in the United States is for Mexicans and Mexican Americans to return to Mexico. María del Consuelo also functions as a redeemer, since she hides Rafael in the kitchen while she tells the authorities who are looking for him that he has left in the opposite direction. María del Consuelo decides to accept Rafael's offer to go to Mexico, so they plan to meet in Cd. Juárez. She saves him from the authorities; he saves her from being further discriminated against in the United States. Fox elaborates on the role that women have in the film: "In *Espaldas mojadas*, betrayal and redemption by women is the primary driving force of the plot: a bad woman makes Rafael cross the border and a good one gives him reason to return again. To be in the United States for the bracero means deprivation of maternal and nurturing love, and only fleeting encounters with prostitutes" (111). The romance serves to unify Mexican Americans, specifically women, to Mexico only if they decide to live in Mexico. I would argue that María del Consuelo is also redeemed: she is saved from the clutches of a Mexican American identity or the lack of a Mexican national identity.

The 1990s saw a reorganization of world power through trade blocks such as NAFTA, and it was also a period of increased migration. José Manuel Valenzuela Arce's conclusion to *Nuestros piensos* best explains how migration forces a reexamination of the nation-building project:

> The phenomenon of migration makes us confront the situation at the end of the century and the end of the millennium that close to a fifth of the Mexican population of Mexican origin lives in the United States; this forces a redefinition of the interpretation of the sociocultural processes that occur in our country (with a profound crisis of the dominant nation-building project) and the *México de afuera* [Mexico on the outside]— that which is constituted by the Mexicans and Chicanos who look for better options in life and fight so that their ascriptions

and cultural heritage do not expose them to exclusion, discrimination, or racism. (245)

Although the nation-building project may be in crisis, as Valenzuela contends, it has not disappeared. The romance can reflect the
changing role of national identity, the nation-building project, and
mexicanidad. Beginning in the 1990s, *El jardín del Edén, Santitos*,
and *De ida y vuelta* offer three distinct alternatives for Mexican
national identity as represented through the relationships developed
in the films. It becomes apparent that a return to Mexico is no longer the only response to migration.

El jardín del Edén

El jardín del Edén focuses on the interconnected lives of a group of
characters who arrive in Tijuana as both permanent and transient visitors. Felipe, a migrant who comes to Tijuana only to cross the border
to the United States, dominates the narrative, but the film also focuses
on a community of women, most of whom are travelers as well. The
crosscutting in *El jardín del Edén* juxtaposes the lives of the various
characters and makes the plot seem fragmented, but the development
of mexicanidad through character profiles provides unity to a film
that otherwise would seem disjointed. *El jardín del Edén* is an expression of mexicanidad and is made to present Mexican national identity
to an audience that may not be Mexican. In an interview, director
María Novaro comments: "In each film I have reflected on one of
the many possible Mexicos. While I must find money from the outside, I must also look for a way to make [these films] attractive to the
exterior—although they may be about Mexican themes" (Romero 85).
As Novaro attempts to reflect on the "many possible Mexicos" within
each of her films, each of her characters represents a stereotype of lo
mexicano. Because of the strong message of mexicanidad, romance
in *El jardín del Edén* never really develops; the only possibility arises
between Mexicans and white, non-Hispanic Americans.

Claire Fox argues that *El jardín del Edén* cannot escape an older
version of mexicanidad that is connected to indigenous imagery and

"deems Chicanos/as to be culturally inauthentic until they return to the mother country and learn proper Spanish" (10). For Fox, the culture-versus-nature message of the film is taken to an extreme: "Indigenous peoples seem to fall on the 'nature' side of the balance, along with the dolphins, rather than being presented also as 'cultural' phenomena" (10). More than mere stereotypes, the film works as a psychological drama within the framework of mexicanidad. The psychological drama revolves around the characters or the archetypes within the film. Just as Novaro reflects on Mexico in each of her films, all of the characters in *El jardín del Edén* come to represent different stereotypes and myths of Mexico and, inevitably, the United States as well.

Felipe represents the millions of farm workers who migrate to the United States each year, but his character also embodies the myth of the *campesino*. Bartra describes the role of the *campesino* as follows: "The hero of this imaginary epic is a singular character because he or she belongs to a race of suffering and aggravated beings. This being is extremely sensible, timid, suspicious, and susceptible. This peasant hero has been closed in a logical dungeon, confined between a past of wild misery and a present of barbarous wealth" (34). Felipe has similarly been ripped away from his land because he is unable to survive in Mexico. The barbarous wealth lies across the border in the United States. Felipe is the singular hero, the only adult Mexican male in the film. Although *El jardín del Edén* has several female characters, it is Felipe's struggle to survive and his migration to the United States that give unity to an otherwise fragmented plot. Unlike Rafael Campuzano or other migrants in Mexican cultural productions, Felipe is a hero not a traitor. As Fox argues, the film does not present migration as a "national betrayal" but, rather, it accepts migratory patterns (10).

The female characters also come to represent different facets of Mexican identity. Jane's character represents the stereotype of the exoticizing *gringa* enamored with indigenous Mexico, especially evident when the camera assumes Jane's gaze. She is also the character that connects Mexican American culture with the indigenous, thus recognizing that Mexico is a multilingual and multiracial nation. The recognition comes from an outsider, an American tourist, so it is through these border relations that this fragmented Mexico is presented. It is only through the outsider's gaze that mexicanidad can be constructed to include Mexican Americans and the indigenous alike. Liz is also something of a stereotype: the Mexican American artist who must travel to Mexico to find her identity. Her Spanish-language abilities are so limited that she accidentally misspells her daughter's name (Guadelupe). This leaves little space for having a Mexican identity outside of Mexico. Regardless of the stereotype of the Mexican American suffering an identity crisis, however, Liz can still be seen as forming part of the community of women in Tijuana. The image of the Mexican American is one that interests María Novaro because she believes that Mexican Americans represent Mexico's future: "More and more I am interested in reflecting on the Chicana condition. When one stops being what one is, one does not get converted into something else; one converts into nothing" (Romero 85). This commentary assumes that there is an essence to being Mexican that Mexican Americans lack. The space that Liz has in the film places her in a void. She is also one of the women who do not develop a love interest. She and Jane may have an attraction, but the film does not give any conclusive details to make the claim that they are more than just friends.

For a film that aspires to question national borders, it is contradictory that the one character in *El jardín del Edén* that is a Tijuana native is negatively portrayed. This signals an inability to accept the culture that is most influenced by the meeting of both countries. Tía Juana's name is reminiscent of the history of the city's name.[6] She is the only character that is not traveling through Tijuana but benefiting from those who are. Tía Juana will do anything to make money, even if it means cheating a child during a game. Besides renting to the travelers, she owns a secondhand store selling used products from the United States.

Among the women in the film, Serena most exemplifies the role of the Mexican mother. She functions only through her children, but most especially through her sons, Julián and Sergio. From the beginning, the film visually connects Serena to motherhood. Serena arrives in Tijuana with her family in an old taxi. As the car stops at their new home, the camera focuses on the car window, which is entirely encompassed by an image of the Virgin of Guadalupe. The window slowly rolls down, and Serena's face becomes visible. The national symbol of motherhood has arrived into Tijuana through Serena. Serena's role as a mother will be discussed at length in the next section.

Impossible Romance

El jardín del Edén does not include a full-blown affair, but it plays with the possibility of a romance. Felipe's and Serena's flirtations with the Americans, Jane and Frank, parallel the relationship of Mexico with the United States. A flirtation exists, but it cannot be developed into an actual relationship. If, as Sommer argues, the romance serves to consolidate the nation, the inability to completely develop a romance serves to mark the subtle divisions between Mexicans and the Americans living and traveling through Mexico. Jane and Felipe have the most intense flirtation. Jane's interest in Felipe leads her to doctor his wounds and to cross him into the United States illegally in the trunk of a car. Frank and Serena do not have the contact that Jane and Felipe do, but the film suggests an interest on Serena's part. Despite the apparent interest, neither of these flirtations lead to romances or committed relationships.

Jane's attraction to Felipe is evident from the moment that she meets him. When she first sees Felipe, the camera focuses on him in slow motion, echoing the shot in which she sees Margarita, the indigenous woman. Jane's desire for the exotic is here translated into a flirtation with Felipe that develops despite their inability to communicate. To thank Felipe for his help with changing a flat tire, Jane and Liz take him to a restaurant to eat. The first shot shows them sitting at the table together while Liz serves Guadelupe some food. Jane and Liz sit at one side of the table while Felipe sits at the other. Felipe speaks as the camera alternates between him, Liz, and Jane. The camera is placed so that Jane's and Felipe's backs appear in each other's front shots, which visually connects them. As Felipe speaks to them, Jane makes comments to Liz about him, and the camera alternates between front shots of Liz and shots of Jane watching Felipe eat. Felipe is shown smiling as Jane asks Liz, "Aren't his teeth wonderful?" The flirtation between Jane and Felipe is obvious from this conversation, especially when Felipe asks who the *tolohache*, a flower sitting on the table, is for. When Jane says that it is for him, he explains in Spanish, "*Tolohache* makes men go crazy." Jane unknowingly acknowledges this chemistry between them and responds, "Fantastic!"

Jane and Felipe subsequently travel to Los Angeles, and Serena's son Julián accompanies them. We see that there is a definite attraction between Felipe and Jane, but the physical contact shown in the film is limited. At the motel, it seems that Jane and Felipe slept together and perhaps consolidated their relationship sexually. The camera starts to move up their bare feet as they sleep in the hotel bed. Felipe's legs are indistinguishable through the shadows, but Jane's are visible. Jane is in her underwear and sleeps in a white-collared shirt. This shirt is different from the clothes that she was wearing the previous night, and we cannot tell whether Felipe is wearing any clothes since he is covered with the sheet. Julián's presence plants some doubt about the couple's sexual contact. He is with them at night, and he sits on one bed as he takes a picture of Jane and Felipe lying on the other. When she awakes, Jane discovers that Julián has left the room, signaling that he was probably with them when they fell asleep. Jane and Felipe would have had to deal with Julián if they had had sex. Whether or not Jane and Felipe slept together, it is clear that their inability to communicate ultimately separates the couple. Jane's concern for Julián's absence brings that issue to light. Jane wakes up Felipe at nearly 5:00 a.m. saying, "Your brother is not here." Later, as they leave the motel, Felipe explains, "*Carnal, carnalillo,* brother—these are terms of endearment." Felipe is not as concerned about Julián's whereabouts as Jane is, so he lies to her, leading her to Oxnard supposedly in search of Julián but really looking for his own family members. In Oxnard, their differences and their inability to communicate become too much for the couple. Felipe becomes infuriated when Jane gives money to a Mixtec woman in the middle of a funeral. Felipe does not like Jane's sense of charity, and Jane cannot understand why giving money would hurt Felipe's pride. Soon after, Felipe abandons Jane as she sleeps in her car.

An attraction also exists between Serena and Frank. At Sergio's baseball game, Serena sees Frank and asks Tía Juana who he is. She responds, "Oh well, he's the gringo who lives close to the place where I go to play Jai Alai, the one that doctored your son Sergito's knee. Don't you think that he is a little interesting?" Tía Juana's comment signals the possibility for a love affair between Serena

and Frank, but Serena does not respond. It is Serena's search for
her son that leads her to Frank. Since Frank is Jane's brother, Liz
believes that he can provide some information that will lead them
to the missing Julián. Because Frank does not initially give Liz and
Serena any information about Jane, Serena returns alone to plead
for Frank's help. Although Serena goes to Frank's house for information, they are not shown directly speaking about Jane. They sit
outside without talking. The lighting, or rather the lack of it, in this
scene is fundamental. They sit in the dark as small patches of light
from behind them barely make them visible, and they look at each
other in the dark. Frank offers his jacket and invites Serena to come
inside the house, but she refuses and decides to leave. She thanks
Frank for the information he has given her about Jane, and she asks
him to help her find her son. Her farewell underlines the purpose
of her visit as obtaining information about the whereabouts of her
son. Although a love affair between the two never materializes, the
possibility is left somewhat open at the end of the film, when Serena
leaves a message on Frank's answering machine to thank him for
his help. Frank never answers the telephone, and the film offers no
indication that the couple will meet again.

The erotic nature of the relationships in *El jardín del Edén* does
not lead to their consummation. This separation between the couples serves as an allegory of the separation between the two nations
and their cultures. The boundary between Mexicans and white,
non-Hispanic Americans cannot be crossed since it would symbolize the dissolution of national boundaries.

Single Mothers and Stand-In Fathers

The women in this film do not have partners and are all single mothers. Their romances do not flourish, and there is a lack of married
couples in the narrative. These women must struggle to help their
families. When Liz and Serena have a conversation about their husbands, Serena asks Liz whether she misses her ex-husband, and Liz
replies that she does not. It is Serena who discusses the difficulties of
living without a husband. Through various flashbacks, we know that
her husband died, but the details of his death are not given. Serena's
main reason for relocating to Tijuana is that she has had trouble

raising her family alone. Serena is a weak mother, unable to control Julián, shown wandering the Tijuana streets at various times of the day. The other children spend a considerable amount of time with their Tía Juana. Overall, Serena is not a strong matriarch. While it would seem that *El jardín del Edén* attempts to form a community of single mothers, ultimately, the attempt fails, and the principal focus of the film remains the male characters.

Although the film shows the community of single mothers, ultimately the adult male characters, Felipe and Frank, come to replace the lost father figures. Ana M. López's analysis of the Mexican melodrama of the 1930s, '40s, and '50s holds true in María Novaro's film: "One could argue that, despite their focus on mothers, these family melodramas are patriarchal rather than maternal because they attempt to preserve patriarchal values rather than the sanctity of the mother. In attempting to reinforce the patriarchy their narrative logic breaks down: the moral crisis created in these films revolves around the fathers' identity and not the mothers', whose position is never put into question" (154). In *El jardín del Edén*, Serena's role in the film is necessary for the inclusion of Julián and Sergio, her sons, but her daughter is marginal within the narrative. The film replaces the absent birth father (Serena's late husband), the lost patriarch, with two surrogate father figures, Felipe and Frank. The inclusion of these surrogate fathers also signals the single mother's inability to function independently.

In *El jardín del Edén*, the rural past and modern society are represented through Felipe and Frank. As Roger Bartra argues, the stereotypes of lo mexicano present an opposition between past and future: "The reconstruction of a rural past confronts the real horror of modern society" (33). With Julián, Felipe's role as a surrogate father becomes explicit when Felipe lies in bed after he has been beaten. The film suddenly goes into a flashback in slow motion. Serena is looking at her husband lying in bed, and the heart monitor goes off, indicating that he is dead. This is Julián's memory of the death of his father, which he associates with Felipe. As an undocumented migrant worker, Felipe comes to represent the portion of Mexican citizens, principally men, who leave Mexico for work but also return for various reasons. Felipe influences Julián, takes him to bars where they watch a couple dance *la quebradita*, a Mexican dance, and teaches him to wear a ranchero's hat with pride. Julián learns about migration through his relationship with Felipe, and this leads Julián to travel with Felipe and Jane to Los Angeles. Although Julián returns to Tijuana to rejoin his family, he is shown with Felipe, at the end of the film, standing on the beach at Playas de Tijuana, overlooking the ocean. Julián is wearing a cowboy hat while Felipe sports a cap, demonstrating the change in their appearances from the beginning of the film. Julián's Mexican identity is reinforced, whereas Felipe learns to Americanize his appearance to improve his chances of entering the United States.

Frank's influence on Sergio is developed as a secondary element to the film, but it provides an alternative for the future of Mexican national identity. After Frank helps Sergio doctor a wound from a fall, Frank is able to discuss his interest in whales with Sergio. Frank explains that no one has placed national limits on the whales' territory and that whales have no nationality. While Frank collects recordings of the whales' sounds, Sergio starts to draw whales, which represents a new generation's interest in a borderless or nationless world. Frank, the figure who most discusses the promise of a borderless future, is also linked to the process of the Americanization of Mexican culture. Frank quietly becomes a father figure for Sergio and coaches him when he plays baseball, the American pastime. Frank stands behind the fence while Sergio is about to bat, and Sergio turns back to look at Frank for instruction.

The development of national identity in *El jardín del Edén* contradicts the message of open borders. The romance between Mexicans and white, non-Hispanic Americans is impossible. As María Novaro suggests, her quest is to reflect on the different Mexicos that are possible. If this is her aim, Mexican national identity is not questioned but imposed. Without the development of any romantic bonds, the women remain single mothers. Their children, as seen through Julián and Sergio, must look for their own father figures. Thus, Felipe and Frank influence Julián and Sergio, who become the two alternatives for the future, Mexico's future. Julián represents the continuation of mexicanidad, and Sergio represents its Americanization. The future of Mexican national identity, even one that thrives in the United States, is favored over Americanization.

Although the physical boundaries of the nation are questioned, mexicanidad stays intact.

Santitos

Although Esperanza (Dolores Heredia), the main protagonist of *Santitos*, does not plan to migrate, her spiritual quest eventually leads her to the United States. She is unwilling to accept the fact that her daughter died and believes that she has been taken to a brothel in Tijuana. Her journey may seem spiritual because she believes that San Judas Tadeo, who appears in the window of her dirty oven, leads her.[7] Although the film centers around spiritual and religious themes, Esperanza's journey is also a physical one that takes her from Veracruz to Tijuana and Los Angeles. One of the distinguishing features of this film is that the migrant is a female rather than a male. Traditionally, migration from Mexico to the United States was primarily male, but this has changed. Today, more women are making the move to the United States, changing the process of migration and perhaps making it a more permanent move than that of their male predecessors. As Pierrette Hondagneu-Sotelo argues, migrant women are more inclined than migrant men to settle in the United States.

While searching for her daughter, Esperanza undergoes a transformation that changes her sexual views. As the film opens, Blanca, her daughter, has already passed away, so Esperanza wears the traditional black as a sign of grief. Her dress and shoes are conservative, and she wears a scarf on her head to go to church to confess. She wears her black dress during most of the first part of the film, while she is still in Veracruz. Although she does not work as a prostitute in Veracruz, she begins to work as a cleaning lady at one of the brothels. It is then that her sexual views start to change as a result of watching couples and by her curiosity. As part of her duties, Esperanza has to clean the rooms that the prostitutes have used with their clients. She takes the sheets off one of the beds and decides to smell them. Her curiosity is demonstrated when she is shown looking through the cracks of a door as a couple enters the room. The two start to undress, and the woman throws herself on her client and says, "Cátchame," a Spanglish word that comes from the English

phrase "catch me." This phrase is to stay with Esperanza throughout the film; the experience marks the beginning of a drastic change
that she makes over the course of the film, involving not only her
appearance, but also her views about sexuality.

Esperanza's journey is highly eroticized, leading her to several
encounters with men. Many of these encounters occur because Esperanza works at different brothels, believing that she may find her
daughter. In *Santitos*, each of Esperanza's relationships is telling of
how Mexican identity is constructed and how it relates to the United
States. As Esperanza arrives in Tijuana, she meets el Cacomixtle, a pimp
who helps her get jobs in Tijuana and Los Angeles. Their uneasy meetings portray the uneasy relationship between regions within Mexico.
Later, Esperanza meets an American judge who helps her migrate to
Los Angeles. Together, they come to represent the exchange between
Mexico and the United States. Finally, unlike *Espaldas mojadas* and *El
jardín del Edén*, *Santitos* portrays a love affair that develops and ends
in Los Angeles and outside of Mexican territory.

El Cacomixtle and Tijuana

Representing Veracruz and Tijuana respectively, Esperanza and el
Cacomixtle have a sexual relationship, which causes her repulsion.
He leads her to work in brothels and other jobs centered on her
sexuality. The film portrays Tijuana's nightlife, especially the bars
and the brothels often associated with the city. Blanca's supposed
abduction is reminiscent of the murders of the maquiladora workers
in Cd. Juárez.[8] Of course, the connection between Blanca's death
and Cd. Juárez only functions by way of stereotypes: although these
murders have occurred in Cd. Juárez, Tijuana is not connected in
any way except that it is also located on the U.S.–Mexico border.
The film is misleading because the end reveals that Blanca was not
abducted. Unfortunately, the revelation that Esperanza's house is
la casa rosada, the place where she can find her daughter, signifies
that Esperanza has been led by rumors or unfounded suspicions that
her daughter is in a brothel. These rumors also affect how she sees
Tijuana and how it is portrayed in the film. Despite the stereotypical portrayal of Tijuana, the sexualized atmosphere helps Esperanza
redefine her sexuality.

The rumors of Tijuana reach the other end of the country, and the sexualized stereotype of the city precedes any other image that it could have. By eavesdropping on a conversation in Veracruz, Esperanza hears about the brothels in Tijuana in which young girls are forced to prostitute themselves against their will. There is nothing to indicate that her daughter is really working at any brothel, but she pursues the information by placing herself in an uncompromising position. Esperanza's sexual naïveté is demonstrated when she asks one of the men for information about the brothel, but the man assumes that she is a prostitute and takes her to one of the rooms. She escapes by jumping on him just as she has seen a prostitute jump on one of her clients, and using the word *cátchame*, as she saw that prostitute do.

When Esperanza arrives in Tijuana, she walks down a street that is lined with bars and enters a cheap hotel, where she meets the devilish-looking pimp el Cacomixtle, who embodies the sexual nature of what Tijuana has to offer. Esperanza's appearance and attitude are more dramatic at this meeting. She goes along with his seduction because she believes that he can lead her to Blanca. This inevitably has an effect on her, which is outwardly visible. In the hotel room, the camera focuses on Esperanza moving from top to bottom down her red nightgown with matching red heels. She is now trying to play her role as a prostitute to convince el Cacomixtle to give her information about other brothels in the area. When the client does not arrive at the hotel, el Cacomixtle takes the opportunity to seduce Esperanza. Esperanza looks into a mirror, accepting the seduction, as el Cacomixtle kisses her neck. Their reflection is shown before the scene ends with a blackout. Although the sexual act is not shown in the film, we can deduce that Esperanza has demonstrated her skill as a prostitute. She submits herself to el Cacomixtle believing that his information will lead her to Blanca, but she has never made it clear that she is looking for her daughter. Convinced that she is a prostitute, el Cacomixtle gives her directions to another brothel by writing the information on her inner thigh. Esperanza then starts to work for la Trini, the madam of a high-class brothel. Along with el Cacomixtle, la Trini represents the sexual nature of the city as one that is connected to animal behavior because she owns a cow that she caresses. El Cacomixtle may not have sexual relations with animals, but his name associates him with a small, fox-like, carnivorous animal. La Trini and el Cacomixtle are the only characters in the film that are from Tijuana, and thus form the only representation of the city and its inhabitants.

When Esperanza finally decides that her quest for her daughter has led her in the wrong direction, she cuts ties with el Cacomixtle. One of her jobs, which el Cacomixtle recommends, centers on the voyeur's experience: she sits in a room, doing whatever she pleases, while men peek through a small window. Her final encounter with el Cacomixtle occurs when she breaks the window he uses as a voyeur to peek into her room. She runs out of the building, and el Cacomixtle is unable to catch her. The problem with the relationship is not just that el Cacomixtle is a devilish pimp, but also that Esperanza seeks his attention based on her own assumptions and naive conclusions that he can lead her to her daughter. Although the representation of Tijuana is limited, the film's virtue is that it shows Esperanza is to blame for naively following the stereotypes she has of the city.

The Judge: Scott Hanes

Esperanza's work at the brothel connects her to an American judge from San Diego, Scott Hanes. In a telephone call that Esperanza makes to her priest to confess, she mentions the relationship: "Things only happen with him, but I do not know if they are sins." What she does explain is that he is attracted to her because she reminds him of his mother. In a flashback, the judge explains, "It's the way you look at me." Despite Esperanza's motherly role, the relationship is clearly sexual. They talk about their families and show each other pictures while lying in her bed at the brothel. At one point, the film shows Hanes about to leave Esperanza's room, and he is getting dressed, buttoning his shirt. The sexual act, although not visually present, is implied. She works as a prostitute, and he is a client. Hanes pays to be her only client, so there are exchanges of large sums of money.

Hanes is directly connected to the process of migration and to the national boundary between Mexico and the United States: he helps Esperanza to cross the border and to find a job in Los Angeles. Crossing the border is relatively easy in her case, as she rides in the trunk of the judge's car, crammed in while she prays to Juan Soldado.[9] With his connection to the law, Hanes is able to take her to the United States without a problem and he is also able to find her employment in an L.A. travel agency. This connection between Esperanza and the judge is significant because it allows her the opportunity to survive in the United States. The relationship between Esperanza and Hanes is a result of a post-NAFTA point of view that allows for some integration between the two countries. The affair between the two is never amorous but serves as a business transaction between two individuals. This relationship can be seen as negative, since Esperanza is a prostitute; she represents Mexico as a prostitute that survives with the help of the American legal system. The relationship also allows Esperanza, as a migrant, to travel easily into the United States. The implication of this relationship is that national identity is contested. If, as Doris Sommer suggests, the romance serves as an allegory to unite the nation, here it signifies its disintegration—one with negative implications considering that it is compared to a relationship between a Mexican prostitute and an American judge.

El Ángel Justiciero: Love at Last

Whereas Esperanza's connection to Scott Hanes allows her to move across national borders, her relationship to Ángel, a *lucha libre* wrestler, demonstrates an acceptance of the ethnic-Mexican community that resides outside Mexican territorial boundaries. In this case, the location is Los Angeles, the second-largest Mexican city by population. El Ángel Justiciero's name is reminiscent of the Mexican film *El chicano justiciero* (Fernando Osés, 1974), which is in the style of the low-budget el Santo films. Unlike Liz, the Chicana artist in *El jardín del Edén*, who is presented as having an identity crisis, el Ángel Justiciero is never portrayed in such a light. In fact, the film never goes into detail about his identity. The image of el Ángel Justiciero first appears when Esperanza is still in Veracruz. The doctor informs Esperanza that her daughter died, and there is a flash of an angel as Esperanza faints. The angel has wings and is dressed in tights, as are worn in *lucha libre*. This small part of the film, which lasts only seconds, connects el Ángel Justiciero to Blanca's death, which convinced Esperanza to go north. Later, Esperanza is watching a television commercial for the next fight of *lucha libre*, and the contenders are el Ángel and la Migra. She sees the image of el Ángel as he raises his wings and stands proudly, and her fascination with saints is translated to this anonymous figure that she sees on television and, later, at the fight.

The fight between el Ángel Justiciero and la Migra directly brings the topic of migration to the arena. La Migra walks into the ring while the public, who are mainly of Mexican descent, screams to show that they do not support the fighter. El Ángel flies into the arena using a cable. He wears his wings, white tights, and boots that bear red and green to complete the colors of the Mexican national flag. The fight begins, and the crowd screams in support of el Ángel Justiciero. At one point during the fight, la Migra throws el Ángel out of the ring, and he lands at Esperanza's feet. Their eyes meet, but he must return to face la Migra. He unmasks la Migra revealing a white, non-Hispanic male with long, blond, curly hair. The arena becomes a space for the audience's catharsis, demonstrated by their screams and disapproval of the fighter portraying la Migra. Justice, as the name of the fighter demonstrates, is to win against the Border Patrol.

After the fight, Esperanza is left alone as the audience has gone. She is holding el Ángel Justiciero's boot. As in the Cinderella fairy tale, Esperanza takes the boot to el Ángel Justiciero. In this case, she is the one looking for her true love and finding him in his dressing room. He invites her to a party that his manager is holding. At the end of the night, when he drops her off, she kisses him and lets him enter her house. She has just met him and has never seen his face. The extent to which her sexual views have changed are demonstrated in the manner in which she handles her relationship with Ángel. Her assertiveness in this scene is played out like a fight, and the bed serves as an arena where the fight is staged. She jumps on Ángel as she first saw the prostitute in Veracruz do with her client and screams, "Cátchame," connecting her to that first voyeuristic experience. Esperanza wins the match with el Ángel Justiciero, and her victory allows her to see his face.

Esperanza's transformation during the film is gradual and ends with her pursuit of Ángel. Her appearance is the first to change, from the black dress to the negligee that she wears to convince el Cacomixtle that she is a prostitute. When she meets Ángel, she wears jeans and a fitted, flowered blouse. Her appearance is not as risqué as it had been during several scenes at the brothels, but she seems confident and comfortable with her sexuality. The relationship that she develops with Ángel is a result of the experiences that she has had during her journey. Esperanza decides to return to her homeland to resolve her daughter's whereabouts, but she leaves Los Angeles without saying good-bye to Ángel. After the journey, she finally comes to terms with the death of her daughter, which is represented in her acceptance that her daughter's spirit is still with her. As in the beginning of the film, the image of her daughter appears to her in the bathroom. Since Esperanza leaves her relationship with Ángel unresolved, he follows her to Veracruz and finds her praying at the church. The film ends with the couple returning to Los Angeles carrying the bathroom wall, which Esperanza associates with the image of her daughter, in the back of the truck. Esperanza thus carries the remnants of her home, which has been fractured by the deaths of her daughter and, previously, her husband.

Veracruz and Los Angeles are united through this couple. Whereas Esperanza represents Veracruz, Ángel represents Mexican culture in Los Angeles. Unlike *Espaldas mojadas*, this film demonstrates an acceptance of the Mexico that lives outside of its territory. Culture in Los Angeles is no less Mexican than that of Veracruz, and they are connected by the same cultural and religious symbols such as the Virgin of Guadalupe. The film portrays Los Angeles as a Mexican city. The year of *Santitos*' release, 1998, is significant because it coincides with the implementation of the reform to the Mexican Constitution that allows dual nationality, an attempt to officially incorporate the ethnic-Mexican population into national politics. The growing acceptance of Mexico as a transnational community is apparent in *Santitos*. The development of Esperanza's relationship with Ángel in Los Angeles is a vision that allows for cultural identification outside of Mexican territory.

De ida y vuelta

In *De ida y vuelta*, Filiberto (Gerado Taracena), the protagonist, returns to Tsurimicuaro, Michoacán, after having migrated to the

United States. When Filiberto returns to his hometown, he must confront the changes that have occurred in his three years of absence. The most significant discoveries are that Filiberto's parents died, that Soledad, his former girlfriend, married his best friend, Luis, and that they have a child together. The deaths of Filiberto's parents signal a break with Mexican national identity, but Soledad's marriage to Luis makes Filiberto come to terms with his feelings about his hometown and about Mexico in general. Filiberto is not the innocent and timeless migrant of *Espaldas mojadas* and *El jardín del Edén*. He is *machista*, racist, and a murderer; however, his virtue is his refusal to continue to participate in Mexico's corruption, which is represented by his brother, by decrying the town's inability to fight back against his brother's control. By the end of the film, Filiberto is left with no other choice than to return to the United States. Migration becomes an alternative to living within the corrupt system in Mexico, even as the promise of the American dream is questioned.

From the beginning of the film, the loss of love becomes a central theme of Filiberto's return to Tsurimicuaro. Filiberto drives a truck crossing the border as the music informs the viewer that the protagonist is returning from the United States. The song's verses repeat the title of the film and foreshadow what will happen upon his arrival into his hometown: "All I want to know is if it's back and forth / How much love I lost / By crossing the border" (Sólo te pido saber si es de ida y vuelta / Cuánto perdí en el amor / al cruzar la frontera). On his way to the town, he passes a funeral procession, which signals the problems that he will soon face. Filiberto's return to the town is complicated by the attempt of Heriberto (a local hacienda owner and Filiberto's half brother) to take control of the land and water in the town. Luis's property is the main target because the land has a spring that can provide the needed water for Heriberto's hacienda. Because of his interest in Soledad, Filiberto is caught in the middle of the dispute. By helping Luis and Soledad, Filiberto has gotten entangled in the fight for land and water, but his main concern is still Soledad. Fleeing from Heriberto's men, Filiberto, Luis, and Soledad sit in the truck in this order from the driver's side to the passenger side. The film places all three together, and just as in the narrative, Luis sits in between Filiberto and Soledad. All three sit quietly while the baby wails. As the sound of the baby echoes in the background, the camera focuses on Filiberto. The cry seems to accompany the expression on his face as he frowns. Filiberto has been shut out of the nation because of his absence.

Filiberto is not the innocent bystander because he has not been faithful to Soledad. Immediately after his discovery that he has lost Soledad, Filiberto runs into his former lover, Bárbara. From their conversation, it is clear that they were lovers while Filiberto was still with Soledad. At one point, she tells him, "I missed you my king." Bárbara gives Filiberto her opinion about Soledad: "I told you. The skinny cow was not going to wait for you." Bárbara indirectly compares herself to Soledad and implies that she is a better match for Filiberto. When Bárbara is about to have sex with him, she comments, "I know how to treat you." Despite Bárbara's attempt to get Filiberto's attention, he only wants sexual intercourse with her rather than a committed relationship. In spite of his infidelity, the film places more emphasis on Filiberto's migration as the reason for the breakup than it does on his *machista* and womanizing ways so that viewers can empathize with his desire for economic advancement.

The American Dream: A Truck

The American dream is embodied in Filiberto's truck, a symbol of his economic progress. The first part of the film, dedicated to the reintroduction to his hometown, also serves to set Filiberto apart from Mexico, specifically from Michoacán. The camera follows the truck after giving an aerial view of the desert and the mountains surrounding the area. Filiberto is introduced to the viewer as the camera approaches the truck from behind and changes its angle to show him from the front. The camera's movements visually suggest Filiberto's return, but the differences between him and his surroundings are quickly marked. Filiberto's truck is placed in the left lane of the highway, next to a wagon and donkey pulling hay going the opposite way. As Filiberto stops at the side of the road, the truck's California license plates are shown. The camera comes from behind the truck to show a man and donkey crossing the road. Filiberto is shown waiting for them to pass with only traces of their silhouettes in the foreground. The camera angle switches, giving Filiberto's view of the old man from inside the truck and marking the economic differ-ences between him and Filiberto. The introductory scene misleads the viewer into thinking that Filiberto has ascended financially in relation to those who have not migrated: it is later revealed that the truck is not Filiberto's.

Filiberto uses the truck as a sign of economic advancement and to boast of his success in the United States. On Filiberto's arrival at the hacienda and first encounter with his brother, Heriberto asks him about the truck: "Where did you steal it from?" Filiberto implies that it is his: "My work cost me, man." Heriberto gives Filiberto the option to use the truck to help at the hacienda, but he refuses. Heri-berto's men later drive a red truck, the same one that Filiberto sees when they kill don Genaro. Filiberto questions Heriberto, "And that one?" Heriberto answers in the same way that Filiberto did: "My work cost me, man." Heriberto's advancement is placed in opposi-tion to Filiberto's. He has not acquired his wealth by migrating to the United States, but rather by using the resources given to him by his father, which allowed him to monopolize the properties in the area. The comparison serves to demonstrate that economic advance-ment is also attainable in Mexico, but through the abuse of power.

Although Filiberto does not admit that the truck belongs to some-one else until later in the film, there are indications that he struggled to enter the United States and to work there. In one scene, Bárbara finds a scar on his waist. She asks Filiberto about it, and his response is, "It is a souvenir from my trip." Later, when Filiberto drives Luis to Morelia, Luis asks about *la migra*. Filiberto responds, "Well, it's difficult but the camp guards were the worst." Filiberto goes on to tell him about how the guards at the asparagus fields deported him, so he had to cross the border again to return to work. Filiberto's story testifies not only to a dangerous border crossing, but also to the difficulties of living as an undocumented worker.

In Mexico City, Filiberto finally must admit to Luis that the truck does not belong to him and that his migration to the United States did not make him as prosperous as he has led others to believe. Soon after he arrives in Mexico City, Filiberto delivers the truck to Julián, the real owner, and Luis is there to see the exchange. When Luis realizes that the truck is not Filiberto's, he questions him, "It wasn't yours?" Filiberto must admit his lie: "Well yes, but not yet." Luis interprets the deception as Filiberto's strategy to get Soledad back: "So that was how you wanted to recover everything that you left behind?" Filiberto never explains the motives for his deception, but driving the truck was a false symbol of his success in the United States. Because Filiberto has misled his friends and family, the American dream is demystified, and the truck becomes a symbol of unattainable progress. Since the truck has two bullet holes from the attack on Luis and Soledad's house, Filiberto must pay Julián back for the damage; the truck therefore becomes a liability rather than an asset.

Back and Forth

De ida y vuelta portrays Mexico City as closed to outsiders such as Luis and Filiberto. Luis is honest and tries to work within the law. He attempts to get the land title through the appropriate legal means, but the bureaucracy does not allow him to find the needed paperwork to save his property. Filiberto works in Julián's business although it is never clear whether the auto parts are stolen, but he tries to make extra money by being dishonest with Julián and buying cheaper parts. Through both perspectives, Mexico City is shown as a place that is unfriendly to indigenous outsiders from small towns. This is a self-critical portrayal of life for internal migrants in Mexico City. Although Luis and Filiberto have different objectives in traveling to Mexico City, neither is able to work within the city's system. The film's representation of Mexico City is connected to its criticism of mexicanidad. Luis's lack of access to government offices and resources ultimately affects the power relations in the small town. On Luis and Filiberto's return to Tsurimicuaro, they find Heriberto has taken over Luis's land and continues to pump water from the spring to his property, since there is no legal authority to stop him. Unable to survive in Mexico City, Filiberto returns to the hacienda to work, but he endures Heriberto's criticisms for helping Luis and must prove to Heriberto that he is not a traitor.

Filiberto tries to prove his loyalty to Heriberto by trying to help gain control of Luis and Soledad's property, but this scene demonstrates that Filiberto is unable to prove his loyalty to anyone because of his family history. Luis and Filiberto start to talk to each other in the distance as they walk through dead corn stalks. This scene

serves to unravel Luis's biases against Filiberto. Filiberto is the first
to yell: "Let's see if you are really such a hot shit, you damn ungrate-
ful Indian." Luis begins to demonstrate his own tension: "You are
a traitor." Luis finally explains why Filiberto is a traitor: "You grew
up like a dog waiting for scraps outside the kitchen door. You are a
bastard." Filiberto's family background is now revealed completely.
Luis continues, "You are exactly like your brother Heriberto. It's in
your blood." Filiberto kills Luis out of anger.

At this point, Filiberto's family background is completely exposed
to the viewer. Filiberto is the son of the cook, more than likely an
indigenous woman. His father was the late don Heriberto, the original owner of the hacienda. Filiberto is, therefore, *mestizo*, but also
symbolically the son of la Malinche and a *malinchista*. Octavio Paz
has described Mexicans as sons of la Malinche, or the result of the
union between Malitzin and the Spaniard Hernán Cortés. Mexico
and mexicanidad are born out of the conquest of the Aztecs. In this
line of thought, a *malinchista* is a traitor. Paz explains: "The malin-
chistas are the partisans who argue that Mexico must open itself
to the exterior: the true sons of the Malinche that is the Fucked
personified" (95). Despite Filiberto's characterization as a traitor,
or as a *malinchista*, I would argue that the complexity of *De ida y
vuelta* rests on the development of the story line and the revelation
of Filiberto's patrimony. By presenting Filiberto's point of view, the
film portrays Mexican society as one that judges migrants unfairly.

Luis's criticism of Filiberto as a traitor and a bastard forces a
reinterpretation of the events that occurred previously. Throughout the film, Filiberto uses "indios" as a derogatory term, implying
that the people from the town are backward, but he has the darkest
skin of all the characters. Although Soledad and Luis are the two
main indigenous characters, they have dark hair but light complex-
ions. Their mode of dress is the most obvious indicator that they are
indigenous. Soledad wears a traditional dress and her hair in two
braids. Luis and Soledad are reminiscent of the characters of *María
Candelaria* (Emilio Fernández, 1944): María Candelaria (Dolores
del Río) and Lorenzo Rafael (Pedro Armendáriz). Compared to
Luis and Soledad, Filiberto has a darker complexion. His skin color
is more marked than Heriberto's, who has pale skin. Heriberto calls
Filiberto "Mico," or monkey, making reference to his darker skin

color. Despite the fact that Filiberto is darker than Luis, Filiberto continually refers to Luis as an *indio* and a *campesino*. Luis and Filiberto's fight in Mexico City most exemplifies the ethnic conflict. After their brawl, Filiberto yells to Luis, "For whatever this damn place is worth . . . if it's still yours. You will never stop being a damn Indian." Filiberto's rejection of the indigenous population is associated with the town's inability to survive and Heriberto's control over the land. In a conversation with Bárbara, Filiberto connects the town and its lack of progress to Heriberto. Filiberto comments, "I hate this town. Damn Heriberto." He also understands that Luis cannot fight against Heriberto's control: "He's an idiot. He's going to get himself killed." As a *mestizo*, Filiberto understands the conflict as an outsider and as one who has been judged a traitor. Although Filiberto rejects the "indios," it becomes clear through Luis's accusations that Filiberto is not accepted within the indigenous community either. Filiberto's rejection of the town and the indigenous population is clear, but the viewer is not shown Luis's rejection of Filiberto until the end of the film.

After Luis's death, Filiberto returns to the hacienda to gather his belongings and leave for the United States. Heriberto orders Filiberto not to leave. Filiberto explains, "I have no reason to be here." Even though Filiberto rejects his brother's control and power, he longs for the lost patriarch. Filiberto tells his brother, "My father was not like you." The comment also serves to empower Filiberto and make him equal to Heriberto. He is able to reject his subordinated position within the hacienda, but to do so he must leave his hometown. In the final scene of the film, Filiberto hitchhikes on the back of a truck. The camera focuses on Filiberto as he looks forward. His decision to migrate to the United States has little to do with the American dream, but rather reflects his disenchantment with Mexico. In a conversation in the background, a man explains that they can cross the border using a *conejo*, literally a rabbit but used here as a person who runs one way to distract *la migra* while the others run the opposite way. The man's explanation of the border crossing is similar to one that Filiberto gives Luis earlier in the film. The conversation serves to remind the viewer that the border crossing is familiar to Filiberto and that the road ahead is not an easy one. In the last few seconds of the film, the music from the funeral procession at the beginning plays again, forming a circular narrative tied to Filiberto's migration. At the beginning of the film, the music serves as a foreshadowing of the news that Filiberto will receive— that his parents died and that his girlfriend married his best friend. The music at the end of the film confirms that those same events signal the death of Mexican national identity.

The Changing Facets of Mexican National Identity

Nineteenth-century romantic literature, as Doris Sommer argues, was used as a foundational fiction to consolidate the nation. The cinematic romance at the turn of the millennium represents the changing notions of national identity. During the 1950s, when the Bracero Program bringing guest workers to the United States was in place, migration between Mexico and the United States increased steadily, yet as *Espaldas mojadas* demonstrates, a return to Mexico was advocated. This film offers us a comparison to understand more recent representations of migration. *El jardín del Edén* is the perfect example of how economic neoliberalism does not necessarily undo Mexican national identity, since the film cannot consummate the romances between Mexicans and white U.S. tourists. The romances in *Santitos* are more related to the type of integration that is associated with NAFTA and the film's international production. *Santitos* presents a couple that connects Veracruz to Los Angeles. The relationship between Anglos and Mexicans is possible, but it can only take place in a brothel as a "business" arrangement. *De ida y vuelta* is completely different, since it does not represent a migrant's journey to the United States but rather his return to his home community. The strategy of placing the film in Michoacán makes the film a reflection or a questioning of the Mexican nation-state from within. Filiberto's chance for romance is lost even before he returns to his hometown.

El jardín del Edén and *Santitos* question the idea of national identity that is tied to territory, but they do not undo national identity altogether. While it may seem that *El jardín del Edén* questions national boundaries, it imposes national identity by focusing on the psychological drama based on character profiles that follow many of the stereotypes of mexicanidad. Migrant networks are accepted, but mexicanidad is not lost. Even in *Santitos*, in which Esperanza decides to live in Los Angeles with Ángel, the Mexican symbols of the nation are still present. Although national identity is still thriving within internationally produced films such as *El jardín del Edén* and *Santitos*, *De ida y vuelta* offers a completely different alternative for Mexican cinema because it assumes a criticism of mexicanidad. *De ida y vuelta* was produced with Mexican national resources, demonstrating that national cinema is not necessarily nationalist.

The 1990s were marked by trade negotiations and agreements changing our perception of the world, but economic integration does not necessarily undo national identity. The representations of migration in Mexican film of the 1990s demonstrate an acceptance of migrant networks and recognition that national identity can encompass the Mexican population outside of national territory. Mexican film is finally demonstrating that migration involves communities outside the borderlands in areas such as Michoacán, Veracruz, and Mexico City itself. The Mexican border genre continues to signal a concern over migration that originates at the center of the country but that, ultimately, excludes the perspectives from the border and the migrant communities. The major development in the genre is that the perspective from Mexico City can be both self-reflexive and self-critical of its own brand of national identity.

2

How to Cross the Border

Instructions for a Fronterizo and for a Migrant

BOTH THE DOMINANT LITERARY PRODUCTION and the criticism in Mexico continue to see migration as having a role in how identity is constructed at the border. In contrast, the representations of migration as depicted within *la literatura de la frontera* do not appear important to border identity. According to *la literatura de la frontera*, migration should be understood as pertaining to several regions in Mexico—the sending communities or native towns of the migrants and the places where migrants cross the border. Not all border areas have large native populations crossing the border. Many Mexican border dwellers see crossing the national boundary as a natural part of their lives but do not question their national identity. Interpretations of Mexican migration to the United States have focused on it as an encounter with the "other," the United States, but migration is also symptomatic of problems within Mexico. Migration, for both political and economic reasons, is also "pushed."[1] To look at migration is to question the fabric of both nations, the United States *and* Mexico. It is easy to place the blame on the United States, where xenophobia and nativism separate the ethnic-Mexican community from mainstream U.S. society, but migration also forces us to look critically at Mexico. The literature of northern Mexico portrays part of the complexity behind the processes of migration.

Repositioning Migration and Mexican Border Literature

Alberto Ledesma argues that the nationalist subjectivity clouds the perspective of migration within Mexican literature. He specifically cites Luis Spota's *Murieron a mitad del río* and Jesús Topete's *Aventuras de un bracero*. Ledesma argues that the representations of migration within Mexican literature are clouded by a nationalistic discourse: "This nationalist subjectivity is principally characterized by repeated references to Mexican patriotism and national loyalty, which romanticize Mexico while simultaneously vilifying the United States. The discourse is also marked by the negative portrayals of *pochos*—Mexican immigrants or the children of immigrants who show evidence of having acculturated to American society. In addition to this nationalist subjectivity, Mexican immigration narratives are also typified by an emphasis on group class consciousness and the trials and tribulations of *los pobres*—poor Mexicans who struggle to survive amid capitalist rapacity" (74). Although Ledesma's observations are pointed, he neglects to mention that these Mexican narratives of migration were both produced in 1948, and representations of migration have become more complex since then. *La literatura de la frontera* serves as an example of how the recent representations of migration have changed.

Javier Perucho has written extensively on the representations of migration and of Mexican Americans within Mexican literature. He lumps together all types of Mexican border writing: "The corpus that comprises the literature of migration—also called 'border literature,' 'desert literature,' 'literature of the North,'—carries with it an eager interpretation and an implicit criticism of empire, articulated through the postcolonial incarnations of the 'barrier'" ("Un espejo"). Perucho classifies literature from northern Mexico and the different names associated with it (*del desierto* and *de la frontera*) as naturally being part of a genre constructed around migration.[2]

Although many representations of migration within Mexico show this concern for national identity, it is not necessarily one that characterizes all *literatura de la frontera*. Debra Castillo and María Socorro Tabuenca Córdoba warn of the colonialism involved in privileging the border fiction of Mexican centrist writers over *literatura de la frontera*:

> This colonialism is made manifest when one accepts the works of these writers as representative of the border, instead of seeking out other texts by writers from the area. As a result, those authors who write from the border find their work displaced from public consciousness in favor of the latest thematically related "border" book by a well-known centrist writer. It is, therefore, signally important to make the distinction between the border as expressed in literature as opposed to the literature actually produced on the border. The differentiation helps prevent the erasure of Mexican border writers and their writings in favor of works by either well-known Mexican or Chicano/a writers. (27–28)

The literature of northern Mexico is doubly marginalized since it is largely ignored within the United States. The interpretations of the border and its metaphors in U.S. scholarship dominate to the point of erasing the perspective of northern Mexico.

The stereotype of the Mexican borderlands as *agringado* and an area where national identity comes into crisis is one of the reasons that the Mexican federal government funded artistic production in northern Mexico. Castillo and Tabuenca Córdoba mark 1985 as a key year; it was then that President Miguel de la Madrid (1982–1988) started a program to promote artistic production in the borderlands, which led to the creation of local literary workshops. Some participating writers refused the imposed classification of "border writers," while others believed that the workshops helped promote local writers. According to Castillo and Tabuenca Córdoba, one of the major publications to result from the government's programs was a series called Letras de la República published by the Consejo Nacional para la Cultura y las Artes. As Castillo and Tabuenca Córdoba describe, the prologues of the series' publications "speak of a sense of regional autonomy and identity that subsists in a tense relationship with Mexico City's efforts to promote a homogeneous (but implicitly centrist) concept of 'Mexicanness'" (23). The relationship between northern Mexico and the center is complex: northern Mexico's literature is both marginalized within the national canon, yet also promoted through nationally funded programs. Although overshadowed by U.S.-based border literature and writing from Mexico City, Mexican border literature has come into its own since the 1980s, creating an artistic space for Mexican border dwellers. Literature in the Mexican borderlands has developed more noticeably than filmic production.[3]

Humberto Félix Berumen outlines three principal points that characterize Mexican border writing, but he particularly focuses on a generation of writers that includes Daniel Sada, Rosina Conde, Luis Humberto Crosthwaite, and Rosario Sanmiguel. As Berumen contends, these Mexican border writers have chosen to write and sometimes publish from the borderlands themselves. The U.S.–Mexico border for this generation of writers is a direct referent within their works, even if indirectly. Berumen explains, "Whether dealing with geography (desert, mountains, or ocean), cities with their colorful and lascivious lifestyles, or the border itself as linguistic and cultural reality, the narrative of this group of writers faithfully records its environment, thus contributing to the interpretation of it" (17). The characteristics that Berumen lists are based on a literary generation, which is sure to change. Berumen argues for a regional literature: "As we know, a literary work's aesthetic value is not determined by its assignment to the social or geographic atmosphere that gives rise to it; instead, it serves as a reference to understand the conditions from which it arises and the way it participates within them" (14). Castillo and Tabuenca Córdoba argue that such perspectives "can be termed *regionalist* and *essentialist*" (27). They posit that it is difficult to speak of the Mexican northern borderlands as a single entity because of the differences between each of the subregions within the northern states. Castillo and Tabuenca Córdoba promote the articulation of textual borderlands "in which a Mexican geographic space would also acquire a generalizable value, not in relationship to the United States or the rest of Mexico or Latin America, but in terms of the bonds existing among the border states" (28).

Many writers from the Mexican border area represent the border as a geographical space that is real and a part of daily life. Castillo and Tabuenca Córdoba argue that *la literatura de la frontera* is characterized by its treatment of the border as an ordinary space more than an abstraction (28). Similarly, Núria Vilanova argues that "the border is, as a point of enunciation, far from the cultural and metaphoric border that has predominated in cultural studies and border studies, where it is fundamentally perceived as an intercultural space, to use Homi Bhabha's concept, by means of which the rethinking of traditional borders takes place, not only in the geopolitical sense, but also metaphorically, referring to other types of borders, such as those between the public and private spheres, or between older or newer cultures, for example" (9). Vilanova distinguishes border writing in northern Mexico from Mexican American literature: "Chicana literature is really a literature of border crossings—in Hicks's sense—of texts that exist between languages, between cultures, between spaces" (10). Although Vilanova's observations are correct for the most part, the representations of migration within *la literatura de la frontera* can incorporate such metaphorical cultural crossings. Migration always implies the crossing of national boundaries.

Migration is not an inherent part of national identity on the border. People cross the border daily without ever questioning their national identity. Olivia Teresa Ruiz describes transborder crossings as a movement that occurs because of the unequal development between Mexico and the United States. Residents on both sides of the border take advantage of their proximity to the other country. From the U.S. side, many people make the trip to Mexico to buy cheaper medicines, and emigrants may visit family members who still live in Mexico. Many Mexican residents find employment on the U.S. side of the border because of better wages. Border crossing in Mexican border literature is a normal occurrence, and Mexican border writers see the transborder phenomenon as part of their daily lives. Although they know that they are crossing a national boundary, it does not cause a questioning of national identity.

Considering that much migration does not originate at the U.S.–Mexico border, migration must be repositioned and understood as a phenomenon that involves many regions. While Mexican migration to the United States involves northern Mexico since migrants come through the borderlands to cross into the United States, migration should also be placed within the context of the sending areas, most of which are not part of the borderlands. Michoacán, Guanajuato, and Jalisco have traditionally had high levels of out-migration, but in recent times, Zacatecas, Durango, Mexico City, Chihuahua, Tamaulipas, Guerrero, and the state of Mexico have had significant emigrant populations.[4] Whereas states like Chihuahua and Tamaulipas form part of the border region and have a significant amount of out-migration, border cities like Tijuana tend to be more of a thoroughfare or a stopping ground for Mexican migrants trying to enter the United States. In Tijuana, migrants from elsewhere in Mexico are more likely to cross the border illegally than is the city's native population. Elizabeth Fussell argues, "For some migrants, moving to the border is part of a strategy of entry into a particular migratory system" (174). According to Fussell, Tijuana natives and longtime residents have more access to legal documentation, but the probability of out-migration from Tijuana is lower than in the interior. Migration does not affect border areas in the same way, and border dwellers may not need or want to migrate.

The representations of migration in *la literatura de la frontera* serve, many times (but not all), to develop a critique of national discourse. The most significant characteristic of *la literatura de la frontera* is that its representations of migration do not contain the nationalist subjectivity that promotes Mexican patriotism and national loyalty, which Ledesma erroneously attributes to *all* Mexican narratives of emigration. National identity in these northern borderlands stories is not threatened, and the culture of Mexico's northern border is not portrayed as *agringado*, or losing its Mexican identity. Mexico is often criticized for its negligent attitude toward its emigrants or for its endemic poverty that forces its citizens to migrate, literally or metaphorically.

The short stories of three distinct writers—Rosario Sanmiguel from Cd. Juárez; Eduardo Antonio Parra from León, Guanajuato; and Luis Humberto Crosthwaite from Tijuana, Baja California—provide alternative perspectives on how migration impacts the Mexican borderlands. Rosario Sanmiguel is the author of *Callejón Sucre y otros relatos*, a collection of short stories that was originally published in 1994. She is one of a few women writers from Cd. Juárez

who have been able to publish in both local and national venues.
Although she has been able to publish in cultural supplements with
national distribution, Sanmiguel has not received the type of attention given to many other Mexican women writers. According to
Castillo and Tabuenca Córdoba, "Although she has paid her dues
and crossed the bridges to the national literary scene, her work has
not become as well known as that of certain of her contemporaries,
including, most obviously, Laura Esquivel" (62). Although Sanmiguel is not recognized within centrist academic circles, Tabuenca
Córdoba has dedicated much of her criticism, including part of *Border Women* (written with Debra Castillo), to the writer. Sanmiguel's
work has not had wide distribution in Mexico, but Arte Público
published a bilingual edition of her short stories, *Under the Bridge:
Stories from the Border / Bajo el puente: Relatos desde la frontera*,
opening up her readership in the United States.

Parra and Crosthwaite both have complex relationships to the
center and to the U.S.–Mexico border. Perucho describes Parra's
background as follows:

> Originally from one of Mexico's central states (León, Gua-
> najuato, 1965), Eduardo Antonio Parra, in his three decades of
> existence, has—because of his father's work wanderings—put
> down roots in Cd. Juárez, Linares, Nuevo Laredo; in Mon-
> terrey, where he got his bachelor's degree in Hispanic letters;
> León, his birthplace; and Mexico City, land of his literary and
> work pursuits and home life, which is why he knows so per-
> fectly the geography, the flora and fauna of the neighboring
> states to the north, as well as both past and present literary pro-
> duction of its writers, and has even commented critically on the
> more outstanding works of Chicano literature. ("Un espejo")

As Perucho mentions, the publication of Parra's work has flourished within the center, giving it a wider distribution than the work
of other Mexican border writers like Rosario Sanmiguel. Both of
Parra's collections, *Los límites de la noche* and *Tierra de nadie* were
published by Ediciones Era, a major publishing house. Crosthwaite
has published out of both local and national venues. *Instrucciones
para cruzar la frontera* was published by Joaquín Mortiz, another

nationally recognized publisher. *Lo que estará en mi corazón (Ña'a ta'ka ani'mai)* was published by Edamex, but this *testimonio* has not had wide distribution. Despite his participation within the national literary scene, Crosthwaite continued to participate in local venues, most noticeably by directing the independent Yoremito, created specifically to publish *literatura de la frontera*.

Both Sanmiguel and Parra describe migration as a key phenomenon for border communities since they set their stories in Cd. Juárez and Nuevo Laredo. Because of Chihuahua's and Nuevo Laredo's migrant populations, it is possible to see how these areas have been impacted by migration. Many of the fronterizo stories tell of families that are inevitably affected by the absence of the parental figures. While Sanmiguel's stories lack the national archetypes, Parra's stories evoke the social consequences of this loss of fathers within the community with a discourse that questions nationalist loyalty. Crosthwaite's writing differs from Sanmiguel and Parra's short stories because he writes from the perspective of a border dweller who can cross the national boundary legally. However, Crosthwaite's short stories are similar to Parra's in their questioning of national structures and imaginaries. Crosthwaite offers an Oaxacan's testimonial to give voice to the migrant. This testimonial presents an alternative perspective which demonstrates that the Mixtec populations endure hardships in Mexico that push them to migrate. I place Sanmiguel, Parra, and Crosthwaite together because their short stories and testimonials question Mexico's exclusionary economic and political structures that incite migration.

Conflicts with Migrant Parents

Terms such as "patriotism" and "motherland" are clear examples of how the nation is connected to paternal and maternal family relations. Literary representations of orphans are usually associated with a crisis within national identity; however, in the stories by Sanmiguel and Parra, this sense of orphanhood is not indicative of a loss of national identity. Sanmiguel's writing does not contain any of the national tropes or archetypes of mexicanidad. Her stories portray the social dynamic caused by the absence of a parent. In "Juntos o

desaparecidos," Gail Mummert delves into the different attitudes surrounding migration within the nuclear family and how they changed
from one generation to another, concluding that the second generation of the family is impacted by the absence of the fathers who
migrated to the United States. According to Mummert, migration
caused a shift in the concepts of conjugality, paternity, and maternity
because of the effects of the absent fathers or migrants from the late
1950s. The absence of these men affected their children and wives,
so the second generation (1980s) views marriage and migration dif-
ferently than does its parents' generation. The second generation
opted to keep families together by migrating together. In other cases,
young men postponed their marriages until after their return from
the United States.[5] Both Sanmiguel and Parra portray the complexity behind the process of migration and the sense of orphanhood
left by the absence of a parent and the conflicts that migration cause
between parents and children.

Sanmiguel's "Las hilanderas," from *Callejón sucre* (republished
in *Under the Bridge*), is principally a story about a young woman's
relationship with her mother. Unlike other Mexican narratives of
migration, "Las hilanderas" does not present the nationalist discourse, but instead presents a critique of why migrants must stay
out of their country. "Las hilanderas" means "the spinners." Both
Fátima (the young woman) and her mother, Manuela, sew and
embroider, but they also are spinners of their own lives. The details
of their migration are not given, but instead implied: the narration
jumps from their departure in Malavid, their hometown, to their
life as housekeepers. After some time working for *la gringa*, Manuela decides to return to Malavid, but she advises her daughter to
remain working for the white American woman. As Tabuenca Córdoba notes, the recurrent conflict in the story is "the lack of communication between mother and daughter and the protagonists'
search for identity and autonomy" ("Rearticulation" 292). Fátima
believes that as her body changes and she becomes an adult she will
understand her mother more, but she does not: "I thought that I
would look like my mother this way, and that would bring us closer
together. It wasn't that way. She continued to live in her world of
voices" (*Under* 58). Fátima attempts to understand her mother's
decision to migrate to El Paso: "I often asked her why we had left

Malavid. To me, the only palpable change was the litany of work-days in the *patrona*'s immaculate mansion. It was useless. She gave me some partial explanation, some reason I couldn't understand" (*Under* 59). It is also her mother's decision to leave Fátima behind to work with *la gringa* as Manuela returns to Mexico. Even after her mother leaves, Manuela is present in Fátima's daily life. Fátima tries to keep her mother's routine: "I never altered the rhythm of domestic work my mother had established" (*Under* 60). However, it is a routine that it would seem her mother herself, who has inexplicably left *la gringa*'s house, cannot keep.

The original version of this short story is somewhat longer than the 2008 bilingual edition. In *Callejón sucre*, Fátima's return to Malavid at the end of the story is also connected to her mother, because her perspective and her living situation change. While watching a film which contains images of the ocean that somehow remind her of her mother and her hometown, Fátima suddenly wants to return to Malavid: "For the first time in all those years I wanted to go back. Inexplicably, I felt a great discouragement and urgency to return" (*Callejón* 45). The Border Patrol detains Fátima and her friends after they return from a night in Cd. Juárez. Fátima has a dream that explains the change occurring within her: "Suddenly the waves grew large, tossing my boat" (*Callejón* 45). The imagery of the ocean in the dream is similar to the ocean that she sees in the film. These images describe a woman who is breaking away from the influence of her mother and forming an independent sense of herself. In both versions of the story, as she is about to wade through the Rio Grande, "Fátima sees her reflection in the water just like the first day, when she crossed with Manuela. The mirror of time brings the face of a girl holding her mother's hand back to her" (*Under* 61). As she crosses the Rio Grande, Fátima is reminded of her initial migration with her mother.

Fátima returns to Malavid by herself as an independent adult. She also breaks the connection to her mother: "she suddenly senses that Manuela is dead" (*Under* 61). Tabuenca Córdoba sees this newfound independence in relation to *la gringa*: "Fátima escapes from the gringa's house and in her companions' decision to continue with the crossing routine. In breaking with the routine, the migrant is given an alternative discourse of power. The alternative discourse of power can be seen in her ability to acknowledge her living conditions in *la gringa*'s house and in the United States: always hiding, always running. She sees that it is better to return to her own town Malavid" ("Rearticulation" 294). Although the decision to return to Malavid is Fátima's way to escape her work with *la gringa*, I would add that the return also gives Fátima an alternative discourse of power in relation to her mother. Fátima is able to return to Malavid by free will, unlike her migration to El Paso, which is imposed by her mother. Fátima marks her identity as an independent woman by breaking from her mother's control. "Las hilanderas" does not contain any of the typical archetypes associated with Mexican national identity, so the figure of the mother does not necessarily represent the motherland. If she did, what Manuela would represent is a country that ousts migrants even when they would prefer not to leave.

Mónica, a young waitress who lives and works in Cd. Juárez, narrates Sanmiguel's "Bajo el puente." Mónica recounts how she first met her boyfriend, Martín, and how she later loses him in a fight with a Border Patrol agent. Martín is both a *cholo* (a gangster) and a *coyote* (a smuggler) who dedicates himself to illegally crossing people through the Rio Grande using an inner tube. He works at the Puente Negro, an old metal bridge used for crossing trains that is located close to the Santa Fe Port of Entry between Cd. Juárez and El Paso. As Mónica narrates, the basis of the dispute between the agent and Martín is the control of the Puente Negro. At the end of the story, Mónica sits on an inner tube as Martín pushes her across the river, but the border crossing is interrupted when Harris, the Border Patrol agent, shoots at them. Both Mónica and Martín die in the river under the black bridge. Although "Bajo el puente" principally tells how the Border Patrol agent murders them, Mónica narrates several secondary story lines, describing her family's history of migration and her father's disappearance.

Tabuenca Córdoba focuses her analysis on how "Bajo el puente" and "Las hilanderas" "criticize white or Anglo hegemony and its discourse of 'purity and integrity'" ("Rearticulation" 295). She argues that the "narrator presents these events as one more element of daily life on the northern border, a commonness that proves violent, as the end of the story demonstrates. The agent shoots the *coyote* upon reaching U.S. territory. This occurrence challenges the image of the agent as a guardian of the nation, because Harris kills the *coyote* to defend his economic and personal interests, not to protect the national sovereignty" ("Rearticulation" 294). "Bajo el puente" does not romanticize the relationships between Mexicans, in this case, the *coyotes*, who fight for control of the border crossing areas. Martín participates in these rivalries, by stabbing one of his adversaries for staring at Mónica. Martín later finds out that the rival *coyote* is collaborating with Harris, which intensifies his distrust of the Border Patrol agent. "Bajo el puente" criticizes the function of the Border Patrol, but it also presents the complex relationships and rivalries between Mexicans along the U.S.–Mexico border.

Mónica, as mentioned, discusses her relationship to migration, her father's disappearance, and her desire to cross the border. Mónica's family migrated to northern Mexico in search of employment. Although her mother is able to find work as a housekeeper, her father leaves Cd. Juárez hoping to find work in the United States, and he never returns. Mónica remembers her father as she contemplates the possibility of migrating with Martín. She is aware that she can only do so illegally: "We were thinking about renting some rooms to live together, just til we went to Chicago, like wetbacks, like the poor people who cross the river with nothing but God" (*Under* 32). She is curious to see "the other side," but she is also reluctant to cross the border because of her father's disappearance: "When Martín asked me if I wanted to leave with him, I didn't answer. The truth is I didn't want to travel hidden in a freight car like my dad must have done just a few days after we arrived here" (*Under* 32).

Sanmiguel demonstrates that not all Mexican border dwellers are familiar with crossing the border. Mónica has never seen El Paso, and she can do so only by crossing the border illegally. Mónica asks Martín to take her to El Paso, "cuz I'd never been to the other side" (*Under* 31). Despite her request, Mónica wavers between crossing the border and avoiding the situation altogether because of her father's disappearance and because she knows of the danger that Martín faces after his initial confrontation with Harris. Martín finally pushes her to cross the river for a day trip to El Paso by putting her on the inner tube that he regularly uses to cross people through the river. Mónica is excited by the prospect of seeing El Paso for the first time: "Despite feeling scared I got excited thinking that we'd stay on the other side the rest of the day, that we were gonna walk the streets of a city unknown to me—all that thrilled me" (*Under* 34). Because Mónica is crossing the Rio Grande with Martín, her story is intertwined with his. Mónica's desire to see the other side places her in the middle of the river when Harris decides to kill Martín, and her family history gives a particular meaning to the end. As Harris shoots toward them, Mónica sees her life flash before her: "I felt like everything was far away, the little kids that played in the dusty streets, my house, Mere's restaurant, the Hotel Sady, the Cathedral, its staircase and its beggars. The day I last saw my father" (*Under* 34). Although everything may have seemed far away to the narrator, the details remind the reader of Mónica's life, especially her own link to migration. The end of the short story is linked to her father's disappearance, marking her attempt to enter the United States as a generational phenomenon. The last sentence poetically describes Mónica's death: "I felt an intense heat in my eyes. The August sun, I thought. I closed them hard, and saw how much silence the river carries" (*Under* 34). The "silence the river carries" makes reference to the unfortunately common occurrence of migrants dying in the Rio Grande while attempting to enter the United States.

Neither "Las hilanderas" nor "Bajo el puente" contains the national references characteristic of the dominant narratives of migration. The migrants in these stories are not concerned about losing their national identity. Sanmiguel portrays migration as a real occurrence; she represents undocumented migration in her stories and distinguishes it from the legal crossings that occur on the bridges that connect Cd. Juárez and El Paso. These stories focus on the migrants who must cross under the bridge without documentation. She describes a migrant community that crosses borders regularly but must face the Border Patrol to do so. Sanmiguel represents migration as a recurring phenomenon in the Cd. Juárez–El Paso area. Fátima and Mónica must grapple with migration and how it affects their families. In Fátima's case, the decision to return to her hometown marks the liberation from her mother's influence. Mónica's death represents the migrants who have drowned in the Rio Grande. Sanmiguel's stories do not judge emigrants, but rather portray their reasons for migrating and the difficulties of crossing the border illegally.

Gang Loyalty

Many of Eduardo Antonio Parra's short stories are set in Monterrey, Cd. Juárez, and Laredo. His stories are characteristic of his own movement and his contact with the U.S.–Mexico border, although he is not native to the area. Parra's connection to Guanajuato must be considered because his native state has traditionally had a large population of migrants. As mentioned previously, Berumen argues that Mexican border writers make reference to the U.S.–Mexico border through the imagery of the landscape (the desert, ocean, etc.) and through language that is characteristic of the borderlands. Because of his connection to northern Mexico, Parra is able produce direct cultural and linguistic references to the U.S.–Mexico border.

Parra's characters do not lose their national identity. Javier Perucho assumes that migration is only a result of the lure of the American dream, and he analyzes Parra's stories accordingly: "Parra's short stories can be read and understood as an acknowledgment of the other (*pochos*,[6] vagrants, transvestites, prostitutes) a welcome into a strange land—in this case the United States—as a way of assimilating the traumas of the new colonization and vassalage. Certainly it also frames a dialogue between two cultures, idiosyncrasies, and traditions: the Mexican and the U.S. American. The writing of Eduardo Antonio Parra is the Mexican mirror in which one considers the other, the mercurial bed where the bedfellows of men without a country and those shut out of the American dream frolic" ("Un espejo"). Although Parra does give space to the "other," his stories are not about the new colonization as Perucho contends. The dynamic within Parra's "El juramento," part of his collection *Los límites de la noche*, is such that the symbolic space of a gang imitates that of Mexico as a nation. As Germán Muñoz argues, gangs play out disputes for territorial and sociopolitical control while offering a sense of belonging (266). More than a site of "dialogue," as Perucho calls it, the story presents the contradictory nature of territorial loyalties that discriminate against migrants considering the common family history of absent migrant family members.

The premise of "El juramento" rests on the gang's oath to hate the United States and *la migra*. The story begins as the group discovers that el Güero, the former leader of the gang and the creator of the oath, has returned after migrating to the United States. The new leader of the gang, Elías, tries to convince José Antonio, the main character in the story, that he must join the group in its punitive action against el Güero. Because of his own desire to migrate, José Antonio questions the pledge that the group made and remembers the day when they made the oath:

> *Repeat after me.* El Güero, as serious as an adult, stretched his hand forward. Immediately, Elías put his on top, then Ricardo; José Antonio smiled and did the same: *since the worst enemy we Mexicans have*—the voices of the three followed el Güero's word for word—*is the gabacho, I promise to fuck each and everyone of them up, whenever I get the chance, by day or night, to avenge the way they abuse our people or kill them when they try to cross the river.* After the oath, he took out his knife—made of deerhorn, his father's last gift—and cut the palm of his hand. The others took the weapon and followed suit. Only Elías asked about the reason for all the drama. El Güero averted his gaze, and his child's voice became husky when he answered, *They killed my old man, too.* (*No Man's* 118)

The oath is written in italics whereas the nonitalic print recounts the event; it is much like a pledge to any country and shows that the gang loyalty imitates blind patriotism.

Parra presents us with a critique of how group loyalties, like blind patriotism, can discriminate against the very people that the group wishes to protect. El Güero's decision to make the oath came after he and José Antonio watched the U.S. Immigration and Naturalization Service (INS) and Mexican officials find and dig up the bodies of migrants who died trying to cross the border. The event triggers the pain and memories of the disappearance of el Güero's father, who died in the river and not at the hands of *la migra* as claimed by the group and even el Güero himself. José Antonio understands the oath and its punitive action to be faulty since all the members of the gang can be considered guilty on some level: "Then José Antonio knew that that was the crime, and that he too had committed it by wanting to leave for the North, and so had his father, and Ricardo's uncles, and Elías' brother, and anyone who'd left as a wetback and stayed to live over there" (*No Man's* 119). Unable to see the contradictory nature of his argument, Elías suggests that el Güero is a traitor: "'I bet the bastard feels right at home over there,' Elías continued ruminating. 'He wanted to be a gabacho, and that's like betraying your country'" (*No Man's* 119). José Antonio believes that Elías's impulse to attack el Güero stems from his need to defend his position as leader of the group rather than a real interest in the oath, which did not concern him originally. Despite the group's oath to defend migrants, they are unable to understand that they themselves now discriminate against the migrant, el Güero.

By the end of the story, the pact taken by the gang has a life of its own. José Antonio tries to warn el Güero of the attack but ends up witnessing and inevitably partaking in the ambush. After beating el Güero, several of the gang members urge José Antonio to run and escape before they are caught, but José Antonio falls and stabs himself with the same knife that they used to take the group's oath: "He remembered his father, El Güero's father, the corpses on the island. The pain near his belly didn't let up and he put his hand there. At first, he thought it was a branch that had lodged there when he fell, but as he slowly sank, a trickle of warm, sticky liquid mixing with the waters of the Bravo caused him to recognize, buried up to the handle, the deer-horn knife El Güero always carried with him, the knife of the blood oath" (*No Man's* 124). The knife, which represents the oath, comes out of nowhere. Although José Antonio never tells his fellow gang members that he wants to migrate to the United States, he eventually dies as part of his judgment for being a traitor to his gang. "El juramento" demonstrates the hypocrisy of judging migrants for having to leave their country. José Antonio dared to break the oath simply by hoping to migrate and by recognizing the hypocrisy of taking such a pact when all the gang members have family members in the United States. By presenting the story from José Antonio's point of view, "El juramento" questions national loyalty and patriotism instead of imposing them.

Families That Wait for Migrants

Much like Sanmiguel's "Las hilanderas," Parra's "La piedra y el río" and "El escaparate de los sueños" from his *Tierra de nadie* describe families that are torn by migration. Gail Mummert's survey respondents in Quiringüicharo, Michoacán, showed that they were deeply affected by the absence of migrant fathers ("Juntos o desaparecidos"). Parra's stories about migration similarly focus on the son of migrants and the loss of the migrant father. "La piedra y el río" recounts how Dolores Cerrillo—who, much like la Llorona, a mythical figure who weeps for her dead children, lives next to the Rio Grande—helps to raise the first-person narrator, a young man who lives with her. They are connected by the loss of a family member, and they form a family between them. Dolores, a legend within her community, waits for her husband, who migrated to the United States in search of work, although years have passed since he first left.

Although Dolores has few friends and few people understand her, the men ask for her blessing before their travel to the United States. Much like in the biblical story of Sodom and Gomorrah, the community imagines Dolores as a pillar of salt: "Only a few know that her name is Dolores Cerrillo; for some she is merely the crazy woman by the river, and almost everyone calls her 'the pillar of salt'. She never moves, so they say, she's like a stone: a stone at the side of the river" (*Tierra* 16). The juxtaposition of the river and the pillar of salt works to allegorize Dolores's plight, as she waits for her beloved and the migrant men who leave their families. The river flows eternally while she remains, forever waiting for her husband to return. The legendary woman becomes more than a legend for the narrator; she becomes his mother figure. The story does not mention the narrator's birth mother, but Dolores clearly fills that void. The story is reflective of how legends, archetypes, and national and community figures are created. "La piedra y el río" overlaps the narrator's perspective with how Dolores is seen by the community. She is both the narrator's mother figure and a national mother for the community that seeks her advice. The image of the rock also describes the narrator who lives with her: "My father went off to the other side that night, and from the next day on I was another pillar of salt, a smaller one, and spent every afternoon beside the old woman" (*Tierra* 16). Just as the woman waits for her husband, the narrator waits for his father. At one point, the young man asks Dolores why she has not gone to the United States to look for her husband, and she responds, "Because it's for men to cross to the other side. If the woman goes with them, they put down roots and never return" (*Tierra* 16). The young man's migration to the United States is expected. He comments, "I suddenly saw myself becoming one of them, with the future opening to the north" (*Tierra* 21). As he mentions, Dolores is the first to realize that he has come of age.

Dolores tells the narrator as a child that the river informed her his father died, but that does not resolve the void that the child feels. As a young man, he attempts to get some information when he migrates to the United States: "In the first months I looked for Zacarías and my father, but nobody could tell me anything" (*Tierra* 21). This inability to find any information about the missing migrants keeps Dolores and the narrator forever tied to each other. The end of the story describes Dolores's death and the legend that she becomes: "When there is a storm, she abandons the current, and in the strings of rain her silhouette can be seen next to a mature man, whom she raised as her own son and who, with a far-off look and his walking stick in hand, listens carefully to her tales as he rests upon a stone" (*Tierra* 26). This time, the legend includes the young man, who suffers the same fate as Dolores. Both are suspended in time, waiting for the migrants to return. Had they received word that their loved ones had died at least they would have been able to mourn their losses. This point is made clear when the child first goes to live with Dolores. She throws a dead fish on the floor for the cats to eat, but her words explain that inability to mourn: "It shouldn't disgust you. It's a good thing that the earth is nourished, too. . . . That's why we must bury everything that was once alive. Whatever doesn't get buried, somehow refuses to die" (*Tierra* 19). The void that Dolores and the young man feel is left unresolved; they are unable to mourn their losses.

The missing, migrant father is at the heart of "El escaparate de los sueños." Parra's portrayal of the American dream is revealing regarding Mexico's lack of opportunities for the poor. According to Javier Perucho, Parra's writing is "a welcome into a strange land—in this case the United States—as a way of assimilating the traumas of the new colonization and vassalage" ("Un espejo"). Parra's story reveals that his protagonist Reyes's dreams are not only about being mesmerized with U.S. culture; they become a form of escape of his reality. Reyes works on one of the international bridges used to cross from Cd. Juárez to El Paso with his friend Tintán, named after the famous comedian from Cd. Juárez. Reyes contemplates his friend's physical appearance to reveal his own situation: "In those sunken eyes, that lifeless gaze, Reyes could see his own unpromising, unexciting future, with nothing to free him from this existence, and he didn't have the heart to go on looking" (*No Man's* 99). While the dream is connected to material items—a house, a car, and a way of living—Reyes daydreams of these things in connection with his father.

Reyes works on the bridge helping people who are crossing with bags to take to El Paso. From the beginning, Reyes is set apart from the people in the cars who are about to cross into the United States. Unlike those people, he does not enjoy the comfort of air-conditioning, and he cannot cross legally into the United States. Reyes is not originally from Cd. Juárez but rather from Guadalupe y Calvo, a small town in the state of Chihuahua. According to Reyes's letters to his father, a drought devastated the town, killing all the animals. Because of his lack of documentation, he has never been able to see El Paso, so he has an idealized image of the city created by his father's stories. His father worked there, and "on his annual family visits he always assured them that everything good in the world came from El Paso" (*No Man's* 98). His father's work allowed the family to receive gifts that they would not otherwise get. These gifts, however, help Reyes to create his idyllic image of the city.

His father disappears after migrating to Chicago, and the family never hears from him again. The absence of his father is a constant obsession for Reyes, especially at the bridge, where there are constant reminders of class differences: "To dispel the image, he thought of his father, whom he had seen so infrequently: always in a good mood, satisfied at having made his family happy at least once a year with his presence and his gifts. He never spent more than fifteen days in Guadalupe y Calvo, but that was enough time for him to return to El Paso convinced it was worth the sacrifice of not seeing them for months at a time. However, the old man's smiling face also reminded him of his absence" (*No Man's* 99–100). Although Reyes's father is mostly absent from the family's day-to-day life, his disappearance affects the family financially. As a consequence, Reyes has to accept old toys and hand-me-down clothes. "El escaparate de los sueños" ends with Reyes's dreams of El Paso. As all the Border Patrol agents leave their stations to attend to a car wreck, Reyes seems to enter El Paso, but the entrance is only part of a fantasy. Reyes recreates the city using his father's descriptions: "While his father's stories about the city of his dreams whirled dizzily through his mind, he stepped up his pace until he was running with all his might" (*No Man's* 109).

Parra's stories do not portray a loss of Mexican identity. The theme of the lost migrant father is a recurring one, demonstrating the local impacts of migration upon the nuclear family. In these stories, the mother's presence or lack thereof is also significant. In "El escaparate de los sueños," Reyes associates his mother's death with his father because she died after the last Christmas that the family spent with the migrant. Nine months after his last visit, the mother died giving birth to Reyes's tenth and final sibling. Reyes does not daydream about his mother in the same way that he does about his father. In "La piedra y el río," there is no mention of the boy's birth mother, but Dolores replaces the mother figure. The children (the sons) are not the only family members left behind. The women must also grapple with the absence of their husbands, but this perspective is secondary to the son's loss. Parra's main focus is on the absence of the father and father-son relationships.

Transborder Crossings and Migration

Unlike Sanmiguel and Parra, who portray the loss of a migrant father, Luis Humberto Crosthwaite gives voice to the migrant father in his quest to improve his family's quality of life. The switch in focus may be attributed to geographical differences between the writers. Chihuahua and Nuevo León are states with some out-migration whereas Baja California is more of a stopping ground for migrants or the place where these internal migrants decide to take up residence. Crosthwaite's work distinguishes migration from transborder crossings, which Olivia Teresa Ruiz describes. These crossings are different from migration because people who live along the border cross the national boundary to work, to go to school, or to visit family. Crosthwaite's *Instrucciones para cruzar la frontera* best portrays the various types of border crossings, including transborder crossings, Mexican migration to the United States, and even the example of a Japanese migrant in Tijuana. In *Instrucciones para cruzar la frontera,* Crosthwaite gives recommendations for crossing the border that are aimed at an audience that can cross the border legally. The narrator urges the reader to carry some type of documentation in order to pass through the checkpoint: "It's necessary to carry a document that states your nationality and your intentions" (9). At the end of the recommendations, Crosthwaite acknowledges that there are many who cross the border through "back ways, hard to get to" (12). This alternative type of border crossing requires a separate set of rules: "To cross in such extreme conditions is a feat of a different kind, requiring a different set of recommendations" (12).

"El largo camino a la ciudadanía" and "Muerte y esperanza en la frontera norte" are two of Crosthwaite's short stories from *Instrucciones para cruzar la frontera* that portray the difficulties that migrants face. "El largo camino a la ciudadanía" focuses on the protagonist's infatuation with becoming a U.S. citizen: "Since childhood he adored everything about the United States, considering it to be the best place in the universe" (25). Although this can be read simply as the lure of the American dream, the protagonist's infatuation with the United States becomes more of an indication of what Mexico cannot offer him—that is, economic opportunity. The well-being of the migrant's family is the reason for his decision to migrate to the United States:

> He wants to be a "migrant" because he knows that it's a first step toward citizenship. It would have been easier if his parents had decided to migrate from the beginning. What's the point of working in the United States if you're not going to seek to become legalized? They had had neither the vision nor the ambition. You quit, and you end up being happy with your Mexicanness. They say that to be Mexican isn't bad, but to be a U.S. citizen is better. What's going to become of my parents when they get old? Who's going to take care of them? In the United States, your life's taken care of. You can get a house, a new car, the best school for your children, free medical service, and a pension from the government. (25–26)

The protagonist equates migration and U.S. citizenship with economic advancement and stability, but migration must be legal in order to attain all the benefits that citizenship will provide. Although he adjusts to his Mexicanness, his infatuation with the United States implies that in Mexico or with Mexican citizenship a comfortable standard of living cannot be attained. What the migrant desires most is economic stability that he feels he cannot attain within Mexico.

Initially, the protagonist wishes to be an American, but later the lure of the American dream starts to lose its appeal. When the migrant receives his green card, he begins to understand that being American has its disadvantages: "He understands that he won't be able to hold the job of his profession in his homeland. Now he must be an auxiliary, a supporting character" (27). The reality is not what he had envisioned. Toward the end of the story, the migrant seems to have accomplished his goal for economic stability and attaining the American dream. "El largo camino a la ciudadanía" demonstrates that migrants may not lose their national identity despite living outside of the country. Here, the American dream is a symptom of Mexico's lack of opportunity. The protagonist goes through a transformation, becoming a U.S. citizen, but his perspective changes as well. The last paragraph reads as follows: "When he is alone, the 'citizen' puts on his old Pedro Infante records, the songs that remind him of his father" (29). The end can be read in two distinct ways. The protagonist must face separation from his family, a result of migration. Part of the reason for the protagonist's infatuation with the United States was his need to provide for his parents in their old age, but the stability comes with the cost of being apart from his family. In another sense, although the migrant achieves his goal of being a U.S. citizen, he has not lost his identification with Mexico. Pedro Infante and his father are direct references to mexicanidad, demonstrating a disjuncture between national identity and citizenship. The protagonist's recollection of his father invokes Mexican national identity in his private space. In the end, although the migrant is a U.S. citizen, the separation from his family enforces his cultural identification with Mexico.

"Muerte y esperanza en la frontera norte" presents three different perspectives about migration: those of the migrant, the Mexican press, and the U.S. press. The migrants come from different areas of the country: "They were from Michoacán, from Oaxaca, from Guerrero, from Zacatecas, from Jalisco" (45). The story begins by telling what the migrants had heard before their travel to the border: "They had told them that in the United States there were great job opportunities, more than in Mexico. They had told them that the work would be tough, but honest. They had told them that they would have to travel north, that to get into the United States was complicated. More so than before, they had told them" (45). The story reflects the fact that migrant networks function by word of mouth and familial connections. The information that they received from other migrants is compared with the information that they were not given. The migrants encounter unexpected bad weather: "Nobody talked about the cold temperatures . . . nobody talked about the snow" (45). The first part of the story tells of the lack of information that the migrants have and how the hope for a better life makes them believe that they can withstand the cold weather.

The narration then switches to newspaper accounts of the Mexican and the U.S. press, telling what happened to the migrants. On April 3, the Mexican press tells us of the migrants' fate that night: "Seven undocumented dead; 37 rescued" (46). The press in the United States focuses on the migrants' rescue: "Immigration Service Rescues Abandoned Illegals" (46). The different accounts by the Mexican and the U.S. press are highlighted throughout the rest of the story. The Mexican press continues to emphasize the deaths of the migrants, warning that crossing the border can be lethal. Both national presses bring up issues that place the blame on the other country. The Mexican press accuses Operation Gatekeeper of causing the migrants' deaths, and the U.S. press blames Mexico for not providing opportunities for their people: "If Mexico can't meet its people's need for work, the most needy will turn to the United States, defying climate and nature" (48). What the story allows us to see is that the reasoning behind the news given by both presses is not incorrect, but each has its blind spots.

Crosthwaite develops the circularity of migration in "Muerte y esperanza en la frontera norte" in a similar way that he does in "El largo camino a la ciudadanía." The circularity demonstrates that migration is a continuing process that will not diminish. The Mexican and the U.S. presses may have different perspectives about migration, but it is the local lore, word of mouth, and the hope for a better future that influence migrants to cross the border. Death is a chance that they must take. "Muerte y esperanza en la frontera norte" demonstrates that migrants' needs and opinions vary from the national and international debates that are played out in the press. Although the United States is commonly criticized within Mexican literature, the critique of the Mexican press portrays a situation in which both countries are negligent. Instead of drawing on the nationalist subjectivity that Ledesma criticizes of older Mexican narratives of migration, "Muerte y esperanza en la frontera norte" demonstrates how discussions of migration within national presses tend to exclude the migrant perspective, and it gives us a context to understand *Lo que estará en mi corazón* as a *testimonio* that seeks to fill the void of the national presses.

Giving Voice to the Migrant

Lo que estará en mi corazón (Ña'a ta'ka ani'mai) received the Premio de Testimonio Chihuahua for the testimonial of Isaías Ignacio (Fidencio) Vázquez Pimentel. The testimonio resulted from collaboration between Luis Humberto Crosthwaite and Fidencio Vázquez, an Oaxacan/Mixtec who migrated to Baja California and the United States, among other places. *Lo que estará en mi corazón* offers an alternative perspective of migration by describing a community that must migrate for basic economic survival. The testimonial goes into detail about the situations that drive migrants to leave their communities, in this case the town of Yucuñuti, Oaxaca. Vázquez's testimonial describes the poverty and exploitation by employers that Oaxacans/Mixtecs encounter on both sides of the border. Although the testimonio directly deals with a local Mixtec identity, the narrator also speaks in favor of all economic migrants who must endure the same conditions.

Lo que estará en mi corazón represents the Mixtec community identity in order to incite political action. For John Beverley, testimonio "represents an affirmation of the individual subject, even of individual growth and transformation, but in connection with a group or class situation marked by marginalization, oppression, and struggle" (35). In this sense, *Lo que estará en mi corazón* attacks the economic and political structures that keep indigenous populations in poverty. As Vázquez argues, "The Mixtecs sleep on a dirt floor while the bosses sleep on their mattresses stuffed with money. Such is life for the Indians of Baja California; such is life for the Indians of all Mexico" (185). Although Vázquez approaches his story from an Oaxacan/Mixtec point of view, in some instances he also speaks on behalf of other migrants: "I decided to help my Mixteca friends who live in San Quintín because I saw that they don't always know how to defend themselves, they come from far away, from Oaxaca, from Guerrero. Some of them aren't Mixteca. Some of them are Zapoteca. Others aren't indigenous at all, but they come from far off just the same, to live better, to be able to help their families. I've seen them; they're like me, sending home their little bit of money to their families in the interior" (184). Although Vázquez speaks of the living conditions of the indigenous in Mexico, his testimonial also describes the difficulties of crossing the border and the threat of being caught by *la migra* within the United States.

Crosthwaite is the transcriber writing from a fronterizo perspective, and Vázquez provides the migrant/Mixtec point of view. The role of the testimonial has been widely debated.[7] Elzbieta Sklodowska warns that the testimonio has been seen as a "seamless monument of authenticity and truth" rather than as a text (98). In *Lo que estará en mi corazón*, Crosthwaite mediates the voice of the migrant. The details of the collaboration are unknown, and the testimonio does not include a prologue or introduction such as the one given by Elisabeth Burgos-Debray with Rigoberta Menchú's well-known and much-debated testimonio.[8] One of the distinguishing features of this testimonio is that it offers a representation of the problems within Mexico and demonstrates that migrants face discrimination and poverty both in the United States and in Mexico. The nationalist subjectivity cannot represent the Mixtec identity because, as José Manuel Valenzuela Arce argues, national identity as imagined by the dominant classes ceases to represent the popular ("Identidades" 114). Valenzuela argues that, although national identity does not represent the subaltern classes, cultural identities persist and may be transnational. In *Lo que estará en mi corazón*, there is a break with Mexican national identity, so the transnational cultural identity is organized around the Mixtec/Oaxacan identity.

The archetype of the migrant and the indigenous Mexican, both used commonly to support Mexican national identity, may not necessarily make migrant and indigenous Mexicans feel included. The testimonial does not reinforce this nationalist subjectivity, but rather questions it. As Vázquez describes his father's first journey to the United States, he struggles to understand the concepts of the boundary line and what a nation is. Vázquez discusses these concepts with his father, who has just returned from the United States. Vázquez asks his father, "What is the line?" (29). His father explains, "The line is where the division is, where we migrate to where the gabachos are, where Mexico ends and the United States begins" (29). In a conversation with his mother, Vázquez asks, "What does 'nation' mean?" and she responds, "Not Mexico, son, it's another nation: the United States" (29), to which Vázquez replies, "Who knows what it is—that's what I would say" (30). The root of Vázquez's problem is that he does not understand what a nation is. Instead of supporting national loyalty or patriotism, Vázquez's descriptions of identity work within local and ethnic schemes of Oaxacan/Mixtec identity.

The movement of a transnational community, as presented in *Lo que estará en mi corazón*, characterizes the Mixtec identity. Gaspar Rivera-Salgado explains the role that ethnic identity plays within indigenous communities as follows:

> Perhaps it appeared at first blush that the great geographical dispersion of indigenous migrant workers was a death blow dealt to communities subjected to this process of integration between the United States and Mexico. Nevertheless, the indigenous communities have responded creatively to the challenge of maintaining the social and cultural fabric so as to allow their viability over these geographic spaces. In the process of migration, the indigenous have strengthened their ethnic identity, which has permitted them to organize and maintain close bonds with their communities of origin. This has allowed them to directly participate in those communities' most relevant matters regardless of where they themselves might be physically.

Vázquez's testimonio demonstrates how the Mixtec community has kept its ethnic identity despite migration. In the first chapter, Vázquez marks a time before the community started to migrate: "No one left my town to go to work. You didn't hear anything about 'we're going to the north, to San Quintín, to Culiacán, to the United States,' nothing. You didn't hear anything" (14). Although Vázquez only mentions San Quintín, Culiacán, and the United States within this quote, throughout the testimonial he also describes his migration to Mexico City, Veracruz, Sinaloa, and Tehuacán, Puebla. Vázquez comments, "The Mixtecs go so far, from Oaxaca to the border between Mexico and the United States" (178). Vázquez's account testifies to the viability of this transnational community as he continually mentions how his friends and family travel with him. The Mixtec identity is one that originates in Oaxaca but is not limited to its geographical limits.

For the Family

Unlike the short stories by Parra and Sanmiguel that focus on the absent father, the testimonio gives voice to the migrant. The title, *Lo que estará en mi corazón*, connects Vázquez's testimonio to his family, his commitment to providing for them, and to his community. A section within the third chapter shares the title of the testimonio. In this section, Vázquez describes how he asked for Suriana's hand in marriage. While it is unclear which family members accompanied him, Vázquez describes his grandfather's and his father's participation in the ritual. The ritual serves two purposes: to assure Suriana's family that Vázquez will not mistreat or leave her and to unite both families as a community. The title of the testimonio not only refers to the section about marriage, but also is part of an expression used during the ritual. The whole expression is as follows: "*Ña'a ta'ka ani'mai, koo'mini*—whatever is in my heart will also be in yours" (84). His father-in-law hands a drink to Vázquez's father, binding the two families together: "My dad takes a drink and then passes the glass, and what was for him, in his heart, is for my father-in-law. The same glass. The same life" (84). Vázquez's description of the ritual and the title of the book connect the migrant's life story to that of his family. His decision to migrate is motivated by his family's welfare and needs regarding his future wife's family.

The narrator starts by describing his family's lifestyle on the communal lands in Yucuñuti, Oaxaca. The people of Yucuñuti make *sombreros* and *petate* to survive. Vázquez takes care of the neighbor's cattle. When he marries Suriana and they start to build a family, the urgency to provide for his family grows. Vázquez's decision to migrate (whether within Mexico or to the United States) is connected to the lack of opportunity in Yucuñuti: "I went back to Mexico [City] because you couldn't make money in the town" (105). Vázquez's decision to travel to the United States is similarly motivated by need: "In Yucuñuti we didn't get ahead, just sewed hats, barely earned enough to eat. I'd do six hats, a dozen; my wife would do eighteen, twenty hats. My wife is a harder worker than I am. We barely had anything to eat; it didn't amount to enough to buy an animal, a cow, to keep a home. It wasn't enough. No way. No way. Now it's the same everywhere. It's the same" (121). Vázquez's testimonial includes not only a male perspective about migration and poverty but also a female one. Throughout the testimonio, Suriana Vázquez is left to fend for herself and for the children while her husband migrates and works within the Baja and Alta California fields. In general, Vázquez narrates his family's struggle to survive. At one point, Suriana Vázquez gets sick: "She was already getting skinny; she was dried out" (112). Unable to go to a medical doctor, Vázquez helps his wife with herbal medicine, which provides her relief. Another time, Froylán, his son, has a hernia. The child gets his operation and recovers.

The testimonio portrays a constant tension between what Fidencio wants or needs and what his wife wants to do or wants him to do. Although Suriana Vázquez is not directly interviewed in the testimonio, Fidencio Vázquez's narration is able to demonstrate that she has a will of her own and that she influences his decisions, and that, at times, she imposes her decisions upon him. Suriana Vázquez arrives in Mexico City to convince her husband that they should go to Baja California. Vázquez argues with her for having come to Mexico City without having told him, but he must comply with his wife's wishes: "I didn't want to go. I didn't want to see the roads of Mexicali, the heat, well, the awful heat there. I was discouraged to see my wife. She came in with her Yucuñuti dress, her little sandals; that's how she always dressed" (148). Although he describes her with her traditional clothes in such a way that she seems backward, he is forced to do what she wants. Vázquez later comments, "What

else could I do? We left for Baja California" (149). The family similarly lives in San Quintín because of his wife's wishes: "It wasn't my
plan to stay in the San Quintín Valley forever; it was my wife's idea,
because her folks aren't in Oaxaca anymore. They died while she
was here, and she said to herself, 'now what am I going to do in my
hometown? There's no one there for me.' She got interested in me
buying a piece of land, and in some places it was easy to do that. But
I didn't ever want to. I did hope to return" (153). Migration, then,
is not determined only by Fidencio Vázquez's need to provide for
his family. His wife is a major factor in their decision to migrate. *Lo
que estará en mi corazón* delves into not only the lives of migrant
men but also those of their families. What this testimonial describes
is a family dynamic in which family members must negotiate their
needs, their migration, and where they decide to live.

The Border as Part of a Conspiracy

Vázquez leaves for the United States by himself as a way to find
some income to support his family. He gives a detailed account of
what it entails to walk across the border through the desert terrain
and vividly explains how he is beaten by a Border Patrol agent. The
most powerful part of Vázquez's account of migration is how he
links the militarization of the U.S.–Mexico border to the agriculture
industry's need for labor.

   In the testimonio, Vázquez crosses the border twice: once by
paying a *coyote* and another time by crossing on foot through the
desert. Although the *coyote* tries to force the Vázquez brothers to
pay him an additional fee, the trip seems relatively easy compared to
Vázquez's second trip. Vázquez explains of the *pasapollos* (the person who smuggles migrants by foot), "El Chupe was cheap; we paid
cash" (142). Vázquez also narrates how he and others crossed the
border by following a *pasapollos* through the desert. He recounts
the conditions of the terrain of the Tecate sierra, and he repeatedly
mentions that it was "nothing but desert." Vázquez describes the
physical pain that he felt after the long walk and night spent in the
wilderness: "I slept curled up tight, and afterward I couldn't stand
up because my feet were asleep, my legs. When the car got there

I couldn't stand. I wanted to stand, but I couldn't. El Chupe was mad because the migra was going to get us, because it was breaking daylight" (142). Vázquez's pain is understandable considering that the group walked five days through the desert and rain, and also had to wade through water. Whatever the method of crossing the border, it is understood that the threat of being captured by *la migra* is always present.

Among the stories about the United States, Vázquez describes how a Border Patrol agent beat him. The beating occurs after the Border Patrol and the police raid the cotton field where Vázquez and several of his family members are working. Vázquez and the other workers start to run, but an agent captures Vázquez:

> He grabs my jacket, reaches out his hand and grabs me. The one who was driving sticks his hand out the window and I hit him and I fall down, well, I fight back. And real quick the other one gets out to grab me, and when I try to stand up, he gives me a whack in the neck with his pistol and another one on the head, and then another, solid and hard, real bad, and another one in the face. It really hurt my Uncle Pablo to see how they hit me. I felt my skin break open. The other agents just watched. They crossed my wrists and put handcuffs on me, and while I was cuffed they hit me again in the head, like eight times, and in the ribs and in the legs with the billy club. (145)

Vázquez's account could be compared to the Rodney King beating, but the difference is that Vázquez is an undocumented worker and his abusers go unpunished. The account clearly describes *la migra*'s excessive use of force. Vázquez also narrates that the agents who beat him were Mexican American: "All of them were Mexican Americans; they say they're Texans. They're Mexicans" (145). The violence against Vázquez demonstrates a lack of solidarity between the Mexican American agents and Mexican migrants.

The raid occurs on the same day that the migrant workers are to get paid for their work. Vázquez attempts to escape because he wants his paycheck: "I didn't want them to pick me up because it was payday, my little paycheck, and I wanted to get a chance to see my money. It was Saturday and we were just about to leave" (144).

The risk of getting caught by the Border Patrol is not just deportation but also represents a financial loss. Vázquez sees the raids as a conspiracy:

> The Border Patrol has an agreement with the bosses: Here's this much money not to take my people, since there's so much work. Then the work is finished and the same boss calls up the Border Patrol: Now I want you to come get these people out of here. That's when the bosses keep the workers' checks. We get paid on Saturdays and the Border Patrol raids us on Fridays. That was the bad part, that they have that arrangement. The Border Patrol never came when there was a lot of work. The Border Patrol knows that all of us up on the little hill are illegals, and every day they see us. Why don't they just come then? Now I've figured it out. I've thought about it. The bosses and the Border Patrol have an arrangement. (157)

For Vázquez, the raids are more than a coincidence because they seem to be made purposefully on the last day of work. Vázquez connects the need for migrant labor to the militarization of the border and to the treatment of undocumented workers. The raids benefit the agricultural sector. The migrant, in turn, suffers from the harsh conditions of crossing the border through the desert and runs the risk, once in the United States, of being caught by the Border Patrol before getting paid for work.

Baja California

Fidencio Vázquez narrates *Lo que estará en mi corazón* from San Quintín, Baja California. His narration tells of a community that not only has been marked by economic hardship and exploitation but also has the ability to mobilize itself politically. In the last chapter, Vázquez describes his involvement in politically mobilizing the Mixtec community in Baja California. The political movement, as described by Vázquez, grew out of the need to change the living and working conditions of the Oaxacan migrant workers in Baja California. In the acknowledgments, Crosthwaite also recognizes a variety of people who were involved both in the book and in the political mobilization of the Mixtec agricultural workers in Baja California. Included in the list are Víctor Clark Alfaro of the Centro Binacional de Derechos Humanos in Tijuana and Benito García Sánchez of the Sindicato Gremial de Obreros Agrícolas, Similares y Conexos (SIN-GOA). The collaborations are significant because they place *Lo que estará en mi corazón* within a greater political project.

When Vázquez and his family arrive in San Quintín, they live in a barn with animals. The family progressively are able to improve their living conditions in San Quintín and live better than they did in Yucuñuti, but they encounter other difficulties. One of Vázquez's complaints is that his employers shortchange him with his paycheck: "One time I got my check and it was short a half-day; to this day they haven't paid me" (158). Vázquez argues that the employers will do anything to save their money and not pay their workers. The employers also hire minors, depending on their height. Because of her size, Vázquez's daughter Leticia starts to work at the age of nine. Vázquez explains how children are paid: "On the Los Pinos ranch they don't pay the children the same. They pay them half, and they work the same as the grownups, and they give the children more crap so that they'll work the same as the grownups. And their parents don't stand up for them; they go along with it because it's a second paycheck, so they live better" (180). Vázquez argues that the employers will do anything to save money, so they do not buy new machinery for work or provide basic living necessities such as showers for the workers.

Finally, the last section of the testimonio, "Mi escuela, mis ojos," is a call to action. Vázquez sees the conditions in which Mixtecs live as part of the abuse against the workers. He blames the greedy ranchers for the poor living and working conditions: "They want all the money for themselves. Since they're already squeezing it all out of the workers, they want more for themselves, even more than they get from the workers" (183). Despite the division in the labor movement and despite the lack of attention by government officials, Vázquez believes that the movement has its positive effects: "But now the bosses are changing. That's the reason for the struggle in San Quintín. The same workers are now starting to stand up for their rights. Now even the most indigenous holds his own; even if he doesn't know how to speak Spanish, even if he only understands

Mixteca, he now knows more or less that the boss is cheating him" (184). Vázquez's testimonial calls for a social change that will affect his community in Mexico and the United States. His hope is that he can return to Yucuñuti one day to be with the rest of his family.

Fidencio Vázquez questions national identity and formulates identity by focusing primarily on the Oaxacan/Mixtec community. Survival in Mexico, as represented in this testimonio, is almost impossible, forcing Vázquez and other migrants to leave their home communities. Many of them have found work in Baja California or by migrating illegally to Alta California, but they must endure exploitation by the ranchers and dangerously cross the U.S.–Mexico border. In *Lo que estará en mi corazón*, although the migrants must face a variety of hardships, they also form a community that is politically conscious and is able to fight for the migrants' rights.

Migration and Mexican Border Literature

Rosario Sanmiguel, Eduardo Antonio Parra, and Luis Humberto Crosthwaite are three distinct Mexican border writers who write about migration. Taken together, the representations of migration in their writing differ from the nationalist subjectivity that Alberto Ledesma criticizes. They present the problems that propel migrants to leave their home communities, and the difficulties that are associated with the absence of a family member (usually a parent) who has migrated to the United States. The desire to migrate to the United States is less a lure of the American dream than a desire to compensate for what the home community cannot offer. All three writers distinguish between legal and illegal migration and between migration and transborder crossings.

In these representations, the borderlands are a place where a variety of identities come together. Baja California is the place where Luis Humberto Crosthwaite's identity as a border dweller meets that of Fidencio Vázquez, a migrant who lives in Baja California but whose sense of community is based on being Mixtec and/or Oaxacan. The border in this case becomes elusive, signifying both the processes of migration and the U.S.–Mexico border. Fronterizo writers struggle to define themselves within a centrist system that both promotes *la literatura de la frontera* and overshadows it. In this sense, the border also represents northern Mexico's self-definition as a literary and cultural movement. How are we to conceive migration within this context? Although the populations of migrants moving into the area and trying to enter the United States affect the border region, migration is not simply an issue of the U.S.–Mexico border. Migration is much more complex, involving originating areas, many of which are in Mexico's west-central region. Mexican migration must be considered a transnational issue, not just one of the U.S.–Mexico border, of the originating states, or of the United States.

3

Rolas de migración

Expressions of Mexicanidad

ONCE THOUGHT TO BE MERELY an import from the United States and Britain, rock music in Mexico is now part of the national culture. Some Mexican bands mix folkloric sounds with rock to make their music sound local, others do not follow such formulas. Although the groups presented in this chapter play different styles of rock, the ways in which they represent identity within their lyrics show that they use many of the old tropes of mexicanidad. Even though most of these bands call for open borders, Mexican national identity thrives within this music. The various groups are from different regions in Mexico: Tijuana, Mexico City, Guadalajara, and Monterrey. Each of the bands lends a local perspective and elaborates on what it means to be from their region, as well as how they identify as Mexicans. As I argue in this chapter, the migrant is an archetype of Mexican national identity within rock. In most of these songs, the musicians do not sing from the point of view of the migrants, because most do not have the firsthand experience of migration. Many of the groups include migrants as part of their community by speaking about them in the first-personal plural.

In the previous chapters, I argued that migration must be understood as a multiregional and transnational phenomenon that involves the migrants' places of origin, the U.S.–Mexico border as a thoroughfare, and the different points of destination. Through this approach, it may seem as though there is a clear dichotomy between Mexico

City and the U.S.–Mexico border; however, in this chapter, I wish to bridge the gap that I have outlined previously. Much like Mexican migration to the United States, rock music is a multiregional and transnational phenomenon, and it includes various bands from different cities in Mexico.

A History of Mexican Rock Music

Once considered an import, rock music has become a Mexican national product. Although the state attempted to control the influence of commercialism, bands in the 1950s formed in border towns to perform for American tourists. These bands copied American and British songs, sometimes performing the English versions of them, sometimes with adapted lyrics in Spanish. Soon after, the border bands took this music to Mexico City, where there was little knowledge of rock music. Eric Zolov in *Refried Elvis* credits border bands such as Los Dug Dugs, Los Yaki, Los Belmont, Los Apson, Tijuana-5, and Javier Batiz and His Famous Finks for the music scene in Mexico City during the 1950s and '60s (94). The scarcity of rock music as a commodity resulted from the Mexican government's high tariff barriers used to discourage distribution of imported goods. As Zolov argues, "The mimicking of foreign rock styles and intonations was not only an attempt to *belong* to a global movement; it also became an act of defiance against a cultural and political structure that limited and denied access to rock as (world) popular culture" (95). Attempts to restrict the music in its foreign form actually resulted in privileging the cultural memory created by the imports rather than the music produced nationally. Zolov further contends that the lack of commodified objects, the albums as well as all the memorabilia associated with the bands, has created a distorted historical musical memory. The "refried" songs initially lacked any political message pertinent to Mexico. Los Teen Tops, for example, translated Elvis Presley's "Jailhouse Rock" as "Rock en la cárcel." As rock music began to express the needs and desires of Mexican youth, bands such as Three Souls in My Mind, which would later become El Tri, began to reflect the nation's local political thought. During these early years, themes of migration were not prevalent.

La Onda Chicana, the Mexican musical and literary movements, drew on foreign music and English lyrics.[1] Despite the acceptance of these foreign influences, as Zolov argues, the musicians started appropriating a nationalist discourse. The band La Revolución de Emiliano Zapata used the revolutionary hero to represent social liberty. Other bands followed suit by picking names that were specific to Mexico. As Zolov notes, "In creating names and images that specifically made reference to the Mexican experience, these groups forged an essential psychic space for youth in which they could reimagine themselves as social actors among the changing, newly constituted reference points of national identity" (181). The music that used national imagery and symbols during the early part of the 1970s functioned by way of transnational companies such as Polydor (now Polygram). Zolov notes that commercialization in this case presented an opportunity to express ideas that were not necessarily in line with the Mexican government. After the Avándaro Music Festival on September 11, 1971, the state halted commercialization, because it was seen as a threat. It became apparent that rock had the potential to mobilize a community of people, and it represented a perceived threat to middle-class values.[2] As Zolov says, "The production and distribution of La Onda Chicana were immediately targeted by the regime. In effect, any song or image related to Avándaro was prohibited by the state" (218). Rock music was forced underground for many years.

Several waves of rock music had emerged by the early 1980s: middle-class bands, *los chavos banda*, and the teenyboppers. First were the middle-class bands, influenced by Argentinean rock and its musicians, Fito Páez and Charly García. Deborah Pacini Hernández and the other editors of *Rockin' Las Américas* explain: "This new generation of rock musicians and their fans had come of age listening to the *rock nacional* genre—both locally produced and imported from other Latin American nations, especially Argentina, Chile, and Mexico" (17). Second, *los chavos banda* from the barrios of Mexico City began to thrive in the early 1980s with punk-influenced rock music. Finally, the commercialized pop rock of Menudo and similar bands took the stage of *Siempre en Domingo* and other nationally aired shows. During the early 1980s, the state could no longer deny the influence of rock music in Mexico, so it created the Consejo

Nacional de Recursos para la Atención de la Juventud (CREA), which incorporated rock music as part of its programming. The state's transformation was accompanied by the support of intellectual circles that had criticized La Onda Chicana, and rock music was finally considered a part of the national culture.

The bands analyzed within this chapter formed part of a wave of music that arrived in the late 1980s and was consolidated by the 1990s. Many bands began mixing rock with Mexican folkloric music to varying degrees. In this chapter, I follow the path that Pacini Hernández and her collaborators in *Rockin' Las Américas* lay out for their collection of articles: "We find it most useful to consider rock as a template within which a variety of sounds and behaviors can be located and still be understood as a coherent category" (5). Although the bands here use various sounds and behaviors, they similarly use national tropes of mexicanidad and represent migration within those archetypes.

Mexican National Identity in Rock Music

Various types of music are associated with Mexican migration to the United States: the *corrido*, ballad, and *banda*, for example. Other studies have already explored how migration is represented in these genres, including María Herrera-Sobek's *Northward Bound: The Mexican Immigrant Experience in Ballad and Song* and Helena Simonett's *Banda: Mexican Musical Life across Borders*. In this chapter, I explore the topic of migration within Mexican rock music. Rock is a great example of how Mexican national identity can thrive in global cultural forms. As I argue in the introduction to this book, the nation-state and national identity work a step below globalization. Despite the transculturation that is evident in the sound of the music, the lyrics recur to old archetypes that reinforce national identity. Although this is not a typical form of music of migration and migrants do not produce it, the songs that I analyze offer complex representations of migration from within Mexico. Along with the first two chapters of this study, this present chapter seeks to demonstrate the extent to which migration has affected Mexican society from within national borders.

Josh Kun has been at the forefront of conceptualizing the flows of audiotopias, the space of songs and music, across the Americas. *Audiotopia* argues for a postnational model of understanding music rather than a nationalist one: "Popular music is, by its nature, a post-nationalist formation. While it may take root in national formations, impact national audiences, and impact the creation of national ideas and politics, music is always from somewhere else and is always en route somewhere else. . . . Music can be of a nation, but it is never exclusively national; it always overflows, spills out, sneaks through, reaches an ear on the other side of the border line, on the other side of the sea" (20). Kun's theoretical framework is based on the notions that *rock en español* does not represent a bounded national iden-tity and that transnational processes function above and beyond the national: "The identities the music both produces and is produced by, and the national spaces it both inhabits and travels across, together refuse conventional, bounded mappings of the nation" (*Audiotopia* 186). Looking from an inverse position, Mexican national identity is not lost within rock music. As a genre, rock music was nationalized in Mexico and no longer represents a "foreign" musical sound.

For many, the involvement of multinational corporations denies the possibility of a boundedness of mexicanidad, but commercial-ization should not and does not preclude national identity. Pacini Hernández and colleagues explain how the multinational corpora-tions cater to the local context: "Today, well-established recording industries located in major urban centers throughout the Americas— Mexico City, Caracas, Buenos Aires, Bogotá, and Rio de Janeiro, as well as New York City, Los Angeles, and, more recently, Miami— constitute multiple nodes of a transnational circuit of production and distribution, and are led by Spanish- and Portuguese-language media conglomerates such as Univisión, Telemundo, Globo, and Venevisión and supported largely with Latin American capital" (19). They also explain that these conglomerates "develop their media strategies with Latin Americans in mind" (19). Commercialization also occurs within Mexico and other Latin American countries.

Tijuana No, El Tri, Maldita Vecindad y los Hijos del Quinto Patio, Molotov, Maná, Control Machete, and El Gran Silencio are all bands that have recorded with major record companies. Commercializa-tion has not limited the ways that these groups have represented national and regional identity. As Pacini Hernández and colleagues point out, "Rockers have assumed their right to belong to the nation and thus have their voices heard as citizens" (20). Tijuana No recorded with RCA; Maldita Vecindad with Sony International, RCA International, and Ariola; Maná and El Tri with Warner Music Latina; Molotov with Universal Music; Control Machete with Polygram Records; and El Gran Silencio with EMI Latin. Their production has not limited how these bands use various tropes of mexicanidad. The Mexican rock bands question national borders, but only to allow for a larger sense of nation that absorbs migrants into the Mexican imaginary. As commercialized products, these rock songs tap into old tropes of mexicanidad that incorporate the Mexican population living in the United States. The migrant, then, serves as another archetype of nationness. These bands portray migration in two narrative voices from the third person, as those who have stayed behind in Mexico seeing their compatriots leave, and in the first-person plural, speaking about issues that affect the community as a whole.

Rock Music as an Interregional Movement

Mexico City is often hailed as the original birthplace of Mexican rock music, but recently fronterizos have reclaimed it as part of the transculturation on the U.S.–Mexico border. Jaime López argues that it is a myth that the *rockenrondero*, or the "rock-and-roller" (also called *rocanrolero*), is from Mexico City: "Just as there is alternative demagoguery and marginal autocracy, there is an underground centralism. This concept of the rock-and-roller is for the most part a myth of the country's capital city and its surrounding areas, which are always centralist. At the beginning, it was the north" (394). Whereas La Onda as a writers' movement was centered in Mexico City, La Onda the musical movement of the 1960s in Mexico was originally from northern Mexico and the southwestern portion of the United States.[3] Although the introduction of rock music to Mexico occurred on the border, Mexican rock from the 1990s is not centered in one city, at the U.S.–Mexico border, or in Mexico City. As seen in other chapters of this study, regional tensions have tended to divide Mexico. While these tensions are evident within Mexican rock music, I would argue that they are minimal because bands from different areas, including Mexico City and the border, collaborate in concerts, CDs, and in a variety of other ways. Whatever the origins of this music, it is now a multiregional phenomenon.

Rock music developed in many Mexican cities: Tijuana, Mexico City, Guadalajara, and Monterrey. Roco, the lead singer of Maldita Vecindad y los Hijos del Quinto Patio, explains the relationship between these major musical centers in Mexico as follows: "It would be difficult to keep demarcating the creative territory of rock in Mexico. I would see it much more logically to talk about a symbolic space, a symbolic territory instead of a geographic territory, because the truth is that an impressive symbolic territory exists through the great dialogue and bridge between Mexico, Guadalajara, and Tijuana that has existed for a long while. This is a symbolic territory, not geographic. Another symbolic territory that I see as very strong is, for example, Monterrey in itself, in its own dialogue, because they have generated their own movement" (Valenzuela Arce, "Roco," 204). I argue that the bands from these various cities have similar concerns about migration, but most of the bands presented in this chapter speak about migration from the perspective of their local context.

Despite the different regional backgrounds, the bands represent their regional and national identities in similar ways through various archetypes. Migration figures prominently in the imagination of these bands. Most of the songs criticize U.S. imperialism and the Mexican government corruption that affects economic and political policy. All the bands in this chapter tend to defend the migrants by telling about their hardships with *la migra* or *los coyotes*. They are, in a sense, defending those they see as part of their own people and nation. The various Mexican national archetypes, therefore, serve to reinforce borders between Mexicans and white Americans yet call for open territorial borders.

Migration and the U.S.–Mexico Border: Tijuana No

Because of the band's commercial success, Tijuana No traveled around the world and reached an audience beyond the U.S.–Mexico border region. Luis Güereña, the lead singer, explained to Frank Barbano of *Retila* that the band played in a variety of venues including Tijuana, Mexico City, Santa Cruz, Berkeley, San José, San Francisco, and countries in Europe such as Spain. Güereña comments, "In reality, it doesn't matter where we play, people of all places understand what oppression is. Most of our followers are in Mexico and California" (43). One of their concerns is migration: "It is very painful for us to see our people escaping from a land that is rich and literally has everything" (41). Güereña blames the Partido Revolucionario Institucional (PRI) for corruption and inability to correctly manage the country's resources in a way that would prevent the migration. As I discussed in chapter 2, fronterizos do not necessarily migrate to the United States. From Tijuana, most migrants tend to come from other parts of Mexico. Although the Tijuana No band members are not migrants, they strategically use their regional identity as a means to speak of migration.

According to Luis Rojo and Cynthia Ramírez, Tijuana is a privileged city in comparison to the rest of Mexico and other countries in Latin America because it is closer to San Diego and Los Angeles than to Mexico City. They argue that Tijuana youth have easy access to new music from the United States, but they do not acknowledge the fact that technology, especially the Internet, allows a wider access to music, making it instantly available in any part of the world.[4] Rojo and Ramírez assume that all the musical influences flow from north to south. Rock music to them is a U.S. musical genre, and they do not consider the influence of other Latin American bands. Josh Kun sees Tijuana No's connection to the United States as more ambivalent: "The identity of Tijuana NO!—which draws musical inspiration as much from U.S. punk bands as from local Tijuana crews—is not nationally constructed; as fronterizos, citizens of the border, they have a relationship to Mexico and for that matter to the United States that is highly ambivalent. To borrow a framework from Zygmunt Bauman, this ambivalence makes them strangers to national unities" ("The Sun" 108). Unlike Kun, I do not believe that crossing national borders causes fronterizos to question their national identities. As Pablo Vila argues in *Crossing Borders, Reinforcing Borders*, they are more likely to see themselves as different from the residents on the other side of the border.

Of the six members of the band, three are originally from Tijuana, but the other three moved to Tijuana from Mexico City at a young age. Tijuana No's music is focused on the social problems of a city located in the U.S.–Mexico borderlands. In an interview with José Manuel Valenzuela Arce, Güereña mentions that the philosophy of the band Tijuana No mirrored those of the band members: "It also applied to our philosophy: like Tijuana, rejecting all the baggage; or rather, Tijuana no to racism, to the gringos, you know, to the exodus of Mexican migrants to the United States caused by the centralism and the country's political system, all the misery that they must flee, and everything that represents the philosophy of the group" ("Luis Güereña" 129). As we see with the songs of Tijuana No, the militarization of the border and the anti-immigrant legislation in California are central to how migration is represented. Tijuana No's music is a product of its city of origin, Tijuana, a space where both Mexican centralism and U.S. imperialism are criticized. Tijuana No combines a variety of musical genres such as punk and ska, which originated in the United States, Britain, and Jamaica. Although the band is influenced by its proximity to the United States, Tijuana No's songs are critical of the United States, as well as its own government in Mexico. The release of the band's second album, *Transgresores de la ley*, with a cover invoking the image of Emiliano Zapata, coincided with the Zapatista protest in 1994. The third album, *Contra-Revolución Avenue*, deals with a variety of issues such as human rights violations and government corruption. The album is a post-NAFTA production released in 1998, which particularly addresses U.S. imperialism.

The imagery on the CD cover of *Contra-Revolución Avenue* addresses the relationship of the two countries through a collage of U.S. and Mexican iconography. The title of the album is strategically placed on a street sign to connect the album to the Avenida Revolución, a street in downtown Tijuana lined with shops for American tourists. Mexican Revolutionary icons Zapata and la Adelita are on the left side of the front cover. The collage also includes a nativity scene depicting Joseph wearing a sombrero and kissing a blonde woman, who looks like an American settler. Mary has a look of terror as Baby Jesus lies next to grenades and cigars strumming a guitar. The iconography on the rest of the insert is much stronger than that on the front cover. The Statue of Liberty rests on top of an Aztec pyramid, portraying Mexico as a country dominated by its neighbor. In another image, a white man with a sombrero fights a snake with a knife; here, Mexico is like a venomous snake vis-à-vis its white neighbor. The images of soldiers with their weapons, knights in shining armor, and Mexican revolutionaries depict U.S.–Mexican relations as combative. At the center of the collage, a specific reference to Tijuana, is a burro painted as a zebra standing in front of a mural. The burros seen on Avenida Revolución are part of the myth tourists have of Mexico and part of a performance by Tijuana natives catering to the tourists. Unlike most of the other iconography used, which refers to Mexican and U.S. national figures and imagery, the collage's image of the burro is a direct reference to the city. *Contra-Revolución Avenue* shows opposition to the tourist culture that is representative of the street.

Although Tijuana No's audience is primarily Latin American and U.S. Latino, "Travel-Trouble" from *Contra-Revolución Avenue* speaks to white, non-Hispanic Americans. The lyrics are in English and seem to target an audience that has the privilege to travel and may be the very tourists that visit Tijuana's Avenida Revolución. The song attacks the high culture ideal that an educated person is one who travels the world. The music that accompanies these verses has a quick beat with a fast, amplified guitar that seems to spiral musically. Güereña sings the lyrics in English without a trace of Mexican accent. The beginning commands its imaginary listeners to travel the world in any way possible, but it leads to a critique of the arbitrary differences between migration and tourist travel. "Travel-Trouble" changes several times to a quicker tempo accentuating certain stanzas. The first change occurs during the verse "No papers, no borders, no visas, no orders." Güerena quickly sings these lines almost in the style of a rap or spoken word. The song sharply criticizes the legal processes and documentation that mark national boundary lines: papers, visas, and orders. Whereas at the beginning of the song the commands to travel can be read more generally, the lyrics later point to a defiance of national boundary lines. The migrants are urged to "erase the lines, just escape." To mark another transition, the guitar switches from its smooth spiraling sound to a quick staccato that accompanies the percussion. By the end of "Travel-Trouble," it is clear that the difference between migration and tourist travel

is one of the limitations imposed by national boundaries. The critique stems from the relatively easy access of U.S. tourist travelers
to Tijuana and the militarization of the border as a means to keep
migrants out of the United States.

When Tijuana No speaks to the white U.S. audience, it calls for
open borders, but it calls for unity among Latin Americans. In contrast to "Travel Trouble," another song from *Contra-Revolución
Avenue*, "Seguimos andando," is aimed at a Latin American audience. This is evident from the first verse of the song: "Presente her-
mano latinoamericano." The song is directed at an "us" that includes
all Latin Americans and U.S. Latinas/os, forming a binary division
between them and white Americans, the gringos. The song is meant
to reclaim the right of undocumented workers in the United States.
"Seguimos andando" addresses the lives of the emigrants in the
third-person plural but includes them within the "us" of the pan-
ethnic identity. While this voice does not assume the experience of
migration, it sympathizes with the difficulties of crossing the border
illegally. A fast-tempoed rap is followed by the repeated rhythm of
a guitar that pauses between stanzas. The song makes reference to
the mythological space of Aztlán and an indigenous past, creating
a fallacy of an era in which national divisions supposedly did not
exist. The reference to Aztlán, though, is nationalist. The image of
the eagle and the serpent on the Mexican flag is a reference to Aztlán within Mexican national culture, and the Chicano Movement
claimed its right to the U.S. Southwest through the myth of Aztlán.
The song's reference to the past is a means to critique the legislation
in California of the 1990s aimed at limiting social services to immigrants. "Seguimos andando" is critical of the United States' role in
the creation of national borders because, as it argues, the country
has much to gain economically by keeping those borders in place.
This point of view is not one-sided; the home countries are also cri-
tiqued for the level of poverty and government corruption.

"Travel-Trouble" shows us that although the band may feel an
affinity to the rock music culture of the United States, it does not
completely identify with U.S. national policies or its national identity. By attacking national boundaries and the policies that keep
them in place, Tijuana No points to the need for them to be reex-
amined and dismantled. The call for "No countries, no flags, no

systems, no politics, no armies" from "Travel-Trouble" points to a critique of national boundary lines that control the flow of human movement. This specific message is aimed at the United States, but this call for open borders does not go so far as to be an appeal for interethnic unity. "Seguimos andando" points to a larger Latin/o American "us" and constructs a division between this expanded pan-ethnic identity and white American culture.

Tijuana No Jams with Kid Frost

In "Stolen at Gunpoint," Kid Frost, a Mexican American rapper from Los Angeles, raps a song written by Luis Güereña of Tijuana No. Fernando Delgado describes how Kid Frost empowers his Chicano identity: "Recovering and rearticulating Chicano cultural memory allows Kid Frost the opportunity to authentically reach out to his audience and community. Such resources also provide a foundation for representing Chicano as an empowered identity, willing and able to address the systemic inequities that circumscribe Chicano communities and create boundaries that appear to be less permeable than the actual border between Mexico and the United States" (399). Because Kid Frost collaborates with Tijuana No, Delgado's observations apply only partially to "Stolen at Gunpoint." Kid Frost and Tijuana No empower a community identity, but in this case it is not the Chicano identity alone. The boundaries here are permeable, and the community is articulated, as in the collaboration, in such a way that Mexican Americans and Mexicans create a cross-border dialogue between Tijuana and Los Angeles. These transnational connections are posited against the anti-immigrant legislation of the 1990s. "Stolen at Gunpoint," refers to the Mexican-American War of 1846–1848 to respond to the xenophobic legislation in California promoted by Governor Pete Wilson during the mid-1990s, such as Proposition 187.

"Stolen at Gunpoint" starts with the sound of a creaking door that changes to scratching, a rap technique produced using turntables. The bass figures more prominently than Tijuana No's characteristic angry guitar, present in its other songs, though the electric guitar is not gone altogether since it is present during the chorus. In "Stolen at Gunpoint," Kid Frost wakes up from a nightmare about mid-nineteenth-century Mexican president Antonio López de Santa Anna's loss of Mexican territory to the United States, a direct reference to the Mexican-American War. As the song argues, Manifest Destiny and the "white man's" need to control the territory are the causes for the tensions between Mexican Americans and white Americans. One of the verses declares, "We arrived here first" (Nosotros llegamos primero). The "nosotros" includes Mexicans living on both sides of the border but is more inclusive to a larger Latino and Latin American community. The song's chorus names the territories that were stolen by the United States: California, Arizona, Texas, Nuevo México, the Alamo, Aztlán, Puerto Rico, and América. The claim for land is a U.S. Latina/o and Latin American demand, which affects America as a greater entity.

Kid Frost directly speaks to ex-governor of California Pete Wilson and attacks the institutions that carry out the type of legislation he promoted: "Fuck the migra. / And the policía. / Fuck John Wayne. / I look up to Pancho Villa." John Wayne and Pancho Villa are two archetypal figures of U.S. and Mexican national identities and their respective political agendas. Francisco "Pancho" Villa was one of the leaders of the Mexican Revolution; he lived and fought in northern Mexico. John Wayne acted in Hollywood, primarily in westerns, and he represents a conservative ideology.[5] In reference to the music video, Josh Kun concludes: "'Stolen' is a fantasy of violent retribution for political injustice, in which the make-believe murder of Pete Wilson hyperbolically stands in for a desired end to legislatively sanctioned nativism and xenophobia" ("The Sun" 106). Although the song clearly supports the premise of the video as Kun presents it, the message goes beyond that to demonstrate that Mexicans and Mexican Americans can have a common cause. As this collaboration shows, the anti-immigrant sentiment can incite the youth on both sides of the U.S.–Mexico border to protest. They form bonds that connect Los Angeles to Tijuana and vice versa.

Imagining Migration from Mexico City

Mexico City's rock music in its inception ran counter to national culture, but it was later supported by various agencies created by the

Mexican government.[6] The bands El Tri and Maldita Vecindad y los Hijos del Quinto Patio are both from Mexico City. Released prior to the implementation of NAFTA, El Tri's song "Indocumentado" demonstrates the influence that migration had before the trade agreement. El Tri's style is based more on blues, whereas Maldita Vecindad is influenced by ska's shuffle rhythm and use of a horn section. "Indocumentado" and Maldita Vecindad's "Mojado" similarly represent Mexico City perspectives on migration, but they do so in differing ways: "Indocumentado" perpetuates the stereotype of the *mojado* who leaves his country to get rich, while "Mojado" focuses on the pain of those who must endure the loss of a family member.

El Tri, previously known as Three Souls in My Mind, participated in the rock movement La Onda and in the Avándaro Rock Festival that took place in 1971. As Three Souls in My Mind, the band lived through the impact of the government's censorship of rock music during the 1960s and early 1970s. Eric Zolov notes that the band was the only vestige of La Onda present in Mexican rock in the 1980s and '90s. The band's strategy involved "taking their music directly to the barrios and transforming their message to reflect the needs and concerns of an audience that differed vastly from the relatively privileged origins of the group's lead singer, Alejandro Lora" (Zolov 250). In the 1980s and '90s, El Tri flourished when the PRI started to support rock music. Zolov further explains, "The PRI not only liberalized access to rock but also directly sponsored rock performances, including those by the confrontational TRI. . . . Alejandro Lora, the lead performer, adopted the name 'TRI' for his own group, which went on to greater fame. The new name was not only a convenient adaptation of the Hispanicized abbreviation for the group—that is, 'the Three'—but a clever play on the 'PRI' as well, and it was used to great effect in their performances" (255). El Tri contested national culture initially (as Three Souls in My Mind), but came to represent it in the 1980s and '90s.

Although Alejandro Lora is originally from Puebla, the band is known for gritty songs that depict life in an urban setting, primarily that of Mexico City. El Tri has two songs about migration, "Chilango incomprendido" and "Indocumentado," but only the latter represents migration to the United States. Both songs were released initially as part of *Indocumentado* (1992), the album of the same title,

and on *Un cuarto de siglo* (1995), a compilation of the band's great-
est hits. In both songs, Lora's raspy voice is reminiscent of the blues.
At times, the electric guitar sounds much like the rock music of the
1950s, particularly Chuck Berry's style. While my primary interest is
the song "Indocumentado," "Chilango incomprendido" presents
an interesting point of comparison because it is about a man who has
left his hometown and migrated to Mexico City. The internal migration is described both as the result of need and as personal choice.
The migrant leaves his home for lack of work. After backbreaking
work in Mexico City, the internal migrant comes to reconsider his
old life back home as easy. "Chilango incomprendido" gives voice
to internal migrants, including Lora, who migrated to Mexico City.

In "Indocumentado," a horn section alternates with Lora's voice,
and Rafael Salgado's harmonica solo adds to the bluesy sound of
the song. The vocabulary of its lyrics is reminiscent of the youth
jargon characteristic of Mexico City. The narrator is a migrant who
has left Mexico City to find work in the United States. The decision to migrate comes when the narrator determines that he needs
to work, though he describes himself as a vagabond.[7] His decision
to move is influenced by his friends' stories of the American dream.
Migration seems to be a get-rich scheme that fails. The migrant
narrator repeatedly acknowledges that his plan to make money was
flawed: "The truth is, it hasn't gone well for me" (La neta me ha
ido de la patada).[8] The inability to speak English, the lack of a place
to go, and a longing for home and family make the narrator's stay
in the United States difficult. The migrant's only advantage is that
his light complexion has helped him avoid being caught by the INS.
He reminds the listener that migrants can be deported at any time,
and that although this migrant of the song has been lucky, it is still
possible to be caught.

The music in "Indocumentado" is obviously influenced by U.S.
musical forms such as rock and blues, but the lyrics are clearly biased
against migration to the United States and the migrants who decide
to make the journey. The ultimate message of the song is that only a
vagabond would decide to migrate to the United States. Lora's voice
clearly positions the imaginary narrator as a rocker. The rocker is
often thought to live by different standards from the rest of society,
as a "rebel without a cause" or as marginal. Because the narrator of

the song is both a rocker and a migrant, laziness and quick money-making schemes are inevitably portrayed as migrant behavior. This type of characterization of migrants has been commonly used in film and literature to warn of the dangers of living within the capitalist society of the United States. One example of this is the film *Espaldas mojadas* (Alejandro Galindo, 1953), which I analyze briefly in chapter 1. "Indocumentado" does not directly tell its listeners that a return home is necessary, as does *Espaldas mojadas*, but the implied message is similar since the only possible outcome is one of hardship. Although El Tri gives voice to the urban experience, especially that of the *rocanrolero*, "Indocumentado" seems to perpetuate national archetypes. The narrative strategy within the song does not acknowledge the real problems that migrants face within their hometowns in Mexico. While a culture of migration may exist, it is undeniable that many migrants leave because of the hardships that they face at home. El Tri's music has come to represent national archetypes despite having once been marginalized nationally.

Maldita Vecindad represents a popular experience. The band's "Mojado," from the self-titled album released in 1989, predates most of the material presented in this chapter. Roco, the lead singer, telling José Manuel Valenzuela Arce of his first encounter with the quotidian experience of migration on his initial visits to Tijuana, notes that emigration had not been as commonplace in Mexico City then as it is now. He explains his concept of the border: "I don't think of Tijuana as border anymore. I think the border with the United States now reaches to Chiapas, that it now extends into all Mexico" ("Roco" 202). "Mojado" demonstrates that migration affects those living in the interior of the country.

"Mojado" portrays the death of a migrant and is structured in two narrative parts: the migrant's departure and his family's discovery that he is dead. According to Kun, "The fatal border-crossing that 'Mojado' documents gives literal voice to one of the thousands of so-called 'silent deaths' that have occurred in the process of crossing the U.S.–Mexico border at designated border checkpoints" (*Audiotopia* 198). Although the song narrates the death of the migrant, my analysis of "Mojado" differs from Kun's because I see the song as giving a voice to people who must endure the loss of a family member. The song's narrative voice is ambivalent because it seems to be narrated by a woman but is sung by Roco, who is male. The narrator speaks to the migrant, remembering his departure, and recalls that her beloved decided to leave because he thought he would find a solution to his financial situation. The narrator describes her beloved's departure: "I saw you leave me / Now I'm alone, alone without you" (Te vi partir / ahora estoy sola, sola sin ti). The narrator must grapple with the migrant's absence, which unfortunately becomes permanent; two days after his departure she discovers that he has died. The narrator tells us of her loss as she continues to talk to the migrant: "You're not here" (No estás aquí). Her reaction is central to the song: "I cry for you" (Lloro por ti). Although she may not have been with the migrant, she is inevitably affected by his absence, which was to be temporary but unexpectedly turned permanent.

Maldita Vecindad's "Mojado" presents the feelings and emotions associated with seeing migrants leave their hometown and family and of enduring their deaths. Many of these migrants disappeared or lost contact with their families in Mexico. The use of a female narrator, sung by a male voice, simultaneously gives voice to both women and men who have experienced the death of a migrant loved one. This narrative strategy differs from El Tri's "Indocumentado," which carries a similar type of title. El Tri imagines the journey to the United States but cannot avoid perpetuating the old trope of migrants within national culture. Maldita Vecindad demonstrates that the people of Mexico City can also be affected by a migrant's death on a personal level. Although in the interview with Valenzuela Roco does admit that Maldita's travels to Tijuana affected how he views migration, he understands that those issues are now important to the rest of the country, including Mexico City. Maldita Vecindad offers us an insight on how migration affects Mexico City without using the tropes associated with centrist representations of migration.

Molotov's Anti-imperialism

Whereas Maldita Vecindad was popular from the end of the 1980s into the early part of the 1990s, Molotov recorded its first album, *¿Dónde jugarán las niñas?*, in 1997, and is associated with the musical production of the turn of the millennium. Fernando Aceves lists

Randy Ebright, born in Ithaca, Michigan, as a member of Molotov: "He was 18 years old, had just arrived in Mexico three years before that from the United States, and he had very little experience. Even so, he fit in well" (103). *¿Dónde jugarán las niñas?* and *Dance and Dense Denso* (2003) were both recorded in California. In 2003, radio stations were asking Universal Music for a version of "Frijolero" that did not contain the offensive language of the original, and this upset the band. In an article by Omar Cabrera, Tito, one of the band members, is quoted as saying: "We want the world to know that Mexicans aren't pro-U.S., even though we exist side by side, that we don't just go along with them. Ours is a clear anti-gringo stance. We know them to be the worst empire in the world." Despite the band's connections to the United States, Molotov openly voices its opposition to the country.

"Frijolero" is presented as a conversation between a Mexican and an American calling on each other to avoid applying ethnic/national stereotypes. The title is the Spanish translation of "beaner," a derogatory term for Mexicans. The accordion alternates with the semi-rapped voice. In contrast to the guitar and drums, the accordion begins playing in longer sequences, at times switching to staccato, accentuating the polka beat. The Mexican speaks first, trying to undo some of the stereotypes about Mexicans, and he complains particularly about being called a beaner. He also defends his reasons for his opinion about the United States. The Mexican points to his country's debt to the United States as one of the reasons for the uneasy relationship between the two countries. He also blames the United States for not taking responsibility for the U.S. demand for and consumption of illegal drugs. The American in the song is white, which is apparent from his accent in both the English verses and in his pronunciation of the double *r*'s in the verses sung in Spanish. The American is similarly upset by the stereotypes that Mexicans have of Americans: "Don't call me gringo, you fuckin' beaner." Instead of the song's resolving the problems between the two men, and in general between the two countries, the name-calling escalates. At times, it is difficult to distinguish between the Mexican and the American. In the first part of the song, it would seem that the Mexican speaks Spanish and the American responds in English in the chorus. Because both are calling each other names, however, it is just as possible that the Mexican is speaking as the American.

The Mexican describes the situation of the migrants to the American by speaking to him using the second person, "tú." The attempt is to make him imagine the hardship of the migrants, some of which is caused directly by the gringos rancheros. He asks, "Would you still call us good-for-nothing wetback?" (Les seguirás diciendo good-for-nothing wetback?). Much like in "Stolen at Gunpoint," the end of the stanza refers to the Mexican-American War and the Treaty of Guadalupe Hidalgo. By pointing to the Mexican-American War, the Mexican in the song attacks the United States, demonstrating that national borders are both permeable and mutable. "Frijolero" initially gives voice to both the white American and the Mexican points of view; but, ultimately, the song focuses on the negative stereotypes of Mexicans and the situation of Mexican migrants in the United States. The difference between the stereotypes of the beaner and the gringo, as presented in "Frijolero," is that the stereotypes of the beaner actually affect the situation of the migrants. Despite commercialization and the band's connection to the United States, Molotov's strongest criticisms in "Frijolero" are directly aimed at the United States. Molotov justifies the Mexican nationalist stance as a direct reaction to the United States.

Guadalajara: Maná

Maná is probably the most well-known band from Guadalajara and from Mexico in general. The group's official website once described Maná's history as connected to the underground movement of Guadalajara and Mexico City: "The history of Maná did not start in one of those laboratories in which future stars are created. On the contrary, its history started in the streets of Guadalajara, in the underground bars of Mexico City at the end of the decade of the seventies."[9] The website also attempted to disassociate Maná from the stereotype of pop groups such as Menudo that were created by the music studios for mass production, although Maná is a pop-rock band. In this section, I argue that Maná's portrayal of migration does not present a critique of political and social structures. Migration figures as a backdrop for the narratives of the songs and as an archetype of Mexican identity. The use of migration is a thematic fad and a trope of mexicanidad joined together.

In the July 27, 2002, issue of *Billboard,* Leila Cobo notes that Maná survives in the Spanish music market and resists crossing over to the English market like other musicians such as Ricky Martin and Shakira. Cobo stresses that Maná's commitment to recording in Spanish is a priority to the band, and she argues that Maná is not seeking to follow market trends. Although the band has decided to continue recording in Spanish, it still follows a specific mold associated with the pop-rock genre. As Joan Anderman of the *Boston Globe* writes, "Maná's catalog is filled with ska-flavored pop rock, which has earned the 10-year-old band frequent and apt comparisons to the Police" (D5). Vocalist Fernando (Fher) Olvera's voice is strikingly similar to Sting's, and the instrumentation follows the same type of logic: rock infused with reggae.[10]

Maná represents Mexico and Mexican national identity musically and with imagery. Although the tempo of Maná's songs is faster than the typical *ranchera*—a Mexican musical form that dates back to the Mexican Revolution—the particular inflection in Fher's voice and the use of acoustic guitars resonate with the musical genre from Maná's home state of Jalisco. Fher's voice may sound like Sting's, but the inflection in Fher's voice combines with the acoustic guitar sounds in "Te lloré un río," for example, mimicking the *ranchera.* In the music video for this song, the *ranchera*-style rock ballad combines with the black-and-white images of mexicanidad, reminiscent of classic Mexican cinema of the 1940s. The setting for the video is a peasant village. Fher dies and appears in a casket being carried by the other band members. The imagery invokes the Mexican archetypes of death and *el adán agachado,* what Roger Bartra calls the stereotype of the sleeping peasant.

Maná makes specific reference to migration in two songs—"El desierto" from *¿Dónde jugarán los niños?* (1992) and "Pobre Juan" on *Revolución de amor* (2002)—which are light ballads that narrate migrants' departures from their home communities for the United States. Neither of these two songs presents a strong critique, the migrant figuring more as an archetype serving the purpose of the love story. "El desierto" is written as a first-person account, and "Pobre Juan" is narrated in the third person. The focus in both

songs is the life of the migrants, the protagonists, and their experience of crossing the border. "El desierto" and, especially, "Pobre
Juan" combine a variety of synthesized sounds including guitar,
drums, and keyboard. "Pobre Juan" also includes a harmonica that
plays between each of the stanzas and during the chorus. "El desierto" is meant to be more of a love song in which the migrant bids
farewell to his hometown than an expression of the hardships that
may lie ahead. Because the song focuses on the farewell and not the
actual migration, it contains little criticism of the conditions that
migrants must endure during their journey to the United States. "El
desierto" reveals itself as dealing more with leaving behind loved
ones than it deals with the desert.

"Pobre Juan," in contrast, narrates the cause of a migrant's death.
The first half of this song tells of the departure of Juan, his need to
provide for his pregnant wife, and his dealings with a *coyote*. The second half focuses on his death. The narration presents a soft critique of
the possible involvement of *la migra* and the *coyotes*. The first stanza
describing Juan's death speculates from the family's perspective on
what might have happened to him. The second stanza offers a concrete scenario about the events leading to his death. The *coyote* betrays
him, kills him, and leaves him to die. "Pobre Juan" targets the *coyotes*
for their treachery. The listeners are given an insight into Juan's death
that even his wife is unaware of: "And María went to look for him /
but she could never find him / he disappeared" (Y María lo fue a
buscar / y ella nunca lo encontró, / desapareció).

"Pobre Juan," part of the *Revolución de amor* album, was released
in 2002, ten years after the release of *¿Dónde jugarán los niños?*
The ten-year time span between the two songs signals an increasing interest in issues of migration in rock music. Neither of these
songs by Maná is as aggressive a musical expression as the songs of
Tijuana No or those of most of the other bands discussed in this
chapter. Maná has reached a large audience, allowing the band to
promote a variety of political causes. The sentimentality of "Pobre
Juan" and "El desierto" makes use of the migrants' plight only as a
narrative strategy, with no critique whatsoever of the nation-state.
The generic use of migration as a theme coincides with the general-
ized form of national identity that Maná presents to its fans. Maná's
use of several archetypes of mexicanidad and its Mexicanization of

Police-style music demonstrate that national identity can persist within commercial music.

Avanzada Regia

Monterrey is touted as an industrial city and a commercial gateway between Mexico and the United States. Although it is not situated directly on the U.S.–Mexico border, it is only an hour's drive from the United States. Monterrey's rock music movement is called la Avanzada Regia, a name that alludes to Monterrey as a mountainous region, and its people are known as *regiomontanos*. The city has a number of rock bands that are nationally recognized and have international audiences. Control Machete and El Gran Silencio are both from Monterrey. *La banda elástica*, a California-based music magazine, explains the Monterrey rock music scene as follows: "Why did such a young and fresh musical sound so different from what was happening in central Mexico arise in Monterrey? Some hypotheses point to three central reasons: 1) the isolation of regiomontano groups from the rock scene of Mexico City and Guadalajara, which allowed them to forge their own personalities; 2) the influence and adaptation of the latest Anglo rock trends, given the pro-U.S. culture that dominates in Monterrey; and 3) the level of the city's economic development, superior to that of the rest of Mexico, which could have stimulated the birth of full-fledged rock bands" (Blanc 39). Despite the transculturation that is evidenced by the various bands' appropriation of American musical forms, the tropes associated with mexicanidad, particularly of *la raza* (the people), still appear within the bands' lyrics.

Monterrey is considered an important center for *norteña* music, a genre characterized by the use of the accordion and the *bajo sexto*, a twelve-stringed guitar.[11] Another musical genre important to Monterrey is *cumbia*, which also uses the accordion.[12] Both *norteña* and *cumbia* are being mixed into the alternative music produced in Monterrey. While the fusion of rock and traditional Mexican music is not new, some of the bands from Monterrey have used rock, hip-hop, and *cumbia* to make a local blend that is becoming popular internationally. Ed Morales in *Living in Spanglish* praises the cultural hybridity that is representative of the music coming from

Monterrey: "One encouraging aspect of the expanding hybridity of Latin alternative is its recent expansion into hip-hop (although some might say it's hip-hop taking over Latin alternative). A mini-boom of rock-rap fusion began in Monterrey, Mexico, by El Gran Silencio, a folk-hip-hop group that had long practiced break dancing and graffiti art, and Control Machete, influenced by L.A.-based Cuban rappers Cypress Hill, who have recently released an album of their gangsta rap in Spanish. Machete actually share a producer with Cypress Hill and have appropriated the defiance of the African American stance, transposing it to the Mexican point of view" (168–69).[13]

Both Control Machete and El Gran Silencio have themes within their music that are related to the U.S.–Mexico border. The idea that Monterrey is an industrial city with a friendly relationship with the United States may be partially true, but Control Machete breaks the stereotype. Control Machete's "Humanos mexicanos" from *Mucho barato* (1997) opens with a brief sample of a *ranchera*. The song uses the scratching of record turntables, a sample of a siren, and heavy bass to mark the rhythm. "Humanos mexicanos" is a response to U.S. xenophobia that holds the United States responsible for the deaths of the Mexican migrants. The reaction to the anti-immigrant sentiment is represented through imagery of gang warfare and words that imitate gunshots. Speaking directly to an imagined listener, U.S. imperialism itself, the speaker takes the identity of the Mexican residing in the United States and reminds the United States that laws and militarization of the border will not deter migration. The migrant belligerently claims the United States for himself and declares, "Your laws don't apply either in your house or in mine" (Tus leyes no me rigen ni en tu casa, ni en la mía). The similarities between Mexicans and non-Latino whites are underlined in the song by the repeated reference to being human. Mexican identity is reaffirmed as a reaction to the anti-immigrant sentiment in the United States.

"Únete pueblo" explicitly calls for unity of Mexican people of both sides of the border. The bass and drums come in before the first sample repeating the phrase, "México, ra, ra, ra." The bass, drums, and tambourine continue as the second sample comes in, and actor Edward James Olmos says, "La Raza, Revolution, El Movimiento." The claim to the Aztec past calls for a unity essentialized through a blood relation. Mexican national identity is counterposed with that of the United States: "It's our nation, not someone else's" (Es nuestra nación, no la de el [*sic*] de al lado). The rap continues to use other tropes of Mexican national identity: Pancho Villa, the indigenous past, *el charro*, and the Mexican Revolution. The two rappers call on the people to unite by repeating the words *únete* and *une* (unite) throughout the song. In two of the verses, they urge their listeners to unite with the movement in the same way that Edward James Olmos does in the sample.

By making reference to the Chicano Movement of the 1960s and '70s, which sought to reclaim the Southwest (specifically the land that had been taken from the Mexicans after the Treaty of Guadalupe Hidalgo), "Únete pueblo" calls for an acceptance of Mexican Americans as part of the nation. The song conjures up the clenched fist, one of the central images used in the Chicano Movement. "Únete pueblo" seems purposely vague in some of its references to Mexicans and Chicanos. The rap presents "an innocent brother" who was born on the wrong side of the border. We can understand this as a call for unity with Mexican Americans who were born in the United States or with Mexican undocumented migrants who are not afforded rights as residents or citizens in the United States. Neither group should be judged for having been born on the wrong side of the border. The references to *el movimiento* are reminiscent of the Chicano Movement, but they also point to a broader unity between Mexicans in Mexico, Mexican migrants, and Mexican Americans.

The title of the second album, *Artillería pesada* (1999), means heavy artillery. Satellite images of Monterrey are used on the inside panel of its CD cover and also within the computer program on the CD, which provides photographs and stories about northern Mexico and Monterrey. The CD insert and program also include a paragraph about the city of Monterrey. According to the CD's description, the heavy artillery referred to is not machinery but people. *Artillería pesada*, as an album, contains many references to migration and to a transnational form of identity. The song "Pesada" continues to elaborate the concept of people as a force of strength. This song is the first on the album, so it marks the tone of the production as a whole. Musically, "Pesada" consists of two looped samples that alternate. The bass is the one continual element that unites the samples and the scratching. Two voices alternate as well: one sings "Artillería pesada," while the other raps the rest of the lyrics. Control Machete emphasizes that the band depends on the artillery of the people, including migrants, who are described as extraterrestrials: "If there's local extraterrestrials / all visitors" (Si hay extraterrestres locales / visitantes todos). According to these verses, the migrant force is missed during difficult times, but their endurance and sacrifice is appreciated even when they are not there.

"Desde la tierra (Tercer planeta)," on the same album, uses the concept of a third planet to address a transnational identity. The song starts with a sample of an acoustic guitar that, along with a heavy bass background, is present throughout the song. The cardinal points are used to call up *la raza*: "To *la raza* in the north / to *la raza* in the south / to *la raza* in the east / to *la raza* in the west" (A la raza acá en el norte / a la raza en el sur / a la raza en oriente / a la raza en el poniente). In *La raza cósmica* (1925), José Vasconcelos argues that a new people were created through the miscegenation of the Europeans and the Aztecs, and the term "la raza" is used by many Chicano/ Mexican American activists and organizations. David G. Gutiérrez explains, "Although La Raza is a term that today has come to mean the entire mestizo population of greater Latin America, in the last third of the nineteenth century Mexican Americans often employed the term to describe the Mexican 'race' on both sides of the new border. Use of group terms such as La Raza varied widely from region to region, but given the historical heterogeneity of the Spanish-speaking population the use of such terminology by Mexican Americans to describe campaigns of protest and resistance in Texas, New Mexico, and California is remarkable" (35). The concept of *la raza* as presented in "Desde la tierra (Tercer planeta)" is of a community found in various places. Since Control Machete's hometown is Monterrey, it is easy to conclude that the use of the word "acá" (here) places the rappers in northern Mexico. Considering Control Machete's contact with the United States, specifically California, *el norte* can also be taken as the United States. Migration is presented as an integral part of how community identity is constructed. The "nosotros" is composed of a variety of people that are from various places and have different opinions, but the symbolic space of *la raza* allows for difference: "We speak different tongues / and grew up in different places" (Hablamos distintos lenguajes / y crecimos en distintos lugares). The song ends by connecting *la raza* to el pueblo. Despite the problems that *la raza* faces, the community still advances and manages to have some type of unity.

Although Control Machete's tone is combative, the band also calls for unifying forms of identity that include Mexicans on both sides of the border. Migration figures in Control Machete's songs as a transnational phenomenon, and it indicates that Monterrey and its inhabitants are closely tied to their *paisanos* who live in the United States. The artillery behind Control Machete is not military but "the people" on both sides of the border.

El Gran Silencio

"Con sangre del norte" from El Gran Silencio's *Libres y locos* (1998) expresses the band's pride in being from northern Mexico and presents two key elements to its music: the band's regional identity and its blending of genres. El Gran Silencio's regional identity and the use of *cumbia* with hip-hop and rock are present in each of its albums. Whereas *Libres y locos* was recorded in New York, *Chúntaros Radio Poder* (2000) was recorded in Monterrey and represents a return to the band's hometown. *Libres y locos*, El Gran Silencio's first commercial production, introduces the theme of crossing borders, but there are few references to migration and to the U.S.–Mexico border in comparison to the band's later productions. The only direct reference to migration in *Libres y locos* is presented within the list of social problems in "Decadencia." The migrants' economic hardship pushes them to go to the United States, "leaving their families, for want of money and imagination" (salen de sus casas por falta de dinero y de imaginación). Out of context, this brief reference to migration might seem to blame the migrants for their lack of imagination in resolving their need for money, but the killing of imagination by commercialization and money is a major concern presented in *Libres y locos*.[14] Lack of imagination is seen as plaguing not only the migrants, but also the rest of the Mexican population. The shift between this album and the following, *Chúntaros Radio Poder*, demonstrates the increasing importance of the theme of migration. (A *chúntaro* is a person of indigenous background with dark skin.)

"La chicana" from *Chúntaros Radio Poder* is a first-person musical account of a man who is going to California to reunite with his Chicana girlfriend. The lack of distinction between Mexicans and Mexican Americans is evident in the radio announcer's introduction, which dedicates the song to all of *la raza* in Los Angeles and all points in between. In the introduction and in the song, *la raza* is united across national borders. The song starts with an acoustic guitar, joined by percussion and the accordion. The first verse is repeated several times as a rap throughout the song: "I leave now for Califas, to see my Chicana, and I don't think I'm coming back here. But if somehow that happens, don't you know I'm gonna take her with me" (Ya me voy para Califas, para ver a mi chicana y no pienso regresar y si acaso me regreso yo conmigo me la llevo). The man must reunite with his Chicana, and he emphasizes that he will not be separated from her even if this entails returning with her to Mexico. The narrator plans to bring his girlfriend across the border into Mexico while transporting *fayuca*, illegal merchandise.[15] The narrator's necessity to migrate is not economic, but rather emotional. The union between the migrant and the Chicana represents a union between Monterrey and California. As discussed in detail in chapter 1, Doris Sommer suggests that the romantic novel in nineteenth-century Latin American literature served allegorically to consolidate the nation. In "La chicana," the romance serves allegorically to unite Mexicans on both sides of the border. The union is necessary for the song's narrator, who feels a connection to the Chicana and to the ethnic-Mexican community in the United States.

The song "I Like to Live en mi tierra" from the same album uses migration to deconstruct the concept of "America" used in the United States. At the core of El Gran Silencio's song is the reference to the lyrics of "America" from *West Side Story* (Jerome Robbins and Robert Wise, 1961). The Puerto Rican women singing in the film use "America" to mean the United States, as it commonly does in the United States. *West Side Story*'s musical styles are revealing as to how *latinidad* is portrayed. As Frances Negrón-Muntaner observes, *West Side Story* "perseveres in a long tradition of representing Latinos as inherently musical and performative subjects, ready to wear their sexualized identity for a white audience at the drop of a hat. Consistent with this history, the 'Puerto Rican music' found in *West*

Side Story is an American-made fusion of a wide range of rhythms with no discernible or specific national origin. In this sense, despite *West Side Story*'s dramatic elements, Latinos are doing exactly what they are expected to do, particularly at a time of significant racial and social unrest in the United States: singing and dancing the night away" (85). El Gran Silencio's "I Like to Live en mi tierra" hispanicizes the concept of "America" by changing the musical style to include an accordion and an acoustic guitar.

In the song, "América" is "mi tierra," a familiar space to the narrator. The reference to *West Side Story* is present in the first verse: "I like to live en mi tierra, I like to live in América." The accordion is of particular relevance because the instrument repeats the melody of the chorus and emphasizes it. The speaker is clearly a migrant singing a love song, presumably to someone residing within Mexican territory. The narrator explains that he struggles as a migrant to support his family, but that he is not the only Mexican in that situation. El Gran Silencio makes reference to the Revolutionary ballad "La Valentina," which contains the following verse: "If I must die tomorrow, let them kill me now" (Si me van a matar mañana, que me maten de una vez). "I Like to Live en mi tierra" changes that verse to show a clear preference to live in the United States: "If I must die tomorrow, let them kill me in English" (Si me han de matar mañana que me maten en inglés). This male voice is unlike those in the scene from *West Side Story*. In the film, the males prefer Puerto Rico to the United States in contrast with the Puerto Rican women, who are most comfortable in "America." Taking this scene into account, "I Like to Live en mi tierra" plays with the intertextual references by changing to a male voice. America is neither the United States, Puerto Rico, nor Mexico, but all of these.

The concept of motherland elaborated in "I Like to Live en mi tierra" is not synonymous with one country, but the places mentioned are of particular relevance to the U.S.–Mexico borderlands, particularly the sending state of Zacatecas and Arizona.[16] Arizona is the place where ranchers have further militarized the border, so the reference to it brings specific debates about migration into context. In a less combative style than Control Machete's "Humanos mexicanos," "I Like to Live en mi tierra" reminds us that migration still occurs despite all the attempts to block it. The song defies any notion of closed borders and presents an identity that crosses them: "I'm a citizen of the world. My life has no borders" (Soy ciudadano del mundo, mi vida no tiene fronteras).

On *¡Súper riddim internacional! Vol. 1* (2003), "Venadito callejero" continues the theme of migration, but the album does not contain as many references to migration as *Chúntaros Radio Poder*. The song is a *vallenato*, a style that was originally Colombian. Lise Waxer defines the genre as follows: "Performed by an ensemble consisting of accordion, vocals, *caja* (small double-headed drum) and *guacharaca* (notched gourd scraper), *vallenato* music is similar to *cumbia* in accenting beats 2 and 4, but places stronger emphasis on the crotchet-quaver rhythmic cell than *cumbia*." "Venadito callejero" has a rapid tempo followed by the accordion. The style of music is lively and unusual for a song about migration made in Mexico. The dedication after the lyrics of "Venadito callejero" in the insert demonstrates that migration is part of El Gran Silencio's community: "Dedicated to all my friends who left to work with the white man, especially Luis el Crudo (R.I.P.) and Gabo Montemayor and all of la raza that paint their colors on the city walls."

The migrant, as in other songs, functions as an archetype that includes those who have left for the United States. "Venadito callejero" is not critical in any way. The difference lies in the fact that El Gran Silencio does not use the Latin pop musical style to express these similar ideas. The use of the accordion, an important element of the *vallenato*, gives the song a more local feel. "Venadito callejero" starts with the quick-tempoed accordion and with the refrain, "se va" (he leaves). The song tells of a migrant's departure by emphasizing this phrase. The point of view of this song is that of someone who is seeing someone else in the community leaving to go to the United States. The migrant in this song leaves because there is no other option. This departure is frustrating but necessary. More than narrating the particulars of one individual's experience, "Venadito callejero" focuses on a more general story that affects all Mexican migrants traveling to the United States.

El Gran Silencio represents *los chúntaros* and their community in Monterrey who are faced with the prospect of migration. Although El Gran Silencio represents a transnational community, the group's music is focused on the perspective of those who are left behind as they watch their compatriots migrate to the United States. Like Control Machete, El Gran Silencio demonstrates that Monterrey is affected by the proximity of the U.S.–Mexico border and by Mexican migration to the United States.

Rock mexicano and the Tropes of Mexican National Identity

The bands discussed here maintain some of the archetypes associated with mexicanidad, and they have in common methods of absorbing the image of the migrant into a larger sense of nation. They similarly express the need to defend migrants from hardship and discrimination. The overlapping of national and regional identities also allows for local stories of migration. Tijuana No uses historical references—the Treaty of Guadalupe Hidalgo and Aztec mythology. Tijuana No and Kid Frost particularly place the immigration debate of the 1990s within a historical context that dates back to the loss of Mexican territory during the nineteenth century. El Tri's image of the undocumented is reminiscent of earlier representations of migration in Mexico that deemed migrants as *vendidos* or "sell-outs" for leaving their country. Maná criticizes the *coyotes* but not the mechanisms that push migrants to leave; instead, it uses the theme of migration as a commercial fad that intersects with the archetypal figure of mexicanidad. Maldita Vecindad, on the other hand, represents the pain of the family when a migrant dies. Molotov uses the stereotypes that Mexicans and Americans have of each other and places them in opposition or in dialogue as two people speaking to each other. Both El Gran Silencio and Control Machete unite Monterrey with the migrants and Chicanas/os living in the United States. Rock music may cross national boundary lines, and it is, as Josh Kun argues, part of a hemispheric movement. These bands demonstrate, however, that historical references still shape how they view the world, that national tropes still exist and can become part of a band's global commercialization, and that they are still imagining themselves as separate from the white, non-Hispanic "them."

4

Diary of a Macuiltianguense

The Transnationalization of Local Identities

RAMÓN "TIANGUIS" PÉREZ, a Mexican undocumented immigrant in the United States, wrote *Diario de un mojado* at the request of Dick J. Reavis, a journalist and editor for *Texas Monthly*. When they met in 1977, Pérez still lived in San Pablo de Macuiltianguis, a town in the state of Oaxaca. Pérez worked as a courier for the peasant leader Florencio Medrano Mederos, who was attempting to regain control of lands seized by agribusinessmen; Reavis followed the peasant movement as part of his work as a journalist and writer. After Medrano Mederos was shot and killed, Pérez and other peasants involved with the leader were jailed and tortured. Upon Pérez's release, he traveled to the United States to escape the persecution that he faced at home. Pérez was not one of the leaders of the movement, but Reavis discovered that the courier could write. He asked Pérez to write first about the peasant movement and later about his travels to the United States. *Diary of an Undocumented Immigrant* was published in 1991 and *Diary of a Guerrilla* in 1999, both translated from the Spanish by Reavis. In 2003, Arte Público Press published the original Spanish version of *Diary of an Undocumented Immigrant* under the title *Diario de un mojado*. In *Diario de un mojado*, Pérez describes his travels from San Pablo de Macuiltianguis to Houston and subsequently to San Antonio, Los Angeles, and the state of Oregon.

Both books are titled "diary," but neither provides specific dates for the events described (the usual hallmark of a diary). Rather, they are written in the style of testimonial memoirs. Pérez reconstructs past events—the peasant movement in Oaxaca and his migration to the United States. He recounts how he found work in each area and how he was able to manage in a country foreign to him. Pérez's migration is circular: at the end of *Diario de un mojado* he decides to return to Mexico. He speaks directly to the reader using the first-person "I," but the book is not merely an individual account of the author's experiences. Pérez also writes about his interaction with other undocumented immigrants, about his hometown's history of migration, and about how the migrant networks link people from his hometown, San Pablo de Macuiltianguis, to different sites in the United States.

Diario de un mojado describes a transnational community that functions in both Mexico and the United States. Pérez participates within a specific migrant network that is linked to his hometown. Transnational processes such as this make it increasingly difficult to place identity within a single national context. In this chapter, I use Pérez's diaries to address what some have called "postnational identities." In its etymology, the term "postnational" implies that we have moved beyond the national; the word literally means "after the nation." I argue that although global processes are affecting our daily lives, we are far from witnessing the demise of the nation-state and national identity. Arjun Appadurai provides a three-part definition of the term "postnational." The first refers to new forms of identity facilitated by the decomposition of the nation-state in a move toward a global order. The second involves the global traffic of images and information that contest the nation-state. Finally, he uses the word to describe "national forms that are divorced from territorial states" (169). In his definition, Appadurai does not assume that the nation-state is obsolete: "These are relevant senses of the term 'postnational,' but none of them implies that the nation-state in its classical territorial form is as yet out of business. It is certainly in crisis, and part of the crisis is an increasingly violent relationship between the nation-state and its postnational Others" (169). Appadurai would probably view Pérez as one of these "postnational Others" because Pérez "contests the nation-state," but I would like to veer away from Appadurai's argumentation. Although transnational communities may contest the nation-state, by using the term "postnational" we imply that the nation has somehow represented these postnational processes. In contrast, as Pérez explains, the indigenous groups in Oaxaca were never absorbed into the Mexican national imaginary.

Alberto Ledesma is one of the few academics who offer us a model that includes representations of migration within Mexican and Chicana/o literatures. Although his essay "Undocumented Crossings" does not focus specifically on the issue of national identity, the subject weighs heavily in his readings of the representations of migration. Ledesma explains his reasons for creating two separate paradigms based on nationalist subjectivity: "First, it shows what structural similarities and differences—major themes, metaphors, and symbols—characterize the way that Mexican immigration narratives are rendered by Mexican and Chicana/o authors; second, it demonstrates how the 'nationality,' if not the 'nationalism,' of the authors influences the style, structure, and/or tone of how undocumented immigration stories are told; and third, it bears out the terms by which undocumented immigrant identity has been defined and constructed by Chicana/o versus *mexicano* narratives" (73). It is clear that Ledesma is critical of any nationalist subjectivity. At the end of his essay, he adds a postscript that analyzes Pérez's *Diary of an Undocumented Immigrant* outside of the two paradigms that he proposes. He lauds this narrative for revealing "much about what it means to live as an undocumented immigrant in the United States" (93). Thus, although Ledesma does not address the issue of national identity or nationalist subjectivity directly within his analysis, his approach is telling because he removes the diary from any national classification.

Without the nation-state, transnational processes would not exist. Although several forms of identity are not and have never been represented by national imaginaries or the nation-state, we cannot forget each of the national contexts. Globalization works by way of the nation-state and not in spite of it. Saskia Sassen argues that the nation-state should not be understood in opposition to globalization, but rather in conjunction with it. Multinational corporations, for example, take advantage of the differences marked by national boundary lines.

This is precisely how outsourcing works: multinational corporations based in a given country take advantage of the fact that a product or service is cheaper to produce elsewhere in the world. My biggest worry with declaring the demise of the nation-state is that we risk forgetting the difficulties that migrants encounter because national boundaries do exist. Undocumented immigrants must live and work in a system that negates their existence but also depends on their cheap labor. They are in a sense invisible, because they do not have the rights that citizenship or even legal residence afford. Their difficulties do not start in the receiving country, in this case the United States; many are pushed to emigrate because their countries of origin cannot provide the economic or political conditions necessary for them to survive.[1]

Neither Mexico nor the United States represents Pérez's identity. However, to fully understand the *macuiltianguense* community, we must examine how it functions within both nation-states without being represented within either national imaginary. I place Pérez's account of migration within the context of other literary texts to argue that *Diario de un mojado* should be considered part of Mexican and Mexican American literary traditions. Although I am principally interested in how Pérez represents his community in *Diario de un mojado/Diary of an Undocumented Immigrant*, I also delve into the ways that lo mexicano is contested within *Diary of a Guerrilla*, which provides the context for the social and political unrest that Pérez witnessed in Oaxaca. In *Diary of a Guerrilla*, Pérez, of indigenous Zapotec background, enters into dialogue with the dominant discourse of *mestizaje* associated with mexicanidad. In *Diario de un mojado*, he demonstrates that his assimilation into U.S. society is partial and that he never comes to identify with U.S. national identity. Finally, I explore how Pérez's community allows him to function within both countries while maintaining his identity as a person from San Pablo de Macuiltianguis, Oaxaca.

Migrant Narratives and National Identity

How do you classify a text that criticizes both Mexico and the United States and refuses any national identity? Traditionally, narratives by migrants that describe their travels to the United States from Mexico are considered part of Chicano/Mexican American literature. Some examples are Daniel Venegas's *Las aventuras de don Chipote* (1928) and Ernesto Galarza's *Barrio Boy* (1971). *Las aventuras de don Chipote* and *Barrio Boy* refer to Mexican cultural identities, and they both describe the living conditions in Mexico that pushed Venegas's and Galarza's families to travel to the United States. Both are narratives which demonstrate that Mexican national identity is imagined outside of Mexico.

Las aventuras de don Chipote is a fictional novel written by Venegas, a Mexican journalist and dramatist who lived in Los Angeles during the early part of the twentieth century. Venegas published various articles and plays in *La Opinión* and *El Heraldo de México*. In the introduction to *Las aventuras de don Chipote*, Nicolás Kanellos argues that Venegas offers us a valuable text to understand Mexican American cultural roots. Because Venegas describes his identity as a Chicano, a term that when the text was first published in 1928 referred to a Mexican immigrant, Kanellos further contends that *Las aventuras de don Chipote* is a precursor to contemporary Chicano literature. Although *Las aventuras de don Chipote* narrates his migration, don Chipote decides to return to Mexico after becoming disenchanted with the idea of making it in the United States. Don Chipote realizes that the American dream is a romantic ideal that is not intended for Mexicans. Kanellos focuses on the Chicano identity, one connected to the immigrant identity, in the context of the novel, which was written and published for the first time before the Chicano Movement. Kanellos offers the novel as a precursor to Chicano literature, associated with the activism of the 1960s and '70s. If we interpret the Chicano identity as part of the Mexican migrant working class, we can also connect it to a Mexican national identity. Although I agree with Kanellos's placement of the novel within a Chicano literary genealogy, the novel should also be included within a Mexican literary history because it elaborates on an alternative model to Mexican national identity from that offered within Mexico.

Instead of a fictional account of migration, Galarza's *Barrio Boy* is a memoir of his childhood in Mexico and a recollection of his migration to the United States. Galarza was a Chicano writer and activist who lobbied for the rights of immigrants, particularly those dealing with farm labor. However, his writing reflects his continued interest in Mexico. *Barrio Boy* tells of Galarza's migration from Mexico to the United States during the Mexican Revolution. Galarza and his family leave Jalcocotán, a town in the Sierra Madre de Nayarit, and travel to Mazatlán, Sinaloa, and to Sacramento, California. Ledesma classifies *Barrio Boy* as a Chicano narrative of migration, but Galarza elaborates on what it means to be *both* an American *and* a Mexican. Although this autobiography narrates Galarza's incorporation into the United States, most of the narration focuses on Galarza's life in Mexico. He expresses his pride in being Mexican and Jalcocotano, and he describes how his identity is affected as he moves from one place to another, not just to the United States but also within Mexico. Galarza's account is a precursor to current representations of transnational communities such as Pérez's *Diario de un mojado* that are organized around town networks.

In comparison to Venegas and Galarza, two different predecessors of the contemporary migrant narrative, Pérez does not elaborate directly about what it means to be Mexican or American. When he does make reference to Mexican and U.S. national identities, it is only to criticize how indigenous groups or *mojados* have been shut out by the state. Instead of elaborating extensively on national identity, Pérez describes his hometown community, which is located in San Pablo de Macuiltianguis but also extends to the Unites States through migrant networks. Despite the contestatory nature of the text, *Diario de un mojado* should be placed within both Mexican and Mexican American literary traditions.

The Collaboration behind the Diaries

Pérez wrote the two diaries himself, but Reavis's mediation is present within the translated texts.[2] A comparison between the original and the translation is only possible with one of the two books because of the availability of *Diario de un mojado* and its translation in published form. In 1998, before the release of the Spanish original, Ledesma commented on the English-language *Diary of an Undocumented Immigrant*:

> At times, the translation by Dick J. Reavis seems too literal and one suspects that some of the nuance of Pérez's observations

might be lost in the process; for example, when Pérez states that "the people I encounter in the streets are all Hispanics, but meeting them doesn't give me much pleasure because a lot of them are walking around looking for work," it is clear that Pérez is alluding to *hispanos* (Spanish-speaking individuals who seem to be of Latin American origin). Pérez is not making any reference to "Hispanic" political conservatives, a connotation that the label has achieved in recent times, especially among Chicanas and Chicanos. Although the label carries political implications that Pérez might have not intended to connote, it is, nonetheless, used in the translation. (92–93)

Ledesma is correct in noting the implications of using the term "Hispanic" instead of Latino, the term that Pérez uses in the 2003 Spanish-language version of the text. The English translation of the title is also problematic from my point of view. The prefix "im" in "immigrant" points to the arrival of the migrant. *Mojado* in the Spanish title does not emphasize either coming or going; however, the literal translation would be "wetback," a derogatory term.

The editing process always presents some type of mediation, and this is visible even in the untranslated, Spanish-language *Diario de un mojado*. I was able to obtain the original manuscript that Pérez wrote by typewriter, and it is evident that some changes were made to the published version. For example, one of the chapters at the beginning of the published book is titled "Fugitivo," but Pérez originally called it "Corriendo." As would be expected, minor changes were made to correct some of the grammatical and spelling errors. Even so, the book—in Spanish as well as in English translation—retains the oral qualities that are present within Pérez's narration.

Reavis's involvement has been central in getting the books published. Without him, the books would not exist. Reavis sought the first publishing contract from Texas Monthly Press. When that press closed, he sent the translated manuscripts to the Houston-based Arte Público Press, which subsequently published both. Through Reavis's intervention, Pérez also published shorter versions of his story in *Texas Monthly* and the *San Antonio Light*.

Pérez takes his readers through his journey into the United States and shows what it is like to be a *mojado*. As Ledesma argues, "What

Pérez demonstrates is the particular way that undocumented immigrants see the world. Their actions are based on necessity, not fancy, and the way that they interrelate with others is determined by how much they are willing to reveal about themselves. Thus, undocumented immigrants are not necessarily suspicious of or hidden from everyone; they recognize each other. Moreover, undocumented immigrants, Pérez shows, help each other out, whether by lending each other money or helping each other find jobs and/or places to stay" (93).[3] Being a *mojado* is just one level of Pérez's multilayered identity. Another is his identification as a person from San Pablo de Macuiltianguis, and he tells of his hometown and how its networks link macuiltianguenses in the United States to those in Mexico and vice versa. Yet another dimension of Pérez's selfhood is his Zapotec identity. These multiple perspectives can only be understood in relation to the two national contexts in question, Mexico and the United States.

The Indigenous within the Mexican National Imaginary

Pérez left Mexico for both political and economic reasons. *Diario de un mojado* narrates his travels to the United States, but it does not go into detail about his reasons for making the journey. *Diary of a Guerrilla*, on the other hand, provides background on Pérez's life in Mexico and his motivations for seeking work in the United States. After the opening of a highway to San Pablo de Macuiltianguis made the area accessible to major timber companies, the competition became too fierce for the townspeople, and they slowly changed their way of life in order to survive. As Pérez recounts, "A time came when the pull of the land wasn't strong enough to keep people from emigrating. The first group went to California with the Bracero Program. Others went to Oaxaca City and Mexico City, especially the unmarried young women, who found jobs as maids" (*Guerrilla* 16). Land was the central issue of the movement that Pérez joined. In his foreword to *Diary of a Guerrilla*, Reavis summarizes how the *campesinos* lost the best land: "The chief issue of the guerrilla movement in Medrano's day, as Pérez explains, was the ownership of land. Mexican law at the time guaranteed the integrity of *ejidos comunales*—farms and other tracts of land owned, not by individuals, but collectively, by the residents of villages in an ancestral pattern that pre-dates the Spanish conquest. Yet the residents of such *ejidos* widely reported that land once theirs had been taken by agribusinessmen—most often cattlemen" (v–vi). The goal of the movement was to gain control of the lost land. In *Diary of a Guerrilla*, Pérez describes how he became involved in the movement and how he was detained for working with Medrano Mederos.

The biggest element omitted in *Diario de un mojado* is Pérez's ethnic background. Only the cover of the book explains that he is Zapotec, a member of one of the indigenous groups in the state of Oaxaca. In *Diary of a Guerrilla*, Pérez dialogues with the dominant narratives of mexicanidad, which posit the Mexican as one descended from the union of la Malinche and Hernán Cortés. This narrative casts true Mexicans as *mestizos* whose mixed heritage comprises both Spanish and indigenous (primarily Aztec) elements. (Octavio Paz's essay "Los hijos de la Malinche" in his seminal text *El laberinto de la soledad* [1950] elaborates on this archetype.) This foundational narrative omits the various indigenous populations that have not been incorporated into the imaginary of the nation and who do not think of themselves as Mexicans. In *Diary of a Guerrilla*, Pérez explains how indigenous people have been marginalized in Mexico: "Ever since the fall of Tenochtitlán, we, the indigenes, have been the fallen tree, and everybody—Spaniards, mestizos, foreigners— has made firewood of us, generation after generation. They made us take gold out of our mines so that they could rob it. The indigenous *campesino* was the rank and file of Don Miguel Hidalgo y Costilla and of Emiliano Zapata, but we were beaten after a few victories. Our people were also the troops of the oppressors. They had made us kill one another and we had come to a point of being helpless" (58).[4] Although the indigenous populations have not been incorporated into the Mexican national imaginary, they have been utilized in the service of national interests. In one of the meetings of the movement that was held at El Zacatal, those involved in the movement understood the loss of their land as continuing an indigenous history of dispossession. Pérez quotes Raúl, one of the leaders and later the president of the Association for Campesino Self-Defense: "We are Chinantecs, Zapotecs, and Mixe, the ancestral inhabitants of this land. Our forefathers were the owners of this land. We have our own customs, our own languages; we are the authentic sons of these lands. All we've been asking for are pieces of land inside our own country! Isn't that a bitter irony?" (*Guerrilla* 57). Raúl claims that the Spanish king in 1711 gave them entitlement to their land.

Pérez clearly does not identify with the way that Mexican national identity has been constructed. As a Zapotec, he believes that his indigenous identity has been omitted by the dominant discourse of *mestizaje* within Mexico. These exclusions, however, are not just in the realm of the imaginary. His people, along with other indigenous groups in Oaxaca, have lost their land to timber companies and agribusiness interests. Their lifestyles changed with the development of roads and the availability of goods that they once supplied for themselves. Many who were unable to adjust within their towns migrated to Oaxaca City, Mexico City, or the United States.

Diary of a Guerrilla describes how Pérez continues to be involved with the movement until Medrano Mederos is killed. Subsequently, Pérez is detained and tortured for being the movement's courier. In an e-mail to me of June 13, 2007, Pérez mentions that he left his hometown because of his involvement in the movement: "In my town, perhaps because they had not worked politically, my *paisanos*, the majority, did not understand our cause, and they stigmatized us as 'guerrillas,' but to them that was the synonym of bandits, crooks, thieves . . . and everything that can be considered a person who only deserves a place below the ground or in prison. My *paisanos* were upset because [it was] our fault the soldiers had entered the town. In addition, there was a General Assembly to determine what to do with us. Expulsion from the town." Pérez complains that the town's distrust toward him affected even his dating. He was engaged for a day until his fiancée's parents found out and disapproved. Pérez does not give these details in either of his books, but his life in his hometown obviously changed dramatically after he was detained.

Once he decides to travel to the United States, Pérez continues to struggle. The Mexican police along the border abuse migrants, as he describes in *Diario de un mojado*:

> To avoid being stopped by the police I have to keep company
> with thieves and maybe murders, who, oddly enough, enjoy

police protection. If the police stop me, I could argue that I'm a Mexican citizen, with a right to be in any part of the Republic, and I could point out that the police don't have the right to suppress my rights unless I'm committing a crime. To be a wetback, to go into the United States illegally, isn't a crime that's mentioned in our Constitution, but whether or not it is, it's not important. Here, he who's going to be a wetback, if he has money, will have trouble with the police, and if he doesn't have money, he'll have even more trouble. (*Undocumented* 21)

Pérez realizes that being Mexican does not naturally create solidarity between him and the Mexican police officer. This scene is similar to one described in Luis Alberto Urrea's introduction to *Across the Wire* (1993), in which fronterizos take advantage of people who are not native to Tijuana. Urrea argues that migrants are in danger of being mistreated and robbed, and raped if they are women. Pérez mentions that his jacket containing $550 is stolen as he naps and waits for the *coyote* to transport him to the United States. He understands that although he is a Mexican citizen, his status as a *mojado* makes him just as vulnerable in northern Mexico as he will be on the other side of the border.

Pérez in the United States

Once Pérez leaves Mexico, he must learn to live and work in a country that is foreign to him. His experience raises issues around assimilation and U.S. national identity. Samuel Huntington, a staunch opponent of immigration, views assimilation as a one-way process in which migrants acculturate to the receiving society: "Americans should recommit themselves to the Anglo-Protestant culture, traditions, and values that for three and a half centuries have been embraced by Americans of all races, ethnicities, and religions and that have been the sources of their liberty, unity, power, prosperity, and moral leadership as a force for good in the world" (xvii). From Huntington's point of view, U.S. national culture remained unchanged until only recently, when new waves of migrants began pouring into the United States. He argues that these recent migrants are reluctant to assimilate into the mainstream and that this challenges a stable U.S. national identity. Huntington's outlook is too narrow to include the variety of ways in which Mexican Americans and other minority groups define what it means for them to be Americans. As Nathan Glazer argues, "Assimilation still works; but today it works in different ways. More easily than in the past, it accommodates more than one identity and more than one loyalty. Immigrants continue to identify with the old country, its institutions and its politics. This is not necessarily cause for regret—for they also forge an identity as Americans" (73). I agree with Glazer to a certain extent, but how immigrants forge an American identity also hinges on whether they are accepted within the United States. In the United States, Pérez learns to live within the system by finding work, but he does not feel that he is American. His resistance to the U.S. national identity is not just a personal choice. At the end of *Diario de un mojado*, when Pérez decides to return to San Pablo de Macuiltianguis, he understands that his assimilation into U.S. culture and society could never be more than partial, even if he were to stay. Pérez comments, "At first it was hard, but afterwards, it wasn't so bad. Now it is time for me to return to Mexico. If I should need to return here someday in the future, I will come back, but only for a short time" (*Undocumented* 233). He decides to return because he is concerned that the Immigration Reform and Control Act of 1986 (IRCA) will affect his quality of life in the United States. The legislation is the immediate trigger for his return, because he knows that he does not want to become a resident of the United States. As an undocumented immigrant, he knows that it will be harder to find work, so his quality of life will deteriorate.

Pérez's integration into U.S. society is partial. He and other migrants are able to follow the demand for labor with the help of friends and family. Pérez works as a carpenter's helper and also washes cars, buses tables, and picks cherries. At the beginning of *Diario de un mojado*, his inability to speak English keeps him from moving outside of migrant circles. Pérez gradually learns enough English to resolve certain problems and to function at work. At one point, he is able to convince a police officer that he is Texan and not an undocumented immigrant and thus avoids being arrested or even deported. He also uses his English abilities to communicate with

white, non-Hispanic women. Although most of his attempts are
futile, he and his friend Miguel manage to spend a night with two
white women.

Mexican Americans are the closest contacts that Pérez has outside
of migrant circles. Some bilingual Mexican Americans, like the sec-
retary at the carpentry shop who translates for him, become intermediaries for him in the United States. Pérez makes friends with his
Mexican American coworkers at the print shop. Javier sells him an
old car for $100, which makes Pérez feel that he is joining U.S. soci-
ety: "I think that my feeling of contentment comes from wanting to
emulate Americans, and I haven't met one of them who doesn't have
a car" (*Undocumented* 108). While owning a car is considered an
American trait, Pérez is only able to obtain the car through a Mexican American. Pérez sees Mexican Americans as different from him
in some ways. He refers to pachucos as "low riders," a term normally
used to describe cars. The world of low riders is still alien to him, but
Pérez tries to imitate it. At one point he dances with a pachuca at
a bar: "Maybe she thought I was a Low-Rider because I was doing
a good job of imitating the *pachuco* guy, or maybe it was my plaid
shirt, which wasn't tucked in at the waist, or maybe it was my low
cut shoes" (*Undocumented* 116). In this exchange, Pérez's attempt to
imitate the pachuco signals his desire to be recognized as one.

While many Mexican Americans help Pérez, some impede his
assimilation into U.S. society. For example, toward the end of the
diary, a Mexican American police officer harasses Pérez: "I ask myself
why the Chicano is determined to harm me. I didn't really expect
him to favor me, just because we're of the same ancestry, but on
the other hand, once I had admitted my guilt, I expected him to
treat me at least fairly. But even against the white man's wishes, he's
trying to make matters worse for me. I've known several Chicanos
with whom, joking around, I've reminded them that their roots are
in Mexico. But very few of them see it that way" (*Undocumented*
215). Pérez starts with the assumption that because he shares cultural roots with Mexican Americans, there is a common identity,
but he discovers that this is incorrect. Ledesma rightly attributes
this type of confrontation to Mexican American attitudes toward
undocumented immigration, a much-debated issue among Mexican
Americans (93–94). Whatever cultural similarities Pérez may have

to Mexican Americans, he learns that they do not necessarily feel sympathetic to him.

Although Pérez does not identify with the dominant discourse of *mestizaje* in Mexico, it is in the United States that we see that he cannot completely disassociate himself and others from Mexico. He may not identify as a Mexican, but he is identified as one, and he identifies others as he would in Mexico. When he is with other *mojados* from Mexico, Pérez identifies mostly as an *oaxaqueño*, someone from Oaxaca. As Pablo Vila argues in *Crossing Borders*, the main classificatory system in Mexico is based on region, and thus differs from the racial/ethnic classification system of the United States (22).

Mixtec populations and other indigenous peoples have also established political and social networks that tie their communities in the United States to their communities in Mexico. Undoubtedly, the migration of these indigenous people does pose particular questions pertinent to ethnic/racial politics in Mexico, but indigenous migrants also fit into the scheme of regional identities. The indigenous identity becomes secondary because the indigenous migrant becomes simply "another Mexican" in the eyes of most people in United States. Jeffrey H. Cohen argues:

> A Zapotec who commutes from Santa Inés Yatzehe to Oaxaca City is an Indian and therefore faces an uphill battle for respect vis-à-vis Oaxacan society. If, on the other hand, that Zapotec migrates to the United States, he or she becomes a Mexican as defined by the larger Anglo American community. The result is that one identity is traded for another, and new kinds of discrimination are encountered once the migrant is in the United States. Nevertheless, the opportunities that are present in the United States do not appear to be limited by the migrants' local or indigenous ethnicity, and the Zapotec becomes "another Mexican." (70)

Although the indigenous identity is transformed in the United States, many indigenous migrants maintain their local regional identities.[5]

In *Diario de un mojado*, Pérez uses the regional system of classification to identify other Mexican undocumented immigrants. He notices the regional diversity of the people in a group of *mojados* waiting for the *coyote* to transport them to the United States: "Most of them are from the northern part of Mexico, although there are a few of us from the south, from Oaxaca, Morelos, Puebla, Chiapas, Tabasco and Mexico City. Everybody is headed for a different place, some to Houston, Dallas, Florida, and Chicago" (*Undocumented* 26). Classifying other Mexicans by their region of origin circumscribes the Mexican identity. Although the migrants are physically located outside of Mexican national territory, they maintain the regional system of classification and identification. In distinguishing between Mexican nationals from different regions, Pérez both demonstrates a familiarity with other Mexicans and marks a difference from them.

Pérez identifies with others in his situation, even when they are other Latin Americans who are not Mexican. He interacts with Central Americans, Argentines, and Cubans. He cannot completely discard national identities, and he does refer to his friends by their national origin. Their national backgrounds do not cause the kind of friction that he experiences with some Mexican Americans, however. All the Latin American migrants, whether from Mexico or other countries, are able to communicate with each other in Spanish. National identity is not completely absent within *Diario de un mojado*, but Pérez can identify with a variety of people, most of them *mojados* like himself. This position allows him to criticize the situations that *mojados* of different nationalities must face both in the United States and in Mexico.

His most extensive and complex interactions are with others from his town of origin, San Pablo de Macuiltianguis. The author's nickname, "Tianguis," a shortened version of his town's name, is a clear reminder of this identity. The connection to his hometown goes beyond identification as he uses his contacts from Oaxaca to circulate within the United States. Pérez's *paisanos* from Oaxaca offer him opportunities to travel to Houston and Los Angeles. They help him find work and a place to live. The concept of community in the diary, therefore, connotes a network of relationships and not merely a town or a place. The case of Macuiltianguis can be compared to that of Aguililla, Michoacán, a town studied by Roger Rouse:

> Through the continuous circulation of people, money, goods, and information, the various settlements have become so closely

woven together that, in an important sense, they have come to constitute a single community spread across a variety of sites, something I refer to as a "transnational migrant circuit." Although the Aguilillan case undoubtedly has its local peculiarities, there is evidence that such arrangements are becoming increasingly important in the organization of Mexican migration to the United States. Just as capitalists have responded to the new forms of economic internationalism by establishing transnational corporations, so workers have responded by creating transnational circuits. (254)

Pérez never identifies completely with the United States, but he gradually incorporates himself into U.S. society by working and living there. He identifies most closely with others who are like him: undocumented immigrants and others from his hometown. If we follow Huntington's notion of assimilation, we cannot say that Pérez fully assimilates into U.S. society. However, scholars such as Glazer have redefined the concept to accommodate the growing need to express multiple national identities. As Robert Courtney Smith argues, "Being more transnational does not necessarily mean being less assimilated" (8). Indeed, it is Pérez's continuing connection to his hometown that allows him to build a new life in the United States. Pérez provides two perspectives on how migration affects his community, defined as Oaxacans and macuiltianguenses, in the multiple sites where they live. On one hand, he describes the impact of migration on San Pablo de Macuiltianguis, a town where there has been a constant movement of people for decades. On the other hand, he provides rich details of how migrant networks function within the United States.

San Pablo de Macuiltianguis and the Culture of Migration

Migration is at the heart of life in San Pablo de Macuiltianguis. The town has a history of migration: "For several decades, Macuiltianguis— that's the name of my village—has been an emigrant village, and our people have spread out like the roots of a tree under the earth, looking for sustenance. My people have had to emigrate to survive"

(*Undocumented* 12). The imagery of the tree roots illustrates the search for sustenance, but it also symbolizes the grounding of the town's identity despite the movement of its people. In this sense, Pérez's description supports Rouse's notion that the space of the community extends outside the geographic location of the town even as it remains tied to that location. Pérez explains that the migration tradition has extended through generations: "One could even say that we're a village of wetbacks. A lot of people, nearly the majority, have gone, come back, and returned to the country to the north; almost all of them have held in their fingers the famous greed bills that have jokingly been called 'green cards'—immigrants cards—for generations" (*Undocumented* 12). Pérez's description points to a tradition of circular migration in which migrants eventually return to their hometowns, only to leave again.

Diario de un mojado includes chapters that describe the town's customs and holiday celebrations, making clear that migration is a part of the town's way of life. Pérez narrates the chapter titled "Navidad" from San Antonio as he imagines the Christmas celebrations at home. He recalls how his hometown fills up with returning migrants who arrive to spend the holidays with their relatives in San Pablo de Macuiltianguis: "During the season, the village fills with the people who have gone off to live in Oaxaca City, Mexico City and other parts of Mexico. Others come from Los Angeles, just to spend the holidays. We also see new faces, of people not born in the village, the children of parents who long ago left to seek adventure in the cities" (*Undocumented* 129). After the holidays, the exodus of the emigrants is dramatic, leaving an empty town. Only children and the very old remain, left behind by an emigrant population composed mainly of younger adults.

Although these people migrate because of financial need, Pérez's descriptions also lend support to the notion that a culture of migration exists. Writing of the Mexican state of Zacatecas, William Kandel and Douglas S. Massey explain: "As migratory behavior extends throughout a community, it increasingly enters the calculus of conscious choice and eventually becomes normative. Young people who grow up and come of age increasingly expect to migrate internationally in the course of their lives" (982). Pérez's description of San Pablo de Macuiltianguis follows this pattern. Kandel and Massey argue that the probability of migration rises dramatically if there is a family history of it, and indeed, Pérez's father traveled to the United States before him.[6] Pérez repeatedly compares his life in the United States to his father's. In "De tal palo, tal astilla," Pérez is having difficulty finding a job. All he has are a few coins, not enough to buy food. He remembers one of his father's stories of being hungry as he attempted to cross the border. His father found himself stranded without money or the promise of work when the *coyote* he hired was killed. Pérez recounts his father's hardship: "The money they had wasn't enough for either hiring another *coyote* or for returning home. Soon they didn't have enough to pay the room in the boardinghouse where they were staying. Upon seeing them in such straits, the woman who owned the place softened her heart and let them sleep in a corner of her entryway" (*Undocumented* 68). His father was left without food to survive and had to depend on the kindness of other migrants.

By comparing his father's hardships to his own, Pérez reveals that he is not on a naive search for the American dream; rather, he is well aware that his migration may not necessarily be profitable and that he may encounter discrimination. Pérez does not say how his family functioned during the times when his father was away in the United States. He briefly mentions that his mother considered his father's migrations as "tiempos malos" and hated hearing even a mention of "el norte" (*Mojado* 84). From this comment, we do not know whether she felt that they were "bad times" because of what her husband had to endure, but it is probable that she had to manage the household by herself while he was gone. Nor do we know when the father worked in the United States, whether he was single or married, and whether his children were already born when he left. Pérez himself never expresses any resentment about living in a household without the father present. His references to his father's migration suggest that Pérez's own journey was motivated by a culture in which migration is seen as an essential part of life in the family and the town.

Macuiltianguenses in the United States

Diario de un mojado's depiction of the macuiltianguense migrant network supports Rouse's assertion that community functions through a series of relations rather than within a specific geographic region. After his initial arrival in Houston, Pérez travels to California, knowing that his uncle will be a source of support. The ways in which the macuiltianguense community interacts are more obvious toward the end of the diary, when Pérez moves to California and comes into contact with a significant number of people from his hometown. Despite migration, the macuiltianguenses are able to maintain ties to their *paisanos* on both sides of the border. The title of one of the chapters, "La parra internacional," explains how this community operates. In California alone, there are macuiltianguenses in Los Angeles, Santa Monica, Santa Barbara, El Monte, San Fernando, San Gabriel, Glendale, Rosemead, Hollywood, North Hollywood, and Encino. As an undocumented new arrival, Pérez depends heavily on help from this established community, which includes some who have lived in the United States for long periods and have become legal residents and U.S. citizens. Although Pérez is able to identify with other *mojados* of various regional and national backgrounds through the shared experience of being undocumented, the macuiltianguense identity does not hinge on legal status. Instead, this community functions through the connection to San Pablo de Macuiltianguis, their hometown.

In California, Pérez moves within migrant circles. His most significant hometown connection is his uncle, who has been in the United States for fifteen years. The uncle takes Pérez into his house and offers him advice on how to live and work in the United States. The uncle is married but his family does not live with him, so his house serves to accommodate newcomers, mostly single males. Pérez lives with three of his *paisanos*, Antonio, Rubén, and Benjamín. He describes the benefits of group living: "We rent big apartments so that four to ten people can live in them, and so as to save money on rent and be able to save money for our returns. It is also so that we can be in a position to help other arriving townsmen" (*Undocumented* 153). The money the men save by living collectively is sent back to San Pablo de Macuiltianguis. As the elder of the group, the uncle offers advice on how to find employment, and the first piece of advice that he gives Pérez is to take English classes. Although Pérez finds it difficult to learn the language, he progressively benefits from his English-speaking skills. The uncle also takes Pérez to a carwash, where he finds his first job in California.

Although Pérez moves mostly within male migrant circles, some women have begun to migrate from San Pablo de Macuiltianguis as well. Pérez describes two of the female migrants: "One has made her home in Los Angeles and now has children who are grown and married. The second, by twists of fate, has wound up living in Tijuana; it is she upon whom the duty falls of helping townsmen who arrive at the border to find *coyotes* who will take them north to Los Angeles" (*Undocumented* 164). The woman in Tijuana is instrumental to the macuiltianguenses who are trying to cross the border. In this manner, she participates within the transnational migrant circuit and is a key link for its continuation. According to Pérez, after these two women came to the United States, other women decided to follow. Many of them had primarily worked in Mexico City as maids. Their move to the United States did not change the type of work they performed, but it represented an increase in salary. This reference to the migrant women offers a limited perspective on female involvement in the process of migration. From Pérez's description, we do not know whether these women came alone or joined husbands who were already living in the United States.[7]

Although Pérez decides to work in the United States temporarily and does not seek to legalize his status, the community of macuiltianguenses also includes legal residents. They legalize their status through a variety of means, including marrying someone who is already documented and using the amnesty provision of IRCA. This group's lifestyles reflect their stable employment: many own their own homes and some even have rental properties. Although the legal residents have severed many of their ties to their hometown, Pérez still includes them as part of the community. This is apparent in his description of the migrants who have children born in the United States: "These townsmen no longer plan to return to Mexico. Their families have grown and their children are attending American public schools. Aside from the family of the first woman who came, the first American citizen to be the child of wetbacks is a young man who is now twenty years old" (*Undocumented* 165). Pérez calls the young man "the first son of mojados." As I argued previously, Pérez does not feel an affinity with many Mexican Americans because he feels that they deny their roots, but in this case the young man is still identified with the *mojado* identity. Despite changes in legal status, permanent settlement, and their children's births in the United States, these established migrants still form part of the macuiltianguense community.

Pérez benefits from the help that his *paisanos* offer, and he is able to help others in turn. At one point Rubén and Benjamín, his two housemates, are caught by *la migra* in Los Angeles and deported to Tijuana. The others who live in the house, including Pérez and his uncle, gather money to pay a *coyote* to bring them back. Pérez also supports his friends and coworkers when they file a claim against the owner of a restaurant because they feel that they are not being paid adequately. Finally, when Pérez decides to return to his hometown, he continues to contribute to the network by recommending one of his *paisanos* to replace him at the restaurant where he is employed. Pérez also carries home several money orders sent by the migrants to their families in San Pablo de Macuiltianguis.

The macuiltianguenses are inextricably linked, and the migrants circulate information about their town. Pérez notes, "Everything that happens in the village is immediately known, since all of us have telephones in our apartments or at work" (*Undocumented* 164). The comings and goings of the macuiltianguenses facilitate the network. Those arriving from Mexico inform the others of the latest news in the town, and those returning to Mexico take money and goods sent by those in the United States. The macuiltianguenses in the United States also form an organization that they call Organización Pro-Ayuda a Macuiltianguis (OPAM). Like other migrant organizations, OPAM contributes to the town in a systematic manner.[8] It collects funds to buy a projector for the town, to support children and the elderly still living there, and to sponsor the annual festivities for Saint Paul, the town's patron saint. Being a macuiltianguense makes one part of a system of relations that involves the town but is not limited to its geographical area. The concept of community includes macuiltianguenses in a variety of sites.

Toward a (Trans)national Reading

Pérez's community and identity can be considered postnational as Arjun Appadurai defines it. However, as I discussed, the "post" in "postnational" may lead us to believe, erroneously, that the nation-state has been dismantled. Even Appadurai, a proponent of the concept, does not make such a claim. Globalization does not have to mean the demise of the nation-state. As Saskia Sassen argues, globalization and the nation-state can coexist. Despite its persistence, the nation-state's breaks and discontinuities result in the exclusion of various groups—in Pérez's case, the indigenous and the undocumented. It would be wrong to consider these processes as postnational ("after the nation") because these indigenous communities were never absorbed into either the Mexican or the U.S. national imaginary.

Pérez openly criticizes Mexican national identity because it is constructed on the concept of *mestizaje*, which is based in turn on the union between la Malinche and Cortés. Zapotecs as well as the other indigenous populations in Oaxaca understand that they are the original inhabitants of the land that has been taken from them. In the United States, Pérez learns to live within the system by finding work, but he does not feel that he is American. His resistance to the U.S. national identity is not just a personal choice. Pérez decides to leave the United States when IRCA is implemented, because he knows that being an undocumented immigrant will become more difficult with the restrictions of the bill.

Read together, *Diary of a Guerrilla* and *Diario de un mojado* offer us a glimpse into the workings of a transnational community. Pérez's local identity comes to represent him and others from his hometown, but the people of San Pablo de Macuiltianguis live within multiple sites. In this context, community is more than a town or geographic space: it functions as a system of relations. The space of this community extends from Mexico to the United States, connecting the hometown in Oaxaca to the various locations where macuiltianguenses live in the United States. It connects people beyond national borders, yet the national contexts—Mexico and the United States—have not disappeared.

5

Artistic Migrations

Mexican Filmmakers Go to Hollywood

AT THE 2007 GOLDEN GLOBE AWARDS, California governor Arnold Schwarzenegger presented the award for best motion picture drama to director Alejandro González Iñárritu for *Babel* (2006). As Schwarzenegger handed the award and the microphone over to González Iñárritu, the director responded, "I swear I have my papers in order, Governor! I swear!" With this single comment, González Iñárritu simultaneously signaled his identification with the Mexican migrant community in the United States and his disapproval of the governor's anti-immigrant legislation in California. *Babel* focuses one of its stories on an undocumented woman and her plight crossing the border trying to return to the United States. González Iñárritu's presence at the ceremony and at the Academy Awards was telling of his position as a Mexican director working in Hollywood. Along with Alfonso Cuarón and Guillermo del Toro, who were also nominated for awards that year, González Iñárritu occupies a space as a director of both Mexican and Hollywood films. As I argue in this chapter, this group of filmmakers has created its own brand of Mexican cinema that survives outside of Mexican territorial boundaries; they are traveling directors creating films about migration. Like *Babel*, Cuarón's *Children of Men* (2006) focuses on the theme of migration; however, the story is set in England many years into the future. From these similarities, the two films then diverge. Whereas *Babel* represents Mexican national identity as part of the web of globalization, *Children of Men* criticizes the British nation-state but presents a broader third-world identity.

The previous chapter primarily analyzed Ramón "Tianguis" Pérez's *Diario de un mojado* and argued that Pérez, as a macuiltianguense and a Zapotec, does not identify with either Mexican or U.S. national identities. Pérez travels to the United States as an undocumented immigrant, and the hardships that he faces there are due to his undocumented status. In the present chapter, I switch focus from economic migration to artistic migration, by which I mean the movement across national borders for the advancement of the arts, in this case, film. This type of migration is also motivated by economic reasons: these artists leave their country to advance their careers. Despite the differences in their works, González Iñárritu and Cuarón both imagine the lives of undocumented migrants.

Directors across Borders

González Iñárritu, Cuarón, and del Toro are only the latest in a long line of Mexican film workers in Hollywood. This movement of workers started early on in Mexico, because the Mexican film industry depended on technology from other countries. Louis and Auguste Lumière, the French film pioneers, were responsible for the initial entry of filmmaking in Mexico. Hollywood later became the model for the Mexican industry as well as a source of funding and talent from which to draw. As Charles Ramírez Berg argues, the connection between Mexico and the United States was solidified during Mexico's golden age of the 1940s: "To the United States, Mexico was a profitable market and a model of capitalistic growth in Latin America. To Hollywood, Mexico was a steady consumer of motion pictures, film equipment, and technology as well as an attractive business partner. In 1943, for example, RKO entered into a relationship with Mexican filmmaking concerns to create Churubusco film studios, the most modern film production facilities in Latin America. Thus, Mexican filmmaking was both exploited and exploiter, dependent on Hollywood just as Latin America was dependent on it" (15). Such connections apply to labor via the migration of actors, directors, editors, screenwriters, and other film workers. The demarcation lines of the Mexican cinema industry have been blurred with the movement of film workers from Mexico to the United States and back.[1]

Mexican cinema was a transnational enterprise from its inception, but we are only now beginning to conceptualize how these transnational flows (re)define the genre. Emilio Fernández, the emblematic figure of the golden age, is an example of the lack of theorization about these flows. As Dolores Tierney argues, "There are no existing studies which sufficiently acknowledge the intersection of the transnational and the local, or the national in Fernández' work" (3). Like his contemporary counterparts, Fernández moved across borders, acting and directing in both Mexican and Hollywood films, taking his expertise garnered in Hollywood to Mexico. The current wave of Mexican film directors in Hollywood should not be understood as a new phenomenon. As Sergio de la Mora notes, "These traveling directors move mostly between Mexico and the United States. They follow the tracks of other Mexicans who have left their mark in Hollywood, including legendary figures of the classic Mexican cinema Dolores del Río, Katy Jurado, María Félix, Pedro Armendáriz, Arturo de Córdova, Emilio Fernández, Gabriel Figueroa, Lupe Vélez, and others. Thus framing the international success of leading figures of the 1990s new cinema as an 'overnight success' overlooks the achievements of their ancestors" (176). The people that de la Mora mentions were actors, with the exception of Emilio Fernández, who worked in Hollywood as both an extra and an actor before working as a director in Mexico. De la Mora correctly adds this recent wave of Mexican film workers to a series of migrations to Hollywood, but I see a change in the type of movement. Whereas contemporary Mexican directors have taken their expertise gained in the Mexican film industry to further their careers in the United States, most of their predecessors started in Hollywood and returned to Mexico.

The connection between Hollywood and the Mexican film industry produced Mexico's first sound film, *Santa* (Antonio Moreno, 1932). As Ramírez Berg notes, Compañía Nacional Productora de Películas (National Film Production Company), a group of investors in Mexico, went to Hollywood, where they found the necessary equipment and personnel to make the film. "They returned with a Spanish actor turned director (Antonio Moreno), a Canadian director of photography (Alex Phillips), and two Mexican actors who were working in Hollywood, Lupita Tovar and Donald Reed" (13). Several directors started their film careers in the United States. As mentioned, Emilio "el Indio" Fernández worked in Hollywood for nine years before directing in Mexico. Fernández directed *Flor silvestre* (1943), *María Candelaria* (1943), and *Enamorada* (1946), all three typical melodramas of the golden age. In Hollywood, Fernández met Miguel Delgado, who assisted Gary Cooper and who later directed many of the Cantinflas films (Ciuk 202). Another of Fernández's friends from Hollywood, Roberto Gavaldón, went on to make *Macario* (1959) after having worked as an extra in the United States. *Macario* was nominated for the Oscar for best foreign film. Finally, Chano Urueta directed Fernández and other actors in *Gitano* (1929), a short film made for RKO in Hollywood (Ciuk 613). Urueta made Mexican films for forty years, including *Los de abajo* (1939).

Other Mexican directors started their careers in the United States for various reasons. After the Cristero War (1926–1929), Joselito Rodríguez, who later directed *¡Ay, Jalisco, no te rajes!* (1941), moved to Los Angeles to study electronics. The rest of his family joined him, including his brothers Ismael and Roberto. The three brothers founded Películas Rodríguez in 1939 (Ciuk 525). Juan, Joselito's son and a filmmaker, was born in Los Angeles and studied film at Loyola University. Ismael Rodríguez is best known for directing Pedro Infante in the Pepe el Toro trilogy: *Nosotros, los pobres* (1947), *Ustedes, los ricos* (1948), and *Pepe el Toro* (1952). Alejandro Galindo, the director of *Espaldas mojadas* (1953) (which I discuss in chapter 1), also worked in the United States in a variety of jobs associated with the film industry, most notably as an assistant to Cecil B. DeMille. Before she created *La negra Angustias* (1949), Matilde Landeta made more than a hundred medium-length films in 16 mm for the *Howdy Doody* children's series in the United States (Ciuk 365).

Although Mexico has its own film schools, several Mexican directors came to the United States to study film, primarily at the University of California, Los Angeles, and at New York University. Many directors who made films during the 1980s and '90s got their training in the United States: Damián Acosta, Rubén Galindo, Pedro Galindo,

Antonio de Anda, U.S.-born Alberto Mariscal, Rafael Rosales Durán, Alfonso Rosas Priego (Enrique Rosas's grandson), and Fernando Pérez Gavilán. Following in his father's footsteps, Ismael Rodríguez Jr. went to Columbia College in New York to study television and film (Ciuk 529). Salvador Carrasco, director of *La otra conquista* (1999), studied at Bard College and NYU in the late 1980s and early 1990s. Fernando Sariñana completed a master's degree in film and television at UCLA in 1989 before creating *Hasta morir* (1994) and *Todo el poder* (1999) (Ciuk 556).

In more recent years, as mentioned, Mexican directors have been starting in Mexico and then moving to the United States to further their careers. After directing *Como agua para chocolate* (1992), Alfonso Arau crossed over to Hollywood to make *A Walk in the Clouds* (1995) starring Anthony Quinn. Later, his son Sergio Arau, one-time member of the band Botellita de Jerez, made a number of music videos before creating *A Day without a Mexican* (2004), which posits a world where Mexican migrants disappear. Although Luis Mandoki completed several feature-length films in Mexico, his most recognizable films are those he made in Hollywood: *When a Man Loves a Woman* (1994) and *Message in a Bottle* (1999). After his debut in Hollywood, Mandoki returned to Spanish-language film with *Voces inocentes* (2004), about a boy in El Salvador during that country's civil war in the 1980s, and he later made the controversial *Fraude: México 2006* (2007), a documentary about the 2006 presidential elections in Mexico.

Del Toro, Cuarón, and González Iñárritu started their film careers in Mexico and moved away after they had established themselves in their home country. Besides his work in animation, del Toro worked with Jaime Humberto Hermosillo on the production of *El corazón de la noche* (1983) and *Doña Herlinda y su hijo* (1984) (Ciuk 197). *Cronos* (1991) was del Toro's first feature-length film and the only one made in Mexico to date. After migrating to the United States, he released *Mimic* (1997), which was his first science-fiction film made in Hollywood. Although del Toro continued making Spanish-language films, *Cronos* is the only one that is thematically liked to Mexico. Cuarón traveled back and forth between Mexican cinema and the United States. After his first film, *Sólo con tu pareja* (1991), Cuarón debuted in Hollywood with *A Little Princess* (1995) and

Great Expectations (1998). He returned to Mexico to direct *Y tu mamá también* (2001). In *Diccionario de directores del cine mexicano*, Cuarón is asked why he went to the United States to work when *Sólo con tu pareja* was such a success in Mexico. He answers, "No, it was before its exhibition . . . Sólo con tu pareja was canned for two years in Mexico for reasons . . . a bit unknown. In reality to make the film I had to burn many 'bridges' that I had in Mexico, and in the U.S. other opportunities were extended that I took" (Ciuk 162). These types of opportunities were also offered to González Iñárritu, which allowed him to make *21 Grams* (2003) after his debut film, *Amores perros* (2000).

The Three as Collaborators

Babel, Children of Men, and del Toro's *El laberinto del fauno* (*Pan's Labyrinth*) were released in 2006. The three can be considered "sister films," using Cuarón's terminology from a 2006 interview with the three directors by Charlie Rose. The three directors are forging a reputation for Mexican cinema and creating an informal way of understanding national cinema. In May 2007, the three directors announced that they had formed a production company and signed with Universal Pictures and its subsidiary, Focus Features International. Their contract includes five films. Cha Cha Cha Films is now credited with the production of Carlos Cuarón's *Rudo y cursi* (2008). With the collaboration of these directors has come a new acceptance that Mexican cinema thrives outside of the country's national borders.

Because of the limited resources for film in Mexico, transnational coproductions have flourished, and many directors have opted for filmmaking in Hollywood. The number of articles about *Amores perros* and *Y tu mamá también* demonstrate how such transnational coproductions are defining the genre.[2] One of the trademarks of this current wave of Mexican films has been the lack of funding by the Mexican government. As Luisela Alvaray explains, "Mexico's new film policies ultimately have not served to support its film industry, but rather have weakened it. In 1990, in accordance with Mexico's neoliberal trend, state production companies CONACINE and CONACITE DOS were shut down, as was the film distributor PELÍCULAS NACIONALES. Soon after, the exhibition network COMPAÑÍA OPERADORA DE TEATROS, also owned by the state, was dismantled. New legislation took effect in 1992 that promised to privatize production facilities and distribution companies and to eliminate protectionist measures, such as screen quotas" (61). Del Toro, Cuarón, and González Iñárritu are creative in discovering alternative sources of funding so that they are not forced to rely on the state.

In addition to these directors, other Mexican nationals have come to the United States to work within the film industry. Apart from the three nominated directors mentioned, the rest of the list of 2007 Oscar nominees shows the influence of this network within Hollywood: Guillermo Arriaga (former screenwriter for González Iñárritu), Emmanuel Lubezki (cinematographer for Cuarón), Guillermo Navarro (cinematographer for del Toro), Eugenio Caballero (production designer for del Toro), and Adriana Barraza (actress in *Amores perros* and *Babel*, for which she received the nomination). Fernando Cámara was the only other Mexican Oscar nominee that year. He received his nomination for sound mixing for *Apocalypto* (Mel Gibson, 2006); however, he previously worked with del Toro on *Cronos*.

Although some would argue that the Mexican filmmakers were elided because they did not win as many of the Oscars as they could have, I prefer to see their presence as a positive movement toward the inclusion and recognition of Mexicans within Hollywood. Whether or not these directors received the awards, they have the power to create and will continue making films that are widely distributed across the globe. The ability to influence and manipulate images is more significant considering that many of the more influential Mexican immigrants in Hollywood have been actors.[3]

Although the three directors have different cinematic styles, their work can be compared in a number of ways. All three have moved away from Mexico, and the theme of migration permeates their films, either directly or indirectly. González Iñárritu's *Babel*—a title that reminds us that linguistic and cultural misunderstandings still occur—focuses on the conflicts between people of various national identities in the face of globalization. One of the story lines portrays a Mexican nanny, Amelia (Adriana Barraza), who works in the United

States, but whose family still resides in Mexico. In contrast, del Toro's films are only indirectly connected to the theme of migration. He stopped making films set in Mexico and turned his attention toward Spain, a change resulting from his disenchantment with Mexico after his father was assaulted in Guadalajara, his hometown. *El espinazo del diablo* (*The Devil's Backbone*, 2001) and *Pan's Labyrinth* are set in Spain during Francisco Franco's dictatorship. Del Toro's interest in the topic is connected to a dear friend of his who was exiled from Spain. The Spanish exile community in Mexico informed the work of del Toro and strongly influenced his depictions of that dictatorship. Although del Toro has apparently lost interest in making films about Mexico, he has not escaped representing national identity. His films can be read as microcosms of Spanish society.[4] Finally, Cuarón sets *Children of Men* twenty years into the future, in a world where most nation-states have fallen except for Britain. The British government militarizes its borders as a means to keep immigrants out of the country. The destruction of the world has led to the possible extinction of the human race, but a pregnant African woman gives the world a glimmer of hope for the future. *Children of Men* looks at the possibility of a universal identity as represented by the Human Project, an elusive organization that seeks to form an alternative society.

In this chapter, I analyze both *Babel* and *Children of Men* and compare how each director approaches the topic of migration within each film. As I argued in chapter 1, Mexican films about migration have tended to reinforce national identity and have moved to incorporate the emigrant into the imaginary of the nation. *Babel* falls into this tradition, except that González Iñárritu is a migrant himself. In contrast, Cuarón does not present Mexican nationalism or national identity in *Children of Men*. This may be due in part to Cuarón's background. He does not live in the United States like his friends do; he lives in London. Cuarón focuses on British nationalism only to deconstruct it and criticize a military state that tries to close its borders and attempts to limit access to immigrants. I do not analyze del Toro's films set in Spain during Francisco Franco's dictatorship, since they are only indirectly about migration.

Both González Iñárritu and Cuarón presented Mexican national identity in earlier films. Analyzing *Amores perros, Y tu mamá también*, and *El crimen del Padre Amaro* (Carlos Carrera, 2002), Jeff

Menne concludes that this group of films "proposes a cultural sense of the national that is valuably detachable from the state apparatus, recognizing that the state sovereignty that gave vitality to past new waves is now flagging; but that the reserves of the national, understood culturally, might still have the power to form communities under the political conditions to come. This is another way of saying that under globalization, the makers of images can more substantially wield political might" (73). *Children of Men* does not delve into Mexican national identity, but neither does Cuarón counter it, instead subsuming it into a third-world identity. *Babel* similarly represents the larger third world, but the director achieves this by allowing space for national identities still to emerge.

Both films explore the topic of globalization, but in distinct ways, as the global and the national combine and overlap. The global is defined as a movement of capital, information, products, and people across the world. Globalization is often heralded as the decline of the nation-state, but the nation-state has not been completely dismantled. As Néstor García Canclini notes, "Not even within the economy can we generalize the idea that globalization substitutes for nations and we live in a world without borders" (53). As I argue in this chapter, González Iñárritu and Cuarón inhabit a filmic space that allows them to be film directors, both national and global at once. Their films are a product of this double position or liminal space in which they work.

Through a Mexican Lens?

Babel is divided into four stories that take place in Mexico, the United States, Morocco, and Japan. González Iñárritu melds a variety of stories to show how globalization can create interconnectedness among disparate peoples. *Babel* was produced with funding from Mexico, the United States, and France; the cast and crew include people from all four of the countries featured in the film. The core of the creative team—including the director, the screenwriter, and the cinematographer—is Mexican. The transnational production and Mexican creative team generate a double or hybrid perspective: in a sense, Hollywood meets Mexican film. Within *Babel*, the global is apparent—because of the settings in distinct countries and the use of four languages—although the national appears throughout the film. The influences of Mexican national identity are obvious and are most apparent in the story line about Amelia and the U.S.–Mexico border. The entire film can be understood within a Mexican film history.

Visually, *Babel* is reminiscent of classic Mexican cinema. The scenes in Morocco and of the desert along the U.S.–Mexico border feature shots that resemble those taken by Gabriel Figueroa in Emilio Fernández's films such as *María Candelaria*. These images capture rural Mexico by focusing on mountains with clouds hovering on top, as Sergei Eisenstein did in *¡Qué viva México!* (1932). By making visual reference to Mexican cinema, *Babel* connects Mexico and Morocco as developing countries. The Moroccan desert eerily resembles the desert that Amelia and the children cross. González Iñárritu describes how his crew survived the climate in Morocco: "For many of us from the Third World, it was a bit easier to tolerate such conditions. The reality of a shepherd in Morocco is not very different from that of one in Mexico. I, as well as Rodrigo Prieto and the Mexican unit of the crew, were delighted with the possibility of understanding their living conditions and their limitations" (94). González Iñárritu sees his cultural proximity to Morocco from a third-world point of view, so his vision of Morocco cannot escape his cultural background. It is inevitable that he approach the film from a Mexican viewpoint.

Paul Julian Smith's study of *Amores perros* provides a background by which to understand *Babel*. *Amores perros*'s complex narrative has often been compared to Quentin Tarantino's *Pulp Fiction* (1994) and *Reservoir Dogs* (1992), but Smith places *Amores perros* as part of the new cinema in Mexico that arose in the 1970s. As Smith argues, "There is scarcely an element of *Amores perros*'s intricate plot, then, that is not anticipated in the crisis of national identity explored in Mexican cinema two decades earlier. What makes González Iñárritu unique, however, is that these elements are not placed within a self-conscious quest for mexicanidad but are rather (as García Tsao wrote) subordinated to the attempt to tell a story as effectively as possible" (38). *Babel*'s structure is similar to that of *Amores perros*, but instead of three stories told in three separate units, the four stories are weaved together throughout the film. They are introduced in the following pattern: Yussef and Ahmed, Amelia and the children, Richard and Susan, and finally Chieko. *Babel* is not organized as a "self-conscious quest for mexicanidad," as Smith notes of *Amores perros*, but the issue of mexicanidad forms part of the nanny's story.

González Iñárritu's perspective as a director can be compared to that of other Mexican directors, but he writes as both a *defeño* (someone from Mexico City) and a migrant. As Norma Iglesias Prieto argues, Mexican films have reproduced a centrist notion of migration as part of an identity crisis on the U.S.–Mexico border, but the gaze within *Babel* does not present one unified point of view. Breaking with centrist representations of the border, González Iñárritu does not depict fronterizos or migrants as losing their Mexican identity or as becoming *agringados*. On the contrary, he highlights their Mexicanness against a background of the United States. The gaze toward Mexico is ambivalent. As a director working in Hollywood, he presents both a romanticized view of Mexico and a negative, hypermasculinized one.

The Migrant as Binational Mother

In *Babel*, the interconnectedness of the different families in Mexico, the United States, Morocco, and Japan is made possible in each case by some type of travel or migration. Richard (Brad Pitt) and Susan Jones (Cate Blanchett) travel to Morocco, where Yasujiro Wataya had visited previously for a hunting trip. Amelia, a Mexican migrant living in the United States, returns to Mexico to attend her son's wedding. Mike and Debbie are the only children to travel across national boundary lines, going with Amelia to the wedding in Baja California. Of all the traveling adults in the film, Amelia is the least privileged and the only migrant; the others are wealthy enough to be tourists in foreign countries. Amelia works for Richard and Susan as a nanny for Mike and Debbie, the couple's children. Amelia's family still resides in Mexico, just on the other side of the border. González Iñárritu explains why he was motivated to include this story within the film: "To me, the character of Amelia was always the incarnation of Julia: the Mexican woman who was working for my family in our Los Angeles home. She has told me about how she has crossed the desert six times and how she was caught by the patrol cars. Julia spent three nights and three days on the desert with[out] seeing a trace of civilization" (García 256). He sees Amelia as a stand-in mother for the two white American children, Mike and Debbie. Part of the dilemma in taking care of the children while Susan is hospitalized in Morocco is that Amelia's son, Luis, is about to get married. Amelia's role as stand-in mother comes into conflict with her responsibilities to her own children, but she tries to balance both by taking the children to her son's wedding. It is Amelia's desire to attend her son's wedding that gives unity to this story line.

The film never shows Mike and Debbie with their parents. Richard and Amelia speak over the telephone while he is in Morocco, when Susan is in the hospital. In one of the telephone calls, Richard speaks to Mike. We see this conversation twice: the first time from Mike's perspective and the second from Richard's. It is not until the end that we see Richard crying on the other end, as he tries to conceal his worry from his son. In Morocco, Richard shows a picture of his children to Anwar, the guide who so generously helps him, and Susan asks to speak to her children as she waits for medical attention to treat her gunshot wound. These scenes show some emotional connection between the birth parents and the children, but their connection to Amelia is much stronger. At the beginning of the film, the children are in Amelia's custody. She cares for them and spends undetermined amounts of time with them. We know at the beginning of the film that she has spent enough time with them that they understand her when she speaks to them in Spanish.

Richard and Susan leave the country as a way to deal with the grief of losing a child, but in the process they leave their surviving children. In contrast, Amelia tries to balance her work responsibilities with those of being a mother. Although Luis is her only child whom we know by name, the film shows Amelia with her daughters, as they help her put on a dress. One daughter pokes fun at Amelia for wearing an older dress that fits her tightly. The playfulness of the conversation demonstrates the intimacy of the family. The viewers know that Richard and Susan live with their children even though the film never shows the family together. Inversely, although we see Amelia interacting with her family, we know that she lives away from them. When she defends her right to stay in the United States to the immigration officer, she mentions that she has lived in the United States for sixteen years. Luis may be an adult, but sixteen years ago he would have been a child. Amelia's absence can be read as a sacrifice for her children; she left her country to provide for them. The major absence in this family is the father figure. The film does not give any details at all about Amelia's past. What happened to the father? Was Amelia always a single mother? Where and with whom did her children live when Amelia worked in the United States? These questions are left unanswered.

The closest adult-child relationships are those that Amelia has with Mike and Debbie. Although Amelia makes several mistakes that lead her to place Mike and Debbie in danger, she claims a personal connection to the children and reinforces the idea that she serves as a stand-in mother. At the end of the film, Amelia defends her right to know about the children's well-being: "I raised these kids since they were born. I take care of them day and night. I feed them breakfast, lunch, and dinner. I play with them. Mike and Debbie are like my own children." This connection between the Mexican migrant and the children demonstrates the transculturation that occurs. It is a given that migrants must adapt to their new environment, but the white American population is also changed by those contacts. *Babel* shows the influence that Amelia has on the family; unfortunately, we do not see how the family reacts after her deportation.

Romantic Mexico

Babel portrays Mexico as an idyllic place, especially in comparison to the other countries in the film. Mexico is shown with romanticized images by way of Amelia's family and her son's wedding. The wedding is contrasted to the previous scene—Yussef and Ahmed tell their father that the police are looking for him. The story lines switch as the brothers begin to brawl; then, we hear Santiago honking his car horn to bring attention to the wedding party. Amelia's family lives in Carrizo, a small town in Baja California. The humble surroundings of the community are most exemplified by the dirt roads and the dust released because of the town's desert climate. The standard of living of the Mexicans in the film is quite obviously not as high as that of the characters living in the United States and Japan, but it is comparable to that of the Moroccans, perhaps somewhat better. Those living in the developed countries, however, are not without their own problems: they have serious issues with communication in their families. Richard and Susan are trying to overcome the pain of losing a child, and Chieko misses her deceased mother and is unable to communicate with her father. The Moroccan brothers, Yussef and Ahmed, seem to get along, but what begins as an innocent competition between them leads ultimately to Ahmed's death. In contrast, Amelia's family are never shown fighting; they are happy as they celebrate the son's marriage. The couple walk down the dirt street followed by their guests, and the music cuts to the party as they dance to the live band. The happiness within the wedding scenes, as González Iñárritu sees this, is a natural part of the Carrizo community: "Even though I was shooting for days and until six in the morning, there was never a complaint out of them. Nothing but smiles and nonstop dancing. For me, them, and the entire crew, the wedding was indeed a fiesta. The people knew one another and that could be felt in the scene" (González Iñárritu 148). González Iñárritu builds on the stereotype of the Mexican fiesta as his way of representing Mexico.

Babel represents Mexico from an unusual perspective, that of a Mexican director's gaze toward his own country and that of a Hollywood film set in Mexico. Mike and Debbie's gaze toward Mexico is similar to Jane's in *El jardín del Edén* (María Novaro, 1994), which I analyze at length in chapter 1. Jane sees Mexico through a romantic lens, the action shot in slow motion when she sees an indigenous person. Mexico is the Garden of Eden, tied to the past. Of course, this is María Novaro's portrayal of the *gringa*. In *Babel*, Mike and Debbie similarly look at Mexico in a romanticized way as they travel there for the first time. González Iñárritu has said that he wanted to film Mexico through the eyes of a child. One of the differences between *Babel* and *El jardín del Edén* is that the films are made for different audiences. Although María Novaro is displaying Mexico to the world, the film is nonetheless in Spanish. *Babel* is made to capture the attention of a large audience, like most Hollywood films.

Mexico is also romanticized in *Babel* through the characters of the couples: Luis and his new wife, Patricia; and Amelia and the older

gentleman who asks her to dance during the party. The diegetic
music from the band in the wedding slowly switches to Chavela
Vargas's version of "Tú me acostumbraste." The nondiegetic song
plays on, as we see the party's movement to the tempo of the band's
music and the lively celebration of the wedding. The film crosscuts
between the festivities and Amelia inside the house with the older
gentleman. The cake is being carried out, and the camera focuses
on the plastic bride and groom. These events do not happen simultaneously; we see several different shots of Amelia sitting in the
party. The images alternate between Amelia kissing the man within
the house and the party outside. The idea that is conveyed in this
sequence is that of romantic love in both the younger couple and
the older one. Romantic Mexico is amorous at all ages.

The Renegade Mexican

Santiago (Gael García Bernal), Amelia's nephew, and his car are the
embodiment of mexicanidad. García Bernal has a secondary role in
Babel, but his character both literally and figuratively drives the plot
of Amelia's story. Most viewers will probably recognize García Bernal
from his previous roles in *Amores perros*, *Y tu mamá también*, and
El crimen del Padre Amaro. García Bernal, therefore, is a participant
within this transnational film network organized by González Iñárritu, Cuarón, and del Toro. As Sergio de la Mora observes, "García
Bernal—'Mexico's new cinema sensation'—is the poster boy for this
revival" (174). García Bernal as an actor plays a variety of roles and represents Mexican masculinity in various ways. As de la Mora explains
through reference to a poem by Marina García-Vázquez, "García
Bernal represents a young, modern, and cosmopolitan middle-class
Latin/o American youth: multifaceted, multilayered, expressive, sin-
cere, intelligent, articulate, 'real,' down-to-earth, capable of expressing complex desires, and boyish. He is both feminine ('a dahlia in full
bloom') and phallic ('deep water-thrust of an octopus'); a precious
gem, he embodies both traditional objects associated with mexicanidad (obsidian used by Aztecs and other Native Americans) and
global modernity (metallic, Bombay)" (164). In *Babel*, García Bernal
does not represent the sexual ambiguities of some of his other roles,

but instead he embodies Mexicanness and machismo through his character, Santiago.

There is some continuity between García Bernal's roles. In *Amores perros*, he played Octavio, a teen at odds with his brother because he is in love with his sister-in-law, Susana. Octavio's desire is to spirit Susana away to Cd. Juárez, the implication being that he wants to migrate to the United States. Menne sees Octavio as being thrust into a global realm:

> Slipping the conventional class identity of national life, Octavio may simply be preparing to join Hardt and Negri's multitude. The film gives us no cause to read his imagination of "possible lives" as liberatory per se. In Octavio's final scene we watch him wait at the bus station for Susana's company; the bus, his opportunity for egress, departs before Susana arrives. His resolve weakened, he neglects to board the bus. The imagination (helped by a fund of media images) that emboldens the global actor may well, as Octavio's case exposes, desolate him. *Amores perros* seems anguished by the fact that the global actor, without company, as yet imagines a sullen emancipation. (79)

For Menne, Octavio is an embodiment of González Iñárritu himself, a man who refuses any national order. It is true that Octavio and González Iñárritu are global actors; this does not mean, though, that they cannot equally be national ones.

Through Santiago in *Babel*, González Iñárritu represents the nation within a global order. From the moment Santiago is introduced, as he helps Amelia and the children into his car, he and the car are connected visually to the Virgin of Guadalupe by means of a sticker of her image that adorns the car's rear window. The camera angle is toward the rear from inside the car, and thus the transparent image of the sticker is superimposed on Santiago and Amelia's faces as they pack the bags into the trunk. This sticker of the virgin serves as a symbol of Mexicanness, both of the car and of the people who ride in it. Although the automobile is usually read as an American cultural symbol, in this film the car embodies Mexican national identity. It is in this car that Santiago transports Amelia and the children into and out of Mexico. Although the car crosses the border, it displays mexicanidad, being driven into the United States as a deterritorialized symbol of national identity. The two border crossings in *Babel* are dramatically different. As the group enters Mexico, the film establishes each person's different vantage point. Santiago and Amelia enter a place familiar to them, whereas Mike and Debbie are going to Mexico for the first time. The film reinforces the children's perspective of Mexico by alternating shots of them as they look out the window with shots of the city of Tijuana as they ride past. Some of the typical Tijuana sites are shown: the international checkpoint, Avenida Revolución, and the famous zebra-painted burros.

Santiago is responsible for taking Amelia and the children to Mexico; he is a tour guide of sorts. Although the children know Amelia, she is a feminine figure, and Santiago may be their first encounter with a Mexican male. Santiago represents Mexican machismo and a facet of Mexico as a nation. De la Mora defines this relationship as follows: "Machismo is intimately linked to State power and to the highly contested gendered social contract extended to Mexican citizens in the post-revolutionary period. Indeed, the machismo attributed to Mexican men (the *charro*, popularized through *mariachi* music and the *comedia ranchera* film genre, or combatants who fought in the Revolution) is among Mexico's most internationally recognized symbols" (6). De la Mora lists the characteristics of the Mexican macho as "virile, brave, sexually potent, and physically aggressive" (7). Santiago embodies the character of a Mexican macho.

The film places special attention on Santiago as a masculine figure set next to Mike, the white American child. Many times when Santiago speaks to Mike, he looks directly at the camera—he looks toward the back seat as he focuses his gaze toward the camera or glances directly at the camera using the rearview mirror—as though these displays of Mexican identity and masculinity are being directed at the viewer. Mike comments, "My mom told me that Mexico is really dangerous." Santiago responds in Spanish, "Yes, it is full of Mexicans." Amelia laughs and tells Mike that it is not true, although it is. She is, of course, responding to Santiago's tone of voice and the implication that Mexicans are bad. This scene draws attention to the fear of Mexico that is instilled in the children by their birth mother, Susan. Santiago responds to these fears, mocking the idea of Mexico and Mexicans as the "other."

Once they arrive in the town, Santiago introduces Mike and Debbie to the other children there, and he entertains them as well. Santiago tells the group of children that he will reward the first one to catch a chicken, and Mike wins this game. The boy is amazed to see how Santiago kills a chicken by twisting its neck. The camera focuses on Mike wide-eyed as the blood spurts from the chicken's neck. Santiago kills the chicken with ease, showing his skill, but it is obvious that Mike has never seen such a sight. Killing the chicken seems archaic, like something out of the past, one that Mike does not understand. At another moment, Santiago shoots his gun, a Mexican custom to commemorate the New Year and, in the film, the wedding. As a display of Santiago's Mexican machismo, the shot underscores his masculinity but frightens Mike in the process.

Later in the night, after the party is over, Santiago's machismo turns aggressive, and he puts Amelia and the children in danger by leaving them in the middle of the desert. It is late, and the wedding has changed from a serene and happy event to a late-night party with drunken people. One woman screams at someone, signaling the change in atmosphere. Santiago and Amelia walk out to the car with the children in their arms. Luis and his new wife walk behind them, and Luis warns Amelia that she should not leave because Santiago is drunk. Amelia insists that she must get the children back to their home, and Santiago denies being drunk. His denial is loaded with a sexualized comment, "Pedo mis güevos" (Drunk, my balls), in a sense exalting his manhood. In a foreshadowing of events, Luis reminds Santiago that he has gotten himself into trouble before.

At the checkpoint for the U.S. Customs and Border Protection, Santiago is belligerent with the agent. When asked where he is coming from, he jokes, "From Mexico." The obvious answer immediately sets the tone for the conversation between him and the agent, making matters worse. Although Amelia has the children's passports, she does not have the parents' written permission to take them out of the country. Their white skin and blond hair make it apparent that the children are not related to the adults, but Santiago carelessly says that they are his nephews. Although Amelia tries to correct him, the comment and Santiago's tone of voice are a red flag for the agent. The agent realizes that Santiago's attitude may be due to alcohol, so he asks him to "step out of the car," but changes his mind and tells him to pull over into another section of the checkpoint. The car, as I have mentioned, represents an extension of Santiago and his Mexican national identity. Instead of pulling over, Santiago speeds away; the sticker of the Virgin of Guadalupe is faintly visible as he leaves. Santiago's resistance to a normal inspection is a way of rejecting U.S. immigration laws and in a sense marking his mexicanidad. This resistance turns into rage, which manifests in his driving. Mike and Debbie cry with fear while Amelia tries to reason with Santiago. He blames her for taking the children to Mexico, but he makes matters worse. This renegade Mexican abandons Amelia and the children in the desert in the middle of the night. His display of machismo places them in danger, never really bringing into question either U.S. national identity or immigration laws.

Unusual Border Crossings

Santiago's aggressive behavior and renegade driving result in the children walking through the desert. In a sense, the children are placed in the shoes of the migrant; they walk with her, though they are U.S. citizens. Although Amelia works illegally in the United States, she has a passport to come and go between the two countries. Many undocumented immigrants in the United States cannot cross the border so easily.[5]

Another odd detail of this journey is that it seems as if they are in the Sonoran Desert, which would have been difficult if they were crossing the border through Tecate. The desert setting serves to tap into the viewer's memory in two ways. The fourteen-mile-long fence dividing Tijuana and San Diego switched the major corridor for crossing, pushing migrants to cross the Sonoran desert through Arizona, a much more dangerous area because of the heat. González Iñárritu's choice of setting, then, conjures up images already in the public's imagination from news reports about the immigration debate and immigrant deaths. These scenes also create a visual reference to classic Mexican cinema. As I have mentioned, the clouds and the mountains in the distance are very similar to those in Emilio Fernández's films marked by Gabriel Figueroa's cinematography. As Amelia walks through the desert, the camera is positioned from below at about a forty-five degree angle, capturing both Amelia and the sky above her. Amelia's red dress reminds us, though, that *Babel* is not a black-and-white film of the golden age. The color stands out as she walks through the brown desert sand and the faded-green shrubs. The red dress is reminiscent of the colors used in *Profundo carmesí* (Arturo Ripstein, 1996), and it contrasts with the opaque brown colors of the desert.

At one point, the camera captures Amelia from below as Mike looks up to her, showing the clouds behind her. The angle allows us to see from Mike's perspective, but it also mimics the style inherited from Fernández and Eisenstein. This is one example of how González Iñárritu is able to film from both perspectives simultaneously, as Mexican and Hollywood director. The camera sits behind Mike's shoulder and mimics his gaze toward Amelia as she tries to attract the attention of the patrol car. The bond between Amelia and the children is so strong that they empathize with her even as they walk through the desert. Mike does not understand what she has done wrong and asks, "Why are we hiding if we didn't even do anything wrong?" Amelia must eventually admit, "I just did something stupid."

Babel makes an ambivalent statement about Mexican migration to the United States. During the desert scenes, the film questions the concept of the border. When Amelia is caught by the Border Patrol, she states, "I didn't cross; I live here." The declaration resonates much like the phrase commonly used by Mexican Americans that refers to the Treaty of Guadalupe Hidalgo and the loss of Mexican land to the United States: "We didn't cross the border; the border crossed us." Like the Mexican American claim to the Southwest, Amelia asserts her right to be in the United States, but this claim rings hollow, as she is deported to Mexico. Amelia is shown with a government official who tells her that she has been working illegally in the United States and that she is better off not fighting the deportation. We see Amelia as her son picks her up on the Mexican side of the border. She still wears the now-battered red dress. The two walk toward each other with the camera hovering behind Luis's back. As they hug, Amelia's tears roll down her cheeks. These last images are of a defeated woman. Since she and her nephew are to blame for her deportation, *Babel* does not present any credible critique of the United States or its immigration policies.

Between Hollywood and Mexico:
Cuarón's Hybrid Style

Alfonso Cuarón's filmic career features his work in Hollywood and for many years in the Mexican film industry. Cuarón studied film at the Centro Universitario de Estudios Cinematográficos (CUEC) at the Universidad Nacional Autónoma de México (UNAM) until he was expelled (Ciuk 161). Although he did not finish his studies, in his time at UNAM he met Emmanuel Lubezki, who would later become his cinematographer. In film school, he made several short films, one of which won an Ariel. *Sólo con tu pareja* was Cuarón's first film, released nearly a decade before González Iñárritu's *Amores perros*. By 2001, when *Y tu mamá también* appeared in film theaters, Cuarón had already worked in Hollywood, so the road film seemed to be Cuarón's return to Mexican film. Cuarón's film career is marked by a continual negotiation between his Hollywood and his Mexican productions. His movement between the two industries undoubtedly influences his cinematic style.

Y tu mamá también reflects his experience with Mexico's national industry and Hollywood's global enterprise. Hester Baer and Ryan Long argue that *Y tu mamá también* inhabits a liminal space between the national and the global: "Mexico's liminal status is reflected in the production and reception contexts of the film, which itself occupies a liminal space between Mexican cinematic tradition and global cinematic styles. Thus, while the film's success results in part from its participation in the tropes of global cinema, it constantly intervenes in these tropes with discourses that insist on the specificity of Mexican national-historical memory in its temporal and spatial dimensions" (151). Cuarón's participation within the global film industry has not led to an obliteration of the national legacy within his work, but has instead blended to create a hybrid aesthetic. In *Y tu mamá también*, the national elements are present within the narrative of the film. Ernesto R. Acevedo-Muñoz concludes that both *Amores perros* and *Y tu mamá también* "directly revise Mexico's 'inevitable' meta-narrative of Malinche and comment on the currency of its cultural and social value in the post NAFTA, globalized economy" (40). With *Y tu mamá también*, Cuarón demonstrates that although he may not focus on mexicanidad in all of his films, he still uses the tropes to represent Mexican national identity.

Children of Men is similar to *Y tu mamá también* in narrative style, in its use of tropes, and as a road film. The narrative of *Children of Men* is incomplete without the mise-en-scène, because most of the background of what led to humanity's possible extinction is written on the walls and displayed on the TV screens in buses, the metro, and in buildings. *Children of Men* uses the mise-en-scène much like *Y tu mamá también* uses voice-over to fill in the gaps of the story. *Children of Men* does not contain any of the Mexican national tropes that *Y tu mamá también* does, but the film does make references to other types of tropes grounded in African identity, as a means to create an umbrella identity for developing countries. *Children of Men* contains several examples of identities that oppose nationalism, yet in these examples a sense of place is not lost. Arjun Appadurai argues, "Carried in the repertoires of increasingly mobile populations of refugees, tourists, guest workers, transnational intellectuals, scientists, and illegal aliens, [nationalism] is increasingly unrestrained by ideas of spatial boundary and territorial sovereignty. This revolution in the foundations of nationalism has crept up on us virtually unnoticed. Where soil and place were once the key to the linkage of territorial affiliation with state monopoly of the means of violence, key identities and identifications now only partially revolve around the realities and images of place" (161). Appadurai is careful not to completely dismiss "the realities and images of place," but he does set identities and identification in opposition to the ways that state sovereignty has been tied to territory. He distinguishes between the fixed territorial boundaries created by the state and the fluidity of identities and identifications. He argues that a sense of place, although not completely disconnected from identity, is less significant to how identities and identifications are constructed. Although it may be true that the sense of place is less significant than it was before, it has not altogether lost its validity. The connections between nationalism and the state are more obvious; the examples of identities and identifications that oppose this nationalism within the film are more fluid and open to interpretation.

Children of Men is not part of third and imperfect cinema in any way; it is a Hollywood production with funding from the United

States, Japan, and the United Kingdom made with technological innovations to create realism, unlike the low-budget productions that were characteristic of Latin American films of the 1970s.[6] Like many high-budget action films, *Children of Men* is recognized for its technological innovation, which allows the camera to capture the action more seamlessly. This is especially evident in the car scene in which Theo, the antihero, travels with Julian and the other Fishes. The roof of the minivan in which they ride was built with a special camera that rotates and captures all the people sitting in the vehicle. Instead of doing shot/reverse shots of conversations, the camera swivels so that there are no cuts between each character speaking. The camera also swivels to film the action taking place outside of the van in such a way that we see the events from the perspective of those in the van. Cuarón is known to be a master of the long take, and he was able to film the scene without any cuts. In another scene, Theo runs through the war-torn Bexhill, a jail or prison for illegal immigrants. He dashes through the streets without any shoes, ducking the passing bullets. In his interview with the Mexican film trio, Charlie Rose asked Cuarón about this particular scene, but the director refused to explain how he achieved this long take. Nevertheless, it is clear that he has both the equipment and high budget that are associated with Hollywood films.

Children of Men lacks the leftist critique of bourgeois society that was the driving force of third and imperfect cinema. The cinematographic style and the production budget of $76 million point to another type of cinema, one that blurs the lines with Hollywood.[7] *Children of Men* does not criticize the economic structures that push globalization, but instead it critiques the violence toward "others" and oppressive anti-immigration laws. The film's main character, however, is not a migrant but an antihero who is disenchanted with the militarized state. The migrant identity grounded in the third world is the alternative for humanity's future.

The World in Twenty Years

Cuarón's *Children of Men* is set in the year 2027 and portrays a devastated world where the first world, with the exception of Britain, has collapsed. A television announcement in the film explains, "The world has collapsed, but Britain soldiers on." This phrase demonstrates the militarization of British society. From the nationalist position, Britain can only survive by means of fences and a strong military presence; nevertheless, immigrants are pouring into the country. On top of those problems, the world has been plagued with infertility. At the beginning of the film, the youngest human dies and the world mourns his death, providing a clear reminder that no children exist. Later, an African woman, Kee (Clare-Hope Ashitey), reveals herself to be pregnant and subsequently gives birth. Humanity's only hope for survival is tightly linked to the woman's female child. This child represents the immigrant population, particularly that of the third world, that must survive against nationalist England. I argue that *Children of Men* breaks with national loyalties and criticizes the nationalist aims of the first world as it tries to limit migration. Theo (Clive Owen), the protagonist, is a representation of a British national who lives in this militarized state and helps Kee. The fences and armed guards are most prevalent in the city where he lives, his disillusionment is physically evident, and he rarely smiles except when he is with Jasper Palmer (Michael Caine), a cartoonist. The restrictions are meant to keep immigrants out of the country, but their effect is also to imprison its citizens.

The British state's excessive territorial limits and restrictions are first shown as Theo goes about his daily life. At the beginning of the film, with credits appearing on the screen, we hear the news announce, "The Homeland Security Bill is ratified. After eight years, British borders will remain closed. The deportation of illegal immigrants will continue." As Theo walks to work, he passes a sign that reads, "Report Illegal Workers." The next line reinforces the restriction as an opportunity for Britain: "Jobs for the Brits." The fences and barbed wire we see throughout the film are visual reminders of the state's militarization. In several scenes in which Theo walks through the streets of London, he passes cages full of people, watched over by armed guards with dogs. These are the most striking images of how the state has literally caught the immigrants and physically separated them from British society. Although the militarization is meant to keep immigrants separate and out of society, it has the added effect of enclosing the British people within their borders. As Theo rides the bus and the metro, the wires on the windows are visible. Although he is free to walk about the city, he seems to be in a cage himself.

While the mise-en-scène displays what has happened in Britain and the rest of the world, Theo shows us how these events affect the people. He lacks any sentiment and caring for his surroundings. As he walks into the coffee shop at the beginning of the film, the people are gathered watching the news that Diego, the youngest human, has died. Theo pushes through the crowd, orders his coffee, and watches the news while he waits. He takes his coffee and leaves the crowd of people behind as they stand there in awe of the death. Theo sets his coffee down and adds some alcohol; shortly after, there is an explosion in the coffee shop. We see that his lack of sentimentality helps to keep him alive, that had he lingered to watch the broadcast, he would be dead or injured. Theo also takes advantage of the situation as he arrives at work and his coworkers are disheartened with Diego's death. Everyone there is watching the news and videos of Diego's life. One woman weeps as she stares at the screen, overcome by her emotion, but Theo's face remains passively blank. He asks for permission to leave work, claiming that he is upset by Diego's death, although he shows no emotion that would indicate this is true. He seems detached, and later he says to Jasper, "That guy was a wanker." Theo represents the disillusioned British citizen who offers no opposition to the state. We learn later in the film that Theo was once an activist, but he lost all hope for the future and stopped protesting for his beliefs.

Theo has not cut all ties with his activist past; he remains friends with the Palmers. Jasper is an older British hippie modeled after John Lennon, and he is married to Janice (Philippa Urquhart). The newspaper clippings on the walls show that Janice was once an activist and advocate for immigrant rights. One headline reads, "MI5 Denies Involvement in Torture of Photojournalist," along with a picture of Janice with a camera in her hands. Janice sits quietly in a wheelchair, staring blankly. A framed picture of Jasper shows that he was an award-winning political cartoonist. This couple is a vestige of the past, particularly of the hippie generation. They seem to live outside of society, though they cannot completely escape it. The Palmers live in the countryside, where the fences seem less restricting. The anti-immigrant fervor, however, is present in all areas of the country, including the rural ones. As Jasper and Theo talk in the car on the way to the house, a bus with bars on the windows passes, full of immigrant detainees. When they arrive at Jasper's house, we see that it is concealed from the rest of the world. In order to enter the property, Theo moves the fake shrubs that hide the entrance. The house serves as a hideaway and retreat from Theo's city life, and it keeps the Palmers at the margins of society.

Theo's conversations with Jasper offer clues as to Theo's past and his disillusionment. As they approach the house, Jasper insists that Theo must have celebrated his birthday, but Theo responds that his birthday was just like any other day: "Woke up, felt like shit, went to work, felt like shit." Theo finally admits that he is not a happy man, and he is also shown reading the instructions for Quietus, a suicide kit administered by the government. The film first shows the commercials for this product on the televisions in Theo's home and in one of the buses. At Jasper's house, Theo reads the instructions for Quietus, and it is finally made clear to the viewer just what the product is. The suicide kit is indicative of how the British government treats its citizens. Quietus, the name of the product, indicates that its purpose is to end life, but the root of the word also shows that it is a way to quiet the population, as in "quiet us."

Children of Men targets British nationalism specifically, but it also presents the United States in more subtle ways. We know from the screen in the metro that Washington, D.C., and New York have collapsed. Julian (Julianne Moore), Theo's ex-wife, is the only American character in the film. The British government wants her for her involvement with the counter-national group the Fishes. We learn that she and Theo had a child who died as a result of a flu pandemic. Theo and Julian were a couple in what is the film's past, but the political events that they protested would have taken place around 2006, the year the film was released. The film contextualizes the destruction of the world within the viewers' present day. The actions and events of the viewers' world are to blame for the future witnessed on the screen, that imagined in *Children of Men*. The mise-en-scène again comes to fill in the historical gaps in the narration of the film. At Jasper's house, Theo turns to look at a picture of himself with Julian and their son, Dylan. The picture of the family is surrounded by other images associated with the Iraq war.

The pictures of the protests show political signs reading, "Not in my name: Stop the War," "Blair must go," and "Bush" with a paint blot on it. To the left of Theo in the picture is a political cartoon of the Statue of Liberty and Uncle Sam in coffins. Theo and Julian are visually placed alongside George W. Bush and Tony Blair during the time of the Iraq invasion.

When Theo reconnects with Julian, it is clear that they are still affected by Dylan's death, which was the reason for their breakup. The loss of that child specifically and the children of the world in general comes to represent a bleak future leading to humanity's death. Without children, parenthood has no meaning. Father and mother figures are often used allegorically to portray the nation, but without children there is no sense of nationhood. This lost sense of nationhood, though, carries concrete references to the film viewers' present and the context of the British and U.S. involvement in the Iraq war. If we consider that Cuarón has represented Mexican national identity in *Y tu mamá también*, we can understand this resistance to national identity in specific reference to Britain and the United States as militarized states.

Alternatives to the State: The Fishes and the Human Project

Children of Men sets the state's control over its borders in contrast to the Fishes and to the Human Project. The Fishes oppose these restrictions and advocate immigrant rights, and the Human Project is an organization working toward the survival of the human race. The Fishes' tactics are much like those of the government that they oppose—they use bombs and violence to fight for their cause. They fight to open Britain's borders and for equal rights for immigrants in Britain, yet they do not offer an alternative to that nationalism or to the state. Although the name of the group could symbolically link it to Christianity, it is more relevant to link the symbolism to the animal itself. While fish have no territorial boundaries, they often travel in schools or groups of other fishes. In a similar way, the Fishes in the film work against territorial boundaries, yet their actions demonstrate the formation of counter-nationalism.

At the beginning, when Julian is introduced, she is the leader of the Fishes. With the collapse of the United States, Julian is also an immigrant, so she fights for her rights as well. She reconnects with Theo because she needs transport papers for Kee. We are first introduced to the Fishes as Theo explains to Jasper that the news blames the group for the explosion at the coffee shop. Later, as three of the Fishes abduct Theo, we see the headlines, "Bomb: Fishes Terror Group Blamed." Next, Theo sits in a small, enclosed room as the Fishes, their identities hidden behind facemasks, begin to talk to him. The scene uses what may be the most elaborate mise-en-scène in the film. The walls and windows of the room are covered with newspapers, giving the headlines of the events that led to the destruction of the world and the creation of organizations such as the Fishes within that context. Some of the headlines read: "Africa Devastated by Nuclear Fallout"; "Raid Nabs Refugee Weapons Cache"; "A Right Royal Ripoff, Charles Should Be Throne Out"; "Fertility Drug Kit"; and "Violent Reaction." At first the camera lingers on the newspapers, and then it focuses on the Fishes and Theo. They uncover his face, and Julian finally reveals her identity. As they start to dialogue, a light sits behind Julian, beaming in Theo's direction. The lighting in this scene is fundamental. We can see that there are windows in the small room because the light shines through them even though they are covered in newspapers. When Julian orders the others to "cut the lights," the windows become more visible, but the newspapers on the walls disappear in the darkness. This use of lighting makes us aware of the headlines that give the context of the fictitious world of the film. The scene encapsulates the history in which the Fishes surfaced and were created as an organization. Unlike Theo and Julian's personal background, which is based in real world events, the Fishes arise from the fallout that has occurred in the created past of the film that is partially explained by the newspapers on the wall of this small room.

While we see the militarization of British society, the Fishes are also violent in their movement to defend migrants from the actions of the state. Julian argues that the Fishes have turned to nonviolent tactics; however, we see later in the film that the other Fishes, primarily Luke, who becomes the leader after Julian's death, organized the attack that kills her. Most of the action of the film revolves around the Fishes, because they are trying to use Kee's baby to further their political projects. When the Fishes, Kee, and Theo meet to discuss how they will proceed after Julian's death, some argue that the baby should stay with them. One woman argues, "She belongs here [with the Fishes]. And this baby is the flag that could unite us all." Julian worked to get Kee to the Human Project, but when Luke becomes the leader of the group the organization becomes more counter-nationalistic. Their aim to control and politicize the birth of Kee's child is the driving force of the film; thus, Theo becomes the hero/ antihero who clumsily battles to save Kee.

The violence that the Fishes generate tells much about their counter-nationalism. By killing Julian, it is clear that they do not support the Human Project or its aims to save humanity in a more general context; the Fishes are more concerned with their own political motives. This is one way that they demonstrate they cannot escape the logic of the nation—they cannot understand working for the greater good of humanity. The Fishes also kill Jasper. As pacifists, Jasper and his wife fought for immigrant rights as well, but their protests seem useless. Janice is in a wheelchair because of her previous political activities, and Jasper finally puts her pain to rest when he gives her a dose of Quietus before the Fishes arrive at their house. While it is obvious that he has contemplated suicide in the past, Jasper also seems aware that he and his wife will die at the hands of the Fishes. A Fish finally kills Jasper for not revealing Kee's whereabouts. In both cases, Julian and Jasper fight for the same reasons as the Fishes, but such counter-nationalism is blind to similar political projects. The Fishes' tactics are aimed at gaining political power.

The Fishes work within the foreground of the film and within British society; the Human Project is more elusive. The future rests on the hope of a non-nationalist society that is represented by the Human Project, an organization attempting to forge an alternative society that may eventually lead to humanity's survival. Except for the boat, *Tomorrow*, that we see in the last scene of the film, we hear about this society only indirectly. Jasper mentions it to Theo; we see flyers and protesters that make references to the organization; and Julian explains to Theo that she needs to get a woman to the Human Project. She is a "mirror" and does not communicate directly with this organization but has contact with it by way of others like her. The Human Project is an almost mythical organization until it is manifest in the form of the boat at the film's end. Unlike the Fishes, the Human Project works outside the logic of the state. In the DVD commentary for the film, Slavoj Zizek refers to the boat *Tomorrow* in the last images of the film as a symbol of the deterritorialized nature of this alternative identity. Despite this, the film does not completely break from the idea of territory with the ending. Although the boat may be a visual representation of deterritorialization, Kee and her baby represent a sense of place that is not altogether divorced from territory.

Third-World Immigrant Identity

Kee and her baby represent a symbolic return to Africa, humankind's birthplace. Although there is no real return to the country, this rebirth of the human race is virtually circular. The film offers a second beginning for humanity by returning to the African people as a source of survival. Although Cuarón adapted the novel by P. D. James, Kee was added specifically because Cuarón wanted the reference to Africa within the film. The film reveals very little about Kee's past, other than to tell that she does not know who the "wanker" is who fathered her child. She never speaks about her native country or about how she moved to Britain, although we do know that she is an immigrant. Kee's character offers an alternative to Theo's disillusionment with the nation.

Kee's baby is born in Bexhill, a former resort town that has been converted into an immigrant detainment facility in the film. The immigrants there are from various places, including Russia, Romania, and the Middle East. Because Britain is the only country to survive the onslaught of wars, epidemics, and other disasters, it draws people of all other nationalities as immigrants. Inside the camp, the immigrants move freely; indeed, many of them seem to lead normal lives. One example is the Russian family with whom Kee and Theo hide with the baby: the house they inhabit seems to be complete, and the family is settled into it. But Bexhill is no resort, nor is it a comfortable place to live. Bearing graphic testimony to this, most of the walls of the buildings in the camp have graffiti written on them.

National differences are still visible, most clearly in the different languages spoken in the facility.

This is the environment and space in which Dylan, Kee's baby, is born. Kee begins to go into labor as she, Miriam (the nurse), and Theo are being transported to the detainment center. Once at the abandoned apartment where she stays with Theo, Kee gives birth to her baby. Although her mother is African, Dylan is born in an immigrant space. Given the United Kingdom's different rules to those of the United States, where citizenship is granted to those born within the country, Dylan would not be a British citizen by virtue of her being born there, nor does *Children of Men* posit that possibility within the story. Instead, she continues the immigrant legacy inherited by her mother and by Bexhill. As a savior of humanity, Dylan is likened to Jesus Christ in several ways: Kee tells Theo about her pregnancy in a barn, making reference to Mary and the manger, and Theo's reaction to her revelation is to say, "Jesus Christ." As the first baby born in eighteen years, she has the ability to save humanity. Dylan also had to be female so that she has the possibility of being a mother.

None of the Fishes live long enough to get to the *Tomorrow*. Julian is killed by the Fishes. The police take Miriam when they enter Bexhill. Theo is the only one able to accompany Kee and her baby off British soil, into the sea, but soon he, too, passes out in the boat and appears to have died. Although he is not technically one of the Fishes, the film makes it clear that he will be considered as such by the police. The Human Project is supposed to be an open society, an organization that allows even the British to join its cause, but only Kee and her baby are able to reach the boat in the end, as the survival of the human race comes to rest on a symbolic return to its original birth. The key to this rebirth lies within the third world and the immigrant population.

Children of Men posits a non-national, universal type of identification that is represented by the Human Project, by Kee, and by her baby. The question of place is present within all three of these, but they each function in various ways. While the state may limit its membership or citizenship to territory, the Fishes and the Human Project are much more inclusive. Kee and her baby represent a return to humanity's inception and to Africa as its cradle. The story of the film follows Theo as protagonist, hero/antihero, and national citizen. Had the story been told from Kee's or the baby's perspective, it would have been structured in a different way, perhaps introducing the pregnant woman from the beginning. The lesson or moral of the story, however, is not for Kee or her baby but for Theo. As the disenchanted citizen, he gains hope for the future by learning of Kee's pregnancy and by seeing the child's birth. This lesson is directed toward a public or viewer who is much like Theo. *Children of Men* reminds Europe and the United States that the future of the world may rest in the hands of the third world and the immigrant population.

Sister Films of Migration

As Cuarón acknowledged, *Babel* and *Children of Men* are sister films. Guillermo del Toro, Alfonso Cuarón, and Alejandro González Iñárritu informally collaborated within their respective films, and they formalized their working relationship with their production company Cha Cha Cha Films. Working in both Mexico and Hollywood, the three directors are blurring the lines between the two. Neither *Babel* nor *Children of Men* is a film about Mexico. Even though *Babel* does contain the story line about Amelia, its other parts are set in different countries: Morocco and Japan. While I resist the idea that this trio of directors completely defines Mexican cinema, I find it difficult to say that these films should not in some way be considered Mexican films. Should a Mexican director be limited to Mexican topics? I think not. However we classify these films and their directors, Cuarón and González Iñárritu are undoubtedly migrant filmmakers, as directors who moved to Hollywood and who also make films about migration. One of the difficulties in defining Mexican cinema and neatly categorizing these directors is that national identity is loosely understood and can overlap with global processes. Both, indeed, are Hollywood directors, and the films analyzed within this chapter are Hollywood films. However, although González Iñárritu and Cuarón work within the Hollywood film industry, they still assert their difference as Mexican directors.

Although *Babel* and *Children of Men* may seem unrelated on the surface, in their subject matter they are connected. Both explore parent-child relationships at length. *Babel* is set in the present whereas *Children of Men* is set twenty years into the future. *Babel* is a snapshot of how communication between people of different nationalities either brings them together or leads to misunderstandings. *Children of Men* hypothesizes about what the effects of current wars and political disputes may be, particularly in Iraq and other parts of the Middle East. *Children of Men* is more effective at denouncing the militarization created by the nation-state, prominently figuring images of cages and armed guards that are reminiscent of parts of our world today. *Babel* offers a critique on Mexican national identity by way of the character Santiago, but the film contains no references to why Amelia left Mexico that would make that critique stronger. It relies on old tropes of mexicanidad to describe Amelia's situation and barely questions the U.S. militarization of the border. While *Babel* represents national identity as resilient, it also points to other ways that people come together despite ethnic and national differences. *Children of Men* presents two connected but different identities that oppose or run counter to the British nationalism of the film: the Fishes and the Human Project. The end of the film favors a third-world identity anchored in Africa, a second beginning of sorts, with an African child being born to save humanity. Cuarón has not left Mexican national identity behind but has instead subsumed it within the umbrella identity of the third world. This identity does not offer much of an alternative, because of the film's setting in a fictitious world twenty years into the future. It serves more as a warning to its audience in the first world to take care of those living in developing countries and the migrants that have moved into militarized states. Both films show that despite the changes globalization may bring, it is impossible to completely erase the old tropes that give us a sense of place and identity.

6

Beyond the First Generation

Mexican Americans Visit Mexico

DESPITE BEING A U.S. CITIZEN and feeling American, I feel that I am also Mexican. I am Mexican American without a hyphen; I embrace both national identities as my own. I have constructed my sense of being Mexican in two ways. First, my mother and my grandfather have always been a significant part of who I am as a person and how I identify. They helped me to define what it was to be Mexican in the United States. My identity is linked to being the daughter of a migrant. Second, we maintain contact with family in Mexico. When I was a child, my mother planned many of my birthday parties and Christmas celebrations so that we could observe them in Cd. Juárez with my aunt, uncle, and cousins who could not cross the border. I also remember our trips to visit family in Guadalajara and Mexico City. My grandfather lived with us when I was a child, but he went back to Cd. Juárez. He no longer went to El Paso, so I visited him. The visits renewed my contact with my aunt and cousins in Cd. Juárez. My sense of family and community has been tied to those who still live in Mexico. Although I do not have dual nationality, I am Mexican culturally.[1] This chapter delves

into the various ways that Mexican national identity is expressed by
the immigrant second and third generations.

Because the ethnic-Mexican population in the United States includes
Mexican migrants as well as those whose families have been in the
United States for generations, we cannot make the generalization
that all Mexican Americans are linked to present-day Mexico. The
participation of the ethnic-Mexican population within transnational
communities should not be taken as a given, but it should not be
dismissed altogether. As I argue in this chapter, many of the children
and grandchildren of migrants, like myself, continue to be involved
with their families' "home" communities. The persistence of Mexican national identity should not be understood as being in opposition to U.S. national identity.

Mexican Americans Looking South?

Américo Paredes understood that people maintain their national identity despite having left their country, as demonstrated in the concepts
of *México de afuera* and Greater Mexico.[2] For those born in the United
States, sometimes that means having cultural pride for a country they
have never visited. Migration does not represent all the ethnic Mexicans in the United States because, as we are often reminded, many of
them were already here. The Mexican Revolution caused the first large
wave of Mexican migration to the United States, but new migrants
have come since. The rate of migration has accelerated within the
past twenty years, and technology makes transnational ties seem even
closer. As Roger Rouse reminds us, this community is represented by
the social space that includes those in Mexico as well as those who
reside in the United States. The children of immigrants participate in
those networks as well. To better understand this dynamic, we must
also understand that there are generational and citizenship differences.
Only children of Mexican nationals can request Mexican citizenship,
so Mexican law excludes Mexican Americans whose families have been
in the United States for several generations. How do Mexican Americans born in the United States participate in transnational processes?

Some Mexican Americans do not have contact with present-day
Mexico. Pablo Vila argues that Mexican Americans from El Paso,

especially those of the third or fourth generation, may have broken their ties to Mexico and identify primarily as Americans (*Crossing Borders* 123). The third- and fourth-generation Mexican Americans feel removed from modern Mexico and more connected to another, older Mexico. Although Vila is correct in noting that many may feel more American, other second- and even third-generation Mexican Americans identify with both Mexico and the United States. In one case, Vila observes how Norma, a Mexican migrant, defines Mexican national identity to include both Mexican migrants and the U.S.-born, ethnic-Mexican population in El Paso: "Despite the fact that she has been living in El Paso for almost ten years she still considers herself a *Mexican*. Not only that, she also feels that *all* her Mexican American neighbors are essentially Mexicans. In this sense, she has constructed a category that includes both Mexican nationals and Mexican Americans; that is, she utilizes 'Mexicano' as an ethnic, not as a national term" (*Crossing Borders* 133). According to Vila, migrants negotiate between the Mexican and the U.S. national systems of identification, but sometimes the second and even third generations do as well.

The second and third immigrant generations tend to identify with Mexico as their parents' country of origin. Alejandro Portes and Rubén G. Rumbaut surveyed students at forty-nine schools, once in 1992 and a second time in 1995, in two separate communities, Miami/Ft. Lauderdale, Florida, and San Diego, California. These students were either U.S.-born or had lived in the United States for at least five years, and they had at least one foreign-born parent. The objective of the study was to see whether these students adopted an American identity and whether their identities changed over time. Portes and Rumbaut's results indicated that most of the children of immigrants in San Diego identified with their parents' home country rather than with an American identity. This identification had grown stronger by the second survey: "In 1992, over 53 percent identified as American or hyphenated American, but only 34.1 percent did so three years later—a net *loss* of nearly 20 percentage points. Meanwhile, both the foreign national-origin and panethnic identifications combined for a net *gain* of almost 20 percentage points. The shift, therefore, has not been toward mainstream identities but toward a more militant reaffirmation of the immigrant identity for some groups (notably Mexicans and Filipinos in California and Haitians and Nicaraguans in Florida) and toward panethnic minority-group identities for others" (157). Very few of the students surveyed in San Diego shifted toward a plain American self-label. More than 71 percent of those identifying with foreign national identity considered identity important to them, and they presented the most stable results, with little change over time. The plain American identity was the least stable. The results indicated that these youth were not adopting the plain American label, but that in fact the opposite had occurred, especially when the children identified with their parents' country of origin. The differences in racial self-identification between the two generations were significant, especially among Mexicans: "Among Mexicans, the children preponderantly racialize their national origin, whereas Mexican parents are more likely to use other (*mestizo*) and multiracial descriptors" (177).

Portes and Rumbaut argue that the racialization of national identity resulted from discrimination. The surveys indicated that two-thirds of those who identified with the pan-ethnic labels or with foreign national terms felt that they had been discriminated against during the 1990s when Proposition 187 was passed in California. The legislation limited social services for undocumented immigrants, but it was later found unconstitutional (181). The reactive formation, according to Portes and Rumbaut, depended on factors including the location where the children were living and the relationship to the parents. The location in this specific study influenced the results: "Like collective consequences of the anti-immigration campaign in that state, direct experiences of discrimination trigger a reaction away from things American and toward reinforcement of the original immigrant identities" (187). The immigrant communities in Florida differed from those in San Diego: "More than two-thirds (67.3 percent) of those identifying by a foreign national origin were in San Diego by the time of our second survey, while about four-fifths (78.7 percent) of those identifying as plain Americans were in southern Florida" (173). As Portes and Rumbaut contend, the results depended on the timing of the second survey, conducted during the discussions about and protests to Proposition 187, which consequently accentuated ethnic differences and reinforced solidarity within the targeted ethnic groups.

A concept of Mexicanness pervades the United States. The feeling is not necessarily one that all Mexican Americans share, since many of them have been in the United States for generations. As mentioned previously, Portes and Rumbaut note that there was a shift toward use of the foreign national identity, including the hyphenated references: "Most of the Mexican shift came from youths who had identified as Chicano, Latino, or Hispanic in the 1992 survey" (160). These youths are not taking on the Chicano identity as readily as other generations did, so they imagine themselves as part of their parents' home country. The work of the imagination is clear here, since many of these children may have never visited Mexico.

The involvement in transnational life can also influence the identity of the second and third generations. Focusing on migrants from the town he calls "Ticuani," Robert Courtney Smith argues that transnational social practices can ease the process of assimilation: "For many second-generation Ticuanenses, adolescence itself is practiced transnationally, even while it is engaged with migration and assimilation pressures. They use Ticuani's communal rituals, such as feasts and dances, to negotiate their place in New York. . . . Ticuani offers the second generation a safe site for rituals and enables parents both to offer their children more freedom and to establish closer connections with them" (14). While Smith acknowledges that transnational life can lead to negative assimilation, especially with the youths that are involved in gang activity, he also argues that transnational connections and trips to Ticuani can be a positive step in the youths' incorporation into U.S. society.

Smith contends that in many cases transnational life can continue even through the third generation, and he attributes the third generation's involvement in transnational life to the pioneer migrant grandmothers. Retirement poses several obvious changes that allow for the grandparents to become caregivers, but the immigrant second generation must also grapple with the limitations imposed by work and family on transnational life. As Smith notes of the migrant community from Ticuani, the third-generation children often travel with their grandparents to visit the hometown. If the grandparents live in Ticuani, the children are sent to spend time with them. Smith uses the example of Xavier, who participates in the town's processions

with his mother: "For him, spending time in Ticuani is as natural as
it is for any small child to visit his grandparents and other relatives.
It seems likely that for Xavier and others like him, Ticuani will always
be a second home. Even if he does not continue to go, Ticuani has
already strongly influenced how he thinks of himself and about what
being Mexican means. If he does return regularly, Ticuanense transnational life may persist into the fourth generation" (201). Smith's
analysis demonstrates that movement across national boundary lines
and contact with the family's hometown in Mexico is possible for
many generations, not just for the first-generation migrants.

Smith's study allows us to view transnational processes beyond
the concepts of citizenship that impose a singular national classification. We must begin to include the children and grandchildren of
migrants in the ways that we conceptualize transnational communities. This does not mean that the children and grandchildren are not
identifying as Americans, but instead that they are formulating their
Mexican identities to coexist with their U.S. national identity. In the
following sections, I explore that ambiguous relationship between
Mexican Americans and Mexico, and how this is represented within
various literary texts.

The Chicana/o Border

The "border" has become the general metaphor for discussions about
race/ethnicity, gender and sexuality, and other identity-related topics. Migration is not excluded from this list of identity issues, even
though clearly not all Mexican Americans migrated and many are
removed from their families' experiences of migration. Joan Penzenstadler explains how the border trope is constructed in various
ways and examines "the literary treatment of the Western frontier,
the U.S.–Mexican border, Aztlán, the territory of *Chicanía*, and
the limits of the barrio" (162). The frontier experience that started
with the Anglo expansion toward the West results in a separation
between the ethnic-Mexican community and the Anglos, and the
barrio comes to represent a separate space. The division between
the Anglo and the Chicano/a experience can be seen as "either/

or," whereby the Mexican American must choose between the two identities, although for some, this ambiguous identity translates to "neither/nor," which means exclusion from both cultures. Penzenstadler also notes that there is an emerging identity of "both/and," where Mexican Americans feel that they are part of both cultures and appreciate bilingualism.

According to Penzenstadler, Chicano/a literature includes representations of migration, the actual crossing of the U.S.–Mexico border, and immigrants: "In Chicano literature, those who cross the border are heroes, not because they have acquired property or knowledge, but because they have simply survived. Their motive is not glory but the welfare of their families. Their accomplishment is relatively unglamorous but no less difficult than that of the pioneers of Anglo myth" (167). Although the representations of migrants may be heroic, Mexican Americans filter their stories of migration, not by lived experience, but rather by the stories that they have heard through others. Alberto Ledesma argues, "Should we not expect some degree of misrepresentation by Chicana/o authors who themselves have to 'assign meaning' to the Mexican immigrant experience? After all, Chicana and Chicano authors who write about Mexican immigration tend to produce narratives that are not about immigrant experiences they lived, more often they must imagine experiences that their parents went through, and thus render stories translated from what others have experienced" (73). Although Ledesma is critical of how the literary representations of migration are distorted by any nationalist subjectivity, both Mexican and American, he also argues that some Mexican American writers are able to posit undocumented migration in a positive light by representing the plight of those who come to the United States. Ledesma further contends that "Chicana and Chicano narratives of immigration concentrate their attention on the redefinition of identity, on the constant adjustments that Mexicans who are now living in the United States need to negotiate their new cultural surroundings" (88). Ledesma's focus is narrower than my own because he analyzes undocumented migration and not transnational communities, but his observations serve as a point of departure. Some Mexican American writers, most especially when they participate in transnational processes, are able to represent the transnational life of migrants within their writing.

Anzaldúa's Borderlands

The experiences of Mexican American writers are not invalid, but they give voice to the experience of Mexican Americans instead of that of the immigrants. One such example is Gloria Anzaldúa's *Borderlands/La Frontera*, in which she defines the new *mestiza* consciousness. Anzaldúa uses imagery of migration as a response to gender and ethnic politics in the United States. Deterritorialization for Anzaldúa must be understood in the context of the U.S.–Mexican War and the Treaty of Guadalupe Hidalgo, which moved the border over the Southwest making it U.S. territory. To Anzaldúa, Mexican immigration into the Southwest is reterritorialization of what was once Mexican territory. Anzaldúa defines what it is to be Mexican as follows: "We say *nosotros los mexicanos* (by *mexicanos* we do not mean citizens of Mexico; we do not mean a national identity, but a racial one). We distinguish between *mexicanos del otro lado* and *mexicanos de este lado*. Deep in our hearts we believe that being Mexican has nothing to do with which country one lives in. Being Mexican is a state of soul—not one of mind, not one of citizenship" (84). She is mostly concerned with the *mexicanos de este lado*, the Chicanos/as. She briefly goes into the economic situation in Mexico that drives migrants to the United States, but she never delves into the effects on Mexico of having such a large portion of its population in the United States.

Anzaldúa's limited dialogue with Mexico is focused on the dominant culture of the center, Mexico City. She refers to la Malinche, la Llorona, and la Virgen de Guadalupe, all significant figures to Mexican national identity. Robert McKee Irwin also points out that the indigenous cultures that she selects are those from the center of the country. The indigenous cultures that existed along the border, many of which still survive today, are completely ignored. Irwin sees this as a recurrent problem in border studies: "While it successfully challenges the 'Anglo-American' bias of American studies by giving a legitimate voice to a Mexican-American point of view, the work of Anzaldúa, like that of many Chicano studies and border studies

scholars in the United States, often seems to paradoxically perpetuate or even reinforce barriers that prevent both dialogue with
Mexican scholars based in Mexico and the study of Mexican texts
that speak to issues of U.S.–Mexico relations and border culture"
(511). Just as Anzaldúa neglects the border culture that exists on
the Mexican side, her representation of migration is limited to a
context within the United States. Although I agree with Irwin's
assertion that Anzaldúa limits her concept of the borderlands to
the United States, Anzaldúa's point of view is influenced by the fact
that her family lived in Texas for several generations. If she cannot
understand the immigrant position completely, it is because she is
far removed from that point of view.

Anzaldúa elaborates the metaphor of the migrant while constructing a Chicana consciousness. The border crossing, as figured
by Anzaldúa, is really not about the crossing of national boundaries but those of racial/ethnic and sexual classifications and cultural norms. She uses the political situation of the migrant as a
metaphor for the problems that homosexuals face in the United
States. A Chicana lesbian, she describes the border within herself:
"Her body, a crossroads, a fragile bridge, cannot support the tons
of cargo passing through it" (96). Anzaldúa similarly describes the
process of attaining the Chicana consciousness as a border crossing: "Every increment of consciousness, every step forward is a
travesía, a crossing. I am again an alien in new territory" (70).
This *travesía* is like the reterritorialization of the Southwest, but
in this case the movement is psychic: "From this racial, ideological,
cultural and biological cross-pollinization, an 'alien' consciousness
is presently in the making—a new *mestiza* consciousness, *una conciencia de mujer*. It is a consciousness of the Borderlands" (99).
Using imagery that connects her to migration, she builds a new
form of consciousness, one that allows her to be proud of her
identity. Anzaldúa could strengthen her position as a feminist if
she included those women in the Mexican border areas, many
who work in the maquiladora industry. Anzaldúa's *mestiza* consciousness does not transcend her position as a Chicana lesbian,
so she limits the possibilities of what a border crossing can represent. Although Anzaldúa's work is significant in that it denounces
discrimination against Mexican Americans, it fails to present the

situation as a transnational phenomenon. To approach migration without crossing the border to see the cultural impact that it has on Mexico tells only half the story.

Selling Mexico from the Inside Out

In the remaining part of this chapter, I analyze two books: *Crossing Over: A Mexican Family on the Migrant Trail* (2001), a *crónica* by Rubén Martínez, and *Caramelo, or, Puro Cuento*, a novel by Sandra Cisneros. Although these two books are of different literary genres, I place them together because they share a biographical aspect that presents Mexican Americans traveling to Mexico. These books provide us with a sense of how Mexican Americans participate within migrant networks and the transnational movements that bind them to Mexico, and they function as interpretations of Mexico made for the United States. Metropolitan Books, a division of Henry Holt, published *Crossing Over*; Alfred A. Knopf, a division of Random Books, published *Caramelo*. Although both books were translated into Spanish, they were originally written in English for a U.S. audience. The translated editions mark the Spanish-speaking as secondary. Writing in English is natural to Mexican Americans educated in the United States, but these particular representations of migration between Mexico and the United States target a general audience that includes U.S. Latinos/as as well as a non-Hispanic public. Both *Crossing Over* and *Caramelo* were written to sell and translate Mexico to the United States.

Guillermo Irizarry's analysis of the translation of two different novels, Rosario Ferré's *The House on the Lagoon* and Roberto Fernández's *Raining Backwards*, provides us with a solid model by which to understand the commercialization of U.S. Latino/a literature within the United States and how language plays a role of cultural and linguistic translation. Irizarry argues that *The House on the Lagoon* was written to translate Puerto Rican culture via a narrative focused on the family. Although Fernández's novel was written in English, the acts of translation within it are inoperative. Whereas Farrar, Straus and Giroux published *The House on the Lagoon*, Arte Público Press published *Raining Backwards*. In other words, Ferré published her novel through a large literary press while Fernández opted for the smaller, less commercial one. Ferré and Fernández previously published in Spanish, so their novels in English represent a market crossover. For Irizarry, the translation of these texts is fundamentally linked to their types of production. Ferré's novel feeds into the translatability of Latin American and U.S. Latino culture within a global market, but Fernández's literal translations of known Latin American and Peninsular literary works written in Spanish renders the novel less consumable for an audience that does not have knowledge of those works. Irizarry places the novels at opposite ends of the spectrum of commercialization and participation within the phenomenon of world literature.

Irizarry's insightful observations leave me with questions about U.S. Latinos/as: What is the role of translation for those U.S. Latino/a writers who primarily write in English? And what role should they have within U.S. markets? Many resist the idea of the commodification of culture and art. Many times we assume that when art and culture become commodities they lose their political and aesthetic value. This type of knee-jerk reaction is natural, but for U.S. Latino/a writers, musicians, and other types of artists, their role in commercial culture is a necessity. Mexican American writers, along with other Latinos, should be represented within the U.S. mainstream because they *are* part of U.S. society. Martínez and Cisneros do not literally translate their works into English, because both books were originally written in English, but they do a cultural translation within their books, one that demonstrates their overlapping identities and their connection to transnational movements. Martínez and Cisneros are, as Penzenstadler would argue, *both* Mexican *and* American. Martínez culturally translates migrant lifestyles and migration patterns. His book is a political project in defense of the *cheranenses*, the migrants that he follows to the United States. Cisneros's quasi-biographical novel follows one family's journey and a girl's quest to find her sexual and national identity. Cisneros uses references to Mexican literature and film and translates them into English, much like Fernández does in *Raining Backwards*. Martínez and Cisneros demonstrate a proximity to Mexican culture. Their knowledge of Mexico is inevitably connected to their families, especially those family members who migrated to the United

States. Their participation in transnational communities does not limit their incorporation into U.S. society.

Rubén Martínez on the Mexican Migrant Trail

Rubén Martínez is a public intellectual and spokesperson for migrants and U.S. Latinos in general. His writing has always had a political bent because he began in the midst of the Salvadoran civil war of the 1980s. Vintage Books, a subsidiary of Random House, published his first collection of essays, *The Other Side*, in 1993. These essays appeared in various newspapers in the United States while Martínez traveled to Mexico and Central America. In 2001, Metropolitan Books published *Crossing Over: A Mexican Family on the Migrant Trail*. More than half of *Crossing Over* is dedicated to the cultural changes in Mexico brought about by migration, specifically in Cherán, Michoacán. In his chronicles, Martínez focuses on the stories of the cheranenses and captures a sense of how those who live in the United States continue to be linked to the town. Martínez decides to follow the Chávez family after the death in a car accident of three brothers: Benjamín, Jaime, and Salvador. Because of the family's loss, migration seems less of a viable option for them, but they must still grapple with the fact that their economic livelihood depends on the income generated during those migrations to the north. Martínez sees this dilemma in one couple, Rosa and Wense, the sister and brother-in-law of those who died. Rosa's commitment to her family keeps her in Cherán while her mother mourns the loss of her brothers, but Wense does not feel this commitment. He misses his lifestyle in the United States and wishes to return as soon as possible. Martínez particularly focuses on this couple because they are at a crossroads in their lives: they must decide whether to stay in Cherán or return to the United States. When they decide to return, Martínez is able to follow them to St. Louis, so he compares Cherán to the various sites where cheranenses live in the United States. Martínez allows us to enter the world of the migrants and their families who form part of the cheranense transnational community.

Despite migration, Martínez recognizes that the people of Cherán imagine themselves as an indigenous population: "Their identity is not a matter of language, not even, strictly speaking, one of bloodlines—*mestizaje* abounds here. In the end, it is a matter of who the people of Cherán think they are. And so Cherán, according to Cherán, is a Purépecha town. Albeit a Purépecha town cruised by late-model pickup trucks blasting hip hop, an Indian town whose homes are crowned by satellite dishes, an Indian town that follows NBA box scores as closely as it does the weather's impact on the cornfields" (55). The Purépecha identity is one that this community chooses over that of being Mexican, and they preserve their identity even though they travel to the United States. Martínez notes, "Ask anyone in Cherán how they identify themselves, and they will say Purépecha before they say Mexican" (55). This type of transnational community demonstrates the variety of identities that can exist both within Mexican territory and outside of it.

Cherán functions much like the community of Aguililla, which was studied by sociologist Roger Rouse. Rouse argues that through the "transnational migrant circuits," the concept of community is no longer tied to a geographical space, but the community can be traced by a series of relations. The concept of home for the cheranenses is pertinent: "On the migrant trail, you create your world and carry it with you. Home is no longer located in a single geographical point. The towns from which the migrants hail are joined with the towns of the north to create a city space of the mind—a migrant lives and works in the States and he visits home at Christmas, New Year's, Easter, and the fiesta. Migration has forged a line of communication between and among these spaces" (139–40). The home is not in a place but rather exists within "the migrant trail." The migrants continue to identify with the town of Cherán, although they forge relationships that extend outside of the town. Martínez quotes Father Melesio's description of the accident as a casualty of a global system: "It's a chain looped over many gears. We can't say that it begins in Cherán or in the United States. It's everywhere at once" (43). Father Melesio's observations reflect the ideas behind *Crossing Over*, which places migration as a process rooted in the social and economic systems of Mexico and the United States.

Although Martínez stresses the indigenous aspect of the cheranense migration, ultimately he still places this identity in the binational context of Mexico and the United States. As Maria Antònia Oliver-Rotger observes, partially citing *Crossing Over*, "Martínez contrasts a 'traditional' Indian, pre-Columbian 'essence' with the 'modern' '[contamination] by the germ of restlessness'" (188). As Oliver-Rotger notes, Martínez uses the trope of the American dream to show how Mexican migrants come to the United States in search of a better life, but "Martínez's evocation of American Dream mythology becomes tragically ironic in light of the migrants' disenfranchisement in the U.S., the high stakes of their journey, and the ambivalence towards assimilation" (189). Martínez divides his chronicle in two by first giving us a glimpse of Cherán and then following the migrants to various locations in the United States.

Although Martínez's aim is to capture the transnational culture of these migrants, and in particular the Chávez family, he cannot avoid comparing his own travel experiences to those of the migrants. Throughout the *crónica*, we learn about Martínez's family history of migration:

> Second generation on my father's side and first on my mother's, I have come back to the line, swimming against the tide, drawn by memory, drawn by the present and by the future. I see the Mexicans pour into Los Angeles, I see them on the banks of the Mississippi in St. Louis. I see their brownness, I see my own. I suppose my sympathy can be summed up simply as this: when they are denied their Americanness by U.S. immigration policy, I feel that my own is denied as well. They are doing exactly what my father's parents and my mother did. They are doing exactly what all Americans' forebears did. (217)

Martínez counts the first generation as those who are born in the United States. If we use the sociological terminology that Portes and Rumbaut and Smith use within their studies, Martínez would be considered part of the second immigrant generation on his mother's side and the third immigrant generation on his father's side. Martínez addresses how ethnic politics in the United States lumps everyone of Mexican heritage together, despite the differences in legal status, citizenship, and generation. Although Martínez is most closely linked to migration through his mother, he writes not as a second-generation Salvadoran immigrant but as a third-generation Mexican immigrant. While this perspective can be understood as privileging the patriarchal lineage, it allows Martínez a direct connection to Mexico and the migrant culture that he is narrating.

In *Crossing Over*, Martínez does not describe visits with family in Mexico as he did in El Salvador in his previous book, *The Other Side*. Nevertheless, we can still think of Martínez's travels to Mexico as part of a transnational process. Martínez continually reflects on his relationship to Mexico through his father's eyes, and he compares his journeys to his father's: "I stare out the window and I become my wide-eyed father in the early fifties, a pudgy teenager with slicked-back hair who devoured the nocturnal landscape from the cramped cab of a 1948 Ford double-axle truck" (23). Martínez explains that his father periodically drove to Mexico to take goods that his grandfather bought in Los Angeles to sell in Mexico. Mexico comes to have various meanings according to each generation: "Mexico was a grand adventure for my father. Having grown up in L.A., he was more the American boy than the Mexican, and so the road must have been exhilarating. For my grandparents, the journey must have been much sadder, filled with dying dreams and ambivalent memories of the Old Country they left behind and to which they returned again and again, never letting go of it entirely and yet never staying" (24). Martínez views his father's relationship to Mexico as distant and different from that of his grandparents, but this description also tells us that his father had direct contact with Mexico. The writer places his travels as parallel to those of his father. They are both U.S.-born with cultural ties to Mexico. Martínez explores the transnational migrant circuits that bind Cherán to the United States, but he reverts to national classifications when he refers to himself and his family.

The references to his father are significant because we see that Martínez shows an ambivalent relationship to Mexico. His comments in an interview with Arturo García Hernández in *La Jornada* illustrate Martínez's connection to Mexico: "From Mexico, which is my father's community, and the United States, which is my community, I have learned many things that I did not expect." Martínez's interview demonstrates the ambivalence that he feels in respect to Mexico and his relationship to the country. He aligns his national identity more clearly with that of the United States, but the two countries are his "two communities, because he belongs to both."

Martínez uses his cultural background to translate Mexican migrant culture into English. This translation is unlike Fernández's and Ferré's because Martínez is known for his writing in English and he established himself within the U.S. literary market. Martínez's translation is cultural. He uses his knowledge of Mexican culture and his own proximity to migration to narrate to a general U.S. public. As Oliver-Rotger notes, "*Crossing Over* plays a key role in informing the general American public that cheap, legal or illegal Mexican labor is subsidizing U.S. industries and that the barriers and risks that exist for people do not exist for capital" (191). Oliver-Rotger does not discuss the production side of Martínez's chronicle, an issue that informs us of the role that the book has in the United States. *Crossing Over* is a more commercial venture than Ramón Pérez's *Diario de un mojado* and Luis Humberto Crosthwaite's *Lo que estará en mi corazón*, texts that I analyze in previous chapters. Because *Crossing Over* was published by Henry Holt's Metropolitan Books, it is, in a sense, a product of the same global forces that Martínez criticizes. Martínez's chronicle crossed over to the Spanish-language market and is reaching Mexican readers as well. This type of publication, along with Martínez's personal appearances on National Public Radio and at universities across the United States, has added to the dialogue about migration, especially the possibility of immigration reform. The immigration debates increased following the publication of the book. Martínez wrote *Crossing Over* at the end of the 1990s, but it is being read in a post-9/11 context in which xenophobia is more marked. The commercialization of this text allowed Martínez to continue to be an international advocate for immigrant rights.

DIVISIONS OF CLASS AND CITIZENSHIP.   Although written in the form of a *crónica*, *Crossing Over* shows the influences of different forms of writing such as testimonial literature, journalism, and autobiography. Juan Poblete informs us as to the various ways in which this text can be read: "Like the testimonio, there is an alliance between popular subjects and an intellectual that attempts to give them a voice in the dominant discourses and channels to which no one has access. Like new journalism and the autobiography, we find a denial of any pretension of neutrality and the incorporation of a point of view and a strong authorial presence. Like an ethnography, here there is also an effort to illuminate a macrosituation by way of its concrete manifestation in a microcontext, more precisely, in the real experience of an extended migrant family" (93). The text is politically motivated since it portrays the social and economic hardships that a migrant community must face. The testimonio as a literary form has been debated because of many claims that it tells a truth and because of the role of the writer as mediator. These types of difficulties are apparent in *Crossing Over*, and they are central to the critiques of the book.

Although her article celebrates Martínez's role as ethnographer-writer, Oliver-Rotger brings up several issues about the power relations between Martínez and the migrants: "As an investigative journalist, he leaves and returns to his home safely like the tourist, the traveler, or the CEO of a transnational corporation" (185). One of the instances that Oliver-Rotger criticizes is Martínez's decision to visit his family for Christmas, because this causes him to miss Rosa's border crossing. He was to cross the border with her, but Rosa decided to leave Cherán during Martínez's absence. Although I understand Oliver-Rotger's criticism, I find it difficult to judge Martínez, because it is natural that he would want to celebrate Christmas with his family. Even if Martínez had crossed the border with Rosa, he would not have been in the same position as her. He would cross as an observer and ultimately without the same level of risk, whereas Rosa would cross out of necessity. In the border crossings that Martínez narrates, he is able to move swiftly across without any problem. In one instance, he talks about the O'odham community that lives on both sides of the Arizona-Sonora border. Martínez describes how he jumps from one side of the border to the other: "I dance a jig back and forth across the line, laughing at it, damning it, and recognizing the mighty power of the very idea of a line that cannot, does not exist in nature but that exists, nevertheless, in political, that is, human terms" (218). Although Martínez is stopped for violating immigration code, he is able to maneuver his way out of the situation: "I flash my credentials, and after a bit of radio repartee between the agents and their supervisors, all is fine and dandy" (218). Martínez is not in the same position as Rosa or Wense.

In chapter 2 I discussed the dynamics of power of the testimonio in relation to *Lo que estará en mi corazón*. The commercialization of *Crossing Over* adds another layer to the power dynamics, which is precisely the importance of the text. If it were not commercialized, the chronicle probably would not circulate, and fewer people would read about the Chávez family. The problems with *Lo que estará en mi corazón* are that few people have heard of the testimonio and that it is almost impossible to buy a copy.[3] The commercialization of *Crossing Over* also means that Martínez makes a living by writing about migrants. I wrote to Martínez to ask about these dynamics. In my e-mail, I asked him: "In order to write, you must eat, but how do you balance that out? How do you avoid doing exactly what you criticize of the U.S. and Mexican societies?" I also asked whether he gave the Chávez family any money from his earnings. In his response (on June 19, 2007), Martínez addresses my question as follows: "Simply put, there is no way to resolve the essential capitalist contradiction of participating in the labor economy while at the same time trying to create an ethical representation of the 'marginal' subject. . . . In some ways the contradiction exists even without the economic aspect." Martínez points to the reflexive nature of his writing that he attributes to new journalism of the 1960s. He acknowledges the contradiction that is inherent in adding his voice to the text, "drawing attention to the writer's character and away from the documentary subject" (Martínez's e-mail). This is one of the qualities that changes this text from what is typically considered a testimonio in the Latin American tradition to a more hybrid form, as Poblete notes, that also includes the *crónica* and the ethnography.

By allowing for those differences to be apparent, Martínez gives voice to an experience that is different from his own. He explores both experiences of border crossing while acknowledging that they are not the same: "We are both nomads, but there is a vast gulf between us. My road is essentially middle-class; I travel because I can. Wense and his migrant brothers and sisters travel because they must" (63). Martínez points to a level of poverty that he cannot comprehend but that he attempts to represent. One of the migrants, Pedro, who survived the accident that killed the Chávez brothers, cries as he begins to speak of his life: "Pedro cries not for the Chávez brothers, that is, he doesn't give their names to his sorrow. Yesterday, his ox died. At first I, the gringo, think this is some kind of joke, but it's not. Eight years that *animalito* had trudged up into the hills and helped Pedro bring back pine and oak from the last free stand of trees in the region. He loved that animal. Because it represented his livelihood in Cherán and because it gave every ounce of its energy so his family might be provided for" (167). By referring to himself as a gringo, Martínez uses citizenship to explain the divide between him and Pedro, but this is also a difference in class.

The differences are apparent to both Martínez and the other migrants, particularly Wense. At one point, Wense shows off his friendship with Martínez, the reporter from the United States, as he speaks to a *norteño* in a bar. Wense dislikes the *norteños*, those migrants who improved their economic and social standing by traveling to the United States. Although Wense has worked in the United States, he has not yet achieved the social status of other migrants. Martínez avoids a confrontation by dragging Wense out of the bar, but this situation leads to a conversation about class. Wense repeatedly tells Martínez, "You don't understand, Rubén, you just don't understand" (162–63). Wense finally confesses what is bothering him by admitting that he is too ashamed for Martínez to meet his family. He describes his poverty: "Because I'm ashamed, because . . . my family is poorer than you can imagine, I'm poor, my family is poor. You think my wife's family is poor, ha! I saw my brother today, his shoes were taped together to keep them from falling apart" (163). Martínez never meets Wense's family, but he travels to the United States at Wense's request. St. Louis is the place where Wense feels most comfortable. His living situation is much better there than it is in Cherán, and he allows Martínez to see that part of his life. Martínez cannot represent Wense's poverty, but he can give voice to the frustration of living in those conditions. Not to allow Wense his personal space would be disrespectful.

Although social class is one of the major differences between Martínez and the Chávez family, citizenship also separates the two. U.S. citizens are afforded more freedom in crossing to Mexico and back to the United States.[4] In his e-mail response to my questions, Martínez acknowledges that he has tried to help the Chávez family; unfortunately, he also understands that help to be limited: "In many ways I feel that I failed the Chávez family because I couldn't get them what they needed—legal status in this country." Martínez's political objective is to cause social change. Added to the issues of class and citizenship, Martínez also tries to complicate the ethnic politics that lumps all Mexicans into the same category. He shows that although his ethnicity is linked to the migrants, specifically the cheranenses, they are still ethnically different from him. Martínez may be an ethnic minority in the United States, but the cheranenses are also ethnic minorities in Mexico because they are Purépecha.

THE CHERANENSES IN THE UNITED STATES.   The generational divisions that I discussed in the early part of this chapter assume that migrants arrive in the United States and can be counted as the first generation. With the movement between Mexico and the United States, those divisions may not exist in that fashion. Many migrants have parents who migrated to the United States but then decided to return to Mexico to raise their families. These generational distinctions are made within the United States as a way of speculating whether the migrants and their families will assimilate into U.S. society. Martínez demonstrates that even those with a family history of circular migration must grapple with the changes that come from permanently moving to the United States. Martínez tells of Raúl Tapia's family history, which includes four generations of migration to the United States. Tapia was the first to establish permanent residence in the United States, but he was not the first in his family to migrate. Martínez speculates as to how the children of these migrants will assimilate into U.S. society and what it may mean for their parents, and he tackles difficult questions about assimilation: Are the migrants assimilating? How are the families changing? What happens linguistically to the children who are born in the United States? Although on the surface it would seem that Martínez is an impartial observer, the ways that he answers these questions are conditioned by his being the son and grandson of immigrants.

Martínez explains how each generation changes as it assimilates into U.S. society, but he also describes the ways that U.S. society changes because of migration and the cultural influences that it brings. Instead of focusing on the Southwest, where Mexican Americans have been living for many generations, Martínez instead goes to the Midwest. The Midwest received a variety of immigrants over the years, but they were mostly European until the Mexicans moved into the area. "Princes of Norwalk," chapter 11 of *Crossing Over*, details how Mexican migration to the United States changed Norwalk, Wisconsin. Martínez describes how different migrant families are adapting to Norwalk and how each generation is being incorporated into U.S. society. Martínez refers to the Enríquez family to explain that "in the span of four generations, the Enríquezes will have gone from being Purépecha-speaking Indians (Santiago's and María's parents), to bilingual Indians speaking Purépecha and Spanish, to bilingual and symbolically trilingual Indians speaking Spanish and English with a smattering of Purépecha, to monolingual and symbolically bilingual Indians speaking English, with a smattering of Spanish and maybe a word or two or Purépecha" (260). Martínez gives an overview of the generational shifts that could occur, but he also acknowledges that the recent waves of migration may present new outcomes: "But that assumes, of course, that this migrant generation will behave like the ones that came before—which is an open question" (260).

Despite these generational differences, the Enríquezes maintain many of the Purépecha traditions. Martínez recounts how the family rehearsed a pre-Columbian dance called *los viejitos*. The Enríquezes decided to perform the dance as a way to promote cultural exchange in Norwalk. Although the children saw the dance performed in Cherán, they had never danced it themselves before this event; therefore, the event in Norwalk reinforced their Purépecha identity. Martínez pays special attention to the youngest Enríquez daughter, Marta, because she is the most Americanized of the group. Although she was born in Cherán, she is growing up in Norwalk. Marta displays the most ease with the dual national identity, that of the overlapping U.S. and Mexican identities: "She speaks accentless English and Spanish and easily travels between her two worlds. In fact Marta is already a crucial link between the rest of her family and English-speaking Norwalk. Her parents and older siblings, who speak a basic migrant's English, are not and probably never will be capable of expressing the complexity of their thoughts and feelings in the new language" (260). Having come to the United States at a young age, Marta acquired the necessary linguistic abilities to be able to help her family.

Martínez also notices the role of interracial marriages between white American women and their Mexican migrant husbands in changing the social and cultural landscape in Norwalk. Martínez partially attributes the marriages to the lack of young white men in the town. These interracial marriages represent the integration of both cultures, which is most apparent in the births of interracial children. Martínez interviews several white American women who are married to Mexican men. Kerry Vian is married to Javier, a Mexican migrant, and they have a son named Chance. Nina Edgerton is also married to a Mexican; she owns a local restaurant. Nina comments to Martínez about the role of the interracial children, "These kids will be less prejudiced, if they're half Hispanic and half American. It's only the American guys that have that prejudice, and I think it's mostly a jealousy thing" (264). The children, then, change the fabric of the community not only by their existence, but also by their attitudes and social outlook.

Martínez focuses on the second generation to show how the children of migrants negotiate between their parents' culture and their new home. Although Martínez mostly chronicles the travels of the first generation, he also gives us a glimpse as to how its children will identify. The second and third generations offer an alternative: "In the end, the joke will be on both the gringo and the Mexican guardians of reified notions of culture. The kids will be neither Mexican nor gringo but both, and more than both, they will be New Americans, imbibing cultures from all over the globe" (191). Martínez already fits the description.

Tapping into the U.S. Mainstream: Sandra Cisneros

Sandra Cisneros is one of the most well-known Mexican American writers. *The House on Mango Street*, her first book, made Cisneros a recognizable figure within the United States. The book is now required reading in classrooms across the country and is considered part of a larger U.S. literary cannon. Arte Público Press first published *The House on Mango Street* in 1984, but Vintage Books later picked it up and published her subsequent books including *Caramelo, or, Puro Cuento*. Cisneros's incorporation into the U.S. mainstream adds to the visibility of Mexican Americans, who have had little access to the U.S. imaginary until recently. *Caramelo* combines the story of a migrant network with a reconstruction of Mexican national identity. The novel uses Mexican history, especially that of Mexico City, to create its background, and it tells of Celaya (Lala) Reyes's travels between Chicago, Mexico City, and San Antonio. Although Lala's father is the only first-generation migrant in his immediate family, his wife and his children also visit Mexico City and his parents.

Cisneros partially based the novel on her own visits to Mexico to see her father's family. In an interview with Ray Suárez, Cisneros explains that the connections that her family had to Mexico were prevalent in Chicago to such a degree that they made Mexico a commuter suburb. She describes how she weaved her family history and that of others into the novel: "Generally if you're a daughter in a Mexican family, no one wants to tell you anything, they tell you healthy lies about your family. But the older I got and the more people recognized me as the writer, family stories started getting passed to me, memoirs, a little bit of gossip, this and that. And I found myself drawing from families' *memorias*, their memoirs." Cisneros plays with the autobiographical twist in the novel by reminding her readers that she is also writing *puro cuento*, mere stories or fiction. Although Cisneros did extensive research on Mexican history, many of her references also include films and music, which add another fictional layer to the novel.

Celaya is a young Mexican American adolescent, nicknamed Lala, who is an active participant within a migrant network. She negotiates between living in the United States and spending her summers in Mexico, and she embraces both cultures. While the novel taps into the workings of migrant networks, it is considerably different from Pérez's *Diario de un mojado*, which I analyzed in chapter 4. As I argued, the diary addresses how the Mexican and U.S. national imaginaries have left the indigenous populations aside for the dominant discourse of *mestizaje*. The Reyes family travels back and forth between the United States and Mexico in the same way that Pérez does, but *Caramelo* embraces the notion of *mestizaje* and uses it to reconstruct Mexican national identity.

The Reyes family has a long tradition of migration. Uncle Old was the first in the family to move to Chicago, and he started a chain of migration that would extend several generations. Narciso, Lala's grandfather, lived temporarily in Chicago, but he returned to Mexico City at his parents' request. Narciso's sons later migrated permanently to Chicago and learned to make their living from Snake, Uncle Old's son, who is an upholsterer. Inocencio Reyes, Lala's father, inherited his way of life from his family: "It could be said Inocencio Reyes lived the life of a person in self-exile, happiest when he could devote himself to his daydreams. Love inspired him to think, as it inspires so many fools. He dedicated his life to this interior inquiry. He did not know he was continuing a tradition that traveled across water and sand from nomadic ancestors, Persian poets, Cretan acrobats, Bedouin philosophers, Andalusian matadors praying to la Virgen de Macarena. Each in turn had influenced their descendent Inocencio Reyes" (199). Inocencio gets his personality and urge to migrate from his ancestors, who extend beyond his Mexican ancestry. The description follows the legacy left by Eleuterio Reyes, his grandfather, who migrated to Mexico from Seville. Although Lala was born in the United States, she forms part of her family's network of migration, and she considers herself to be a Mexican. Her journey is south toward Mexico. The title of chapter 51 explains her identity: "All Parts from Mexico, Assembled in the U.S.A or I Am Born." When others say that she does not look Mexican, Lala asserts her Mexicanness: "I don't know what you're talking about when you say that I don't look Mexican. I *am* Mexican. Even though I was born on the U.S. side of the border" (353).

When the Reyeses move to San Antonio, they meet Mexican Americans who do not participate within migrant networks and who have been in the United States for many generations. Although these Mexican Americans socialize with and live in the same neighborhoods as the migrants, Inocencio distrusts them. Mars is a friend of Inocencio's from when he served in the military. It is he who helps Inocencio find a home and a place for his business when they move to San Antonio. When the friendship is strained, as Lala explains, Inocencio blames his problems on Mars: "Father had a big fight with Marcelino Ordóñez of Mars Tacos to Went that ended with Father cursing his old friend Mars of long ago, cursing all Chicanos for acting like Chicanos and giving Mexico a bad name" (379). Lala makes the same type of distinction even though she was born in the United States. When she visits her friend Viva, she notices that the house seems more settled than that of her family, and she attributes the difference to Viva's long connection to San Antonio. One of the reasons that she likes her boyfriend, Ernesto, is that he understands the migrant way of life because he returns to Monterrey with his family. By marking these differences, Lala shows that she identifies with Mexican transnational communities, those that continue to have contact with Mexico.

Although the story of the Reyes family goes back several generations, Zoila, Lala's mother, is introduced when she meets Inocencio in chapter 50, in the middle of the novel. From Lala's description, we know that Zoila was born in the United States, but we are never given her family's history. Juanita Heredia argues that Lala has a hybrid identity caught between Chicago and Mexico City and between her paternal grandmother and her mother. However, the novel privileges the Awful Grandmother's voice over that of Zoila. It follows the father's lineage. Lala's grandmother interjects in Lala's narration to give her own perspective of the stories being told. Lala and her grandmother retell the Reyes family history, but Zoila's side of the family is completely omitted. Cisneros wanted to write a novel about Mexico as a commuter suburb, and she does so by way of the Reyes family.

Despite her strong identification with Mexico, Lala opts to live in Chicago, a city where her overlapping national identities can coexist. Uncle Old describes Chicago in Mexican terms, conjuring up the images of *mestizaje*. He says, "And so, I wound up here in Chicago, a city cursed with not one but two bad words for a name: 'the fucked one' and 'the one who shat'" (137). The "fucked one" refers to *chingado*, the term used in Mexico to describe the conquest and the relationship between Hernán Cortés and la Malinche, the indigenous woman who was his translator. Uncle Old associates Chicago with one of the strongest symbols of mexicanidad, and he takes the city's name from the root of *cagar*, to shit. As I argue in *"Revista Generación*: Mexican Regionalism and Migration in Tijuana and Chicago," Chicago is absorbed into the Mexican imaginary and its regional system of classification. The representations of migration within *Generación*, a literary and cultural magazine, demonstrate how Mexico is represented as a deterritorialized nation. *Caramelo* presents a similar representation of Chicago as a Mexicanized city but from an inverse perspective. If Mexico is a commuter suburb, then Chicago is the center. From their perspective as second-generation immigrants, Cisneros and her novel's character Lala are both from Chicago, so the city is their primary locus or referent.

RECREATING MEXICANIDAD. Cisneros dialogues with Mexican national identity as a way to include the second generation in the Mexican imaginary of the nation. In addition to weaving some of her family history into the novel, she also uses various Mexican cinematic and literary references to construct the narrative. Cisneros makes particular use of Mexican films of the golden age, mainly of the 1940s. Many of the characters in the novel are modeled after those in Mexican films, *telenovelas*, and literature. A note in chapter 83 states, "A famous chronicler of Mexico City stated Mexicans have modeled their storytelling after the melodrama of a TV soap opera, but I would argue that the telenovela has emulated Mexican life. Only societies that have undergone the tragedy of a revolution and a near century of inept political leadership could love with such passion the telenovela, storytelling at its very best since it has the power of a true Scheherazade—it keeps you coming back for more" (409). *Caramelo* is a fictional novel tinged with autobiographical and biographical elements. Cisneros uses the stories from novels and films to create her own. These intertextual references serve to reconstruct the Reyes family's story, but also a romanticized Mexican national identity.

Cisneros seems to be conscious that she is reinventing and recreating a sense of Mexican national identity. The last paragraph in the chapter titled "Pilón" gives us an insight into the various ways that Mexican national identity is constructed within *Caramelo*. Lala concludes the following: "And I don't know how it is with anyone else, but for me these things, that song, that time, that place, are all bound together in a country I am homesick for, that doesn't exist anymore. That never existed. A country I invented. Like all emigrants caught between here and there" (434). Both Lala and Cisneros seem to be speaking here to the reader to acknowledge the ways that immigrants and their children imagine Mexico. *Caramelo* demonstrates that Mexican Americans also use many of the dominant archetypes of mexicanidad, which are borrowed from Mexican film and literature.

Lala and others describe Inocencio as similar to Pedro Infante, an actor who embodied the ideal masculine type and the hero who supports his family. Infante's most famous role was that of Pepe el Toro in Ismael Rodríguez's films *Nosotros, los pobres* (1947), *Ustedes, los ricos* (1948), and *Pepe el Toro* (1953). Inocencio is thought to be the responsible father figure. Zoila tells Lala toward the end of the novel that Inocencio has another daughter, Candelaria, whom he had out of wedlock. Lala believes that her father must have tried to make up for his prior mistakes by being a good father to her and her brothers. Despite his irresponsibility in Candelaria's case, Lala sees Inocencio as a hard worker and a loyal father. The star persona goes along with the ideal that men must be "feo, fuerte y formal"—ugly, strong, and formal.

Aunty Light Skin is associated with the nightlife of the cabarets. Although she does not describe herself as a *cabaretera* to Celaya, she does admit that she met Tongolele, a *rumbera*, or dancer, in night-clubs, the same night that she met her supposed husband. The ways that the aunt recounts the story and that Lala imagines it show how Cisneros used intertextual references to create the story. Lala imagines the scenario as a scene from a film: "Everything shot in deep shadows, high contrast, plenty of profiles and silhouettes. A black-and-white *churro* of a movie with one hair on the lens flickering on the screen. Tongolele is a tropical rainstorm, a steamy jungle, a black panther in heat. Her dressing room door inhales and exhales from the pressure of 3,129 Mexican men pushing to devour, sink their teeth, lap up blood, swallow her heart whole. Ton-go-le-le! Ton-go-le-le! Ton-go-lee-leeeeeeee!" (268). Lala hears her aunt's story and immediately associates it with a *cabaretera* film. Her imagination adds the visual tones of the "black-and-white *churro* of a movie." Cisneros leads her readers on a similar journey through the imagination. For those readers who have watched many of the classic Mexican films or read Mexican literature, the intertextual references tap into an established set of images, story lines, and character types.

Candelaria, Inocencio's illegitimate daughter, is reminiscent of the title character in *María Candelaria* (Emilio Fernández, 1944). Lala learns from her mother that Candelaria is her half sister when her father is in the hospital. Candelaria seems to be a secondary character until the revelation, but she is significant in many ways. The title of the novel refers precisely to Candelaria's skin color; the story is at root about how Inocencio and Zoila's relationship is affected by the Awful Grandmother's intrusion when she tells Zoila about Inocencio's eldest daughter. Candelaria's mother is indigenous, so Candelaria's skin color is indicative of her *mestizaje*. In *María Candelaria*, Dolores del Río played the young woman who is judged by

her community for being the daughter of a prostitute. The actress's
light skin would seem to be inappropriate for an indigenous woman,
but she is more than likely a *mestiza*. Because her mother was a
prostitute, María Candelaria's father could be anyone, even a white
man. Much like Dolores del Río's character, Candelaria is judged
for her father's past mistakes. Although she is not killed like María
Candelaria, Candelaria represents Inocencio's dishonesty. He was
not disloyal to Zoila, because the affair happened before they even
met; his mistake was that he never told her that he had a daughter.

The question of *mestizaje* is central to the narrative. Eleuterio
Reyes, Lala's great-grandfather, moved to Mexico from Seville and
married Regina, who had indigenous features. Narciso and Inocencio follow the pattern of *mestizaje* by marrying indigenous-looking
women. Although they are *mestizos* themselves, they carry the Spaniard facial features. Celaya indirectly speaks of the *mestizaje* of her
family: "I come from a long line of royalty. On both sides. The Reyes
have blue blood going back to Nefertiti, the Andalusian gypsies, the
dancing-for-their-dowry tribes in the deserts of North Africa. And
that's not even mentioning my mother's family, the Reynas, from
Monte Albán, Tenochtitlán, Uxmal, Chichén, Tzin Tzun Tzán.
I could go on and on" (353). Although Inocencio's grandmother and
mother are not of Spanish descent, it is this lineage that the Reyeses
use to describe their cultural background. Zoila's family comes from
areas associated with indigenous populations and pre-Columbian
roots: the Aztecs, the Mayas, and the Purépechas. Although Lala
is a *mestiza*, she is light skinned. Candelaria, however, has caramel-
colored skin, and she looks more like a *mestiza*.

Through a touch of magical realism, Lala, as mentioned, retells
her family's story while her deceased grandmother, Soledad, interjects. Her grandmother's name is reminiscent of Octavio Paz's *El
laberinto de la soledad*, an essay which argues that the Mexican character is locked in a maze of solitude. The dialogues between the
Mexican American and the Mexican grandmother remind us that,
although Mexican Americans may travel to Mexico and participate
in migrant networks, such relationships can be tense. The deceased
grandmother is suggestive of the characters in Juan Rulfo's short
stories and his novel *Pedro Páramo* (1955). Rulfo's novel follows
Juan Preciado, who returns to the town of Comala in search of his

father, Pedro Páramo. In his quest for his father, Preciado finds himself among ghosts. Comala is much like a purgatory. In *Caramelo*, Soledad is trapped in purgatory. Her sin was that she purposefully told Zoila about Inocencio's illegitimate daughter in order to break up their marriage. *Caramelo* is her story as told by Lala as a means to redeem her grandmother's past and get her out of purgatory.[5]

The Awful Grandmother's conversation with Lala is meant to teach her to avoid getting pregnant and getting married in the same way that Soledad did. Juanita Heredia offers a positive reading of Lala's connection to other women: "What she inherits in this transnational feminist lineage is an independent spirit that allows her to challenge patriarchal attitudes about a woman's servile place in society. Rebellious by nature, Lala becomes independent when she travels to Mexico City, not in search of roots, but sexual and spiritual freedom and assert her transnational gender identity" (353). More than a novel about Lala's discovery of her "sexual and spiritual freedom" as Heredia contends, the novel in my view is about making wise choices about love and sexuality during adolescence. The reason that the grandmother's ghost appears is to warn Lala not to repeat her mistakes. The Awful Grandmother tells Lala, "I can't bear it. Why do you insist on repeating my life? Is that what you want? To live as I did? There's no sin in falling in love with your heart and with your body, but wait till you're old enough to love yourself first. How do you know what love is? You're still just a child" (406). Heredia assumes that Lala is an adult, but she is only an adolescent in high school by the end of the novel. The grandmother wants to break the cycle of accidental pregnancies. Lala gets her second chance, because she does not get pregnant.

The conversation between Celaya and her grandmother is also symbolic of the ambivalent and sometimes difficult relationship between Mexican Americans and Mexican nationals. Lala and Soledad both love Inocencio, but they do not get along with each other. Soledad does not like that her grandchildren's ways show the influence of the United States, which is evident in their use of Spanglish. Soledad also fights for Inocencio's attention, so she sees Zoila and Lala as the competition. The Awful Grandmother, the ghost, explains to Lala that she was jealous, so she deliberately told Zoila about Candelaria: "Look, I didn't mean to hurt anyone, Celaya, I swear to you.

But then I didn't understand how your father loved me. And I was so afraid. He came to visit less and less, and he had all you children to love" (408). Although Soledad might feel resentful, Inocencio, as the migrant, keeps Lala and Soledad connected to each other. Lala finds some reconciliation with her grandmother: "I've turned into her. And I see inside her heart, the Grandmother, who had been betrayed so many times she only loves her son. And I love him. I have to find room inside my heart for her as well because she holds him inside her heart like when she held him inside her womb, the clapper inside a bell. One can't be reached without touching the other. Him inside her, me inside him, like Chinese boxes, like Russian dolls, like an ocean full of waves, like the braided threads of a *rebozo*" (424–25). Despite the problems with her grandmother, Lala recognizes that their lives are intertwined with each other through their love for Inocencio. The migrant connects his family in the United States to that in Mexico and vice versa.

THE SUBTLETY OF U.S. NATIONAL IDENTITY.   Although the migrant networks are a specific cultural reference that may be unfamiliar to many of *Caramelo*'s readers, the novel appeals to a more general audience by making the Reyes family's travel much like that of any American family. The Reyes clan's visit to the grandmother's house is a U.S. cultural trait. Cisneros invokes the commonly repeated phrase within the United States "Are we there yet?"—used by children to ask whether they have arrived at their destination, often the grandmother's. The automobile is another marker of U.S. identity and the center of the family road trip. Despite the Reyeses' pride in being Mexican, it is clear that they are also proud Americans.

Inocencio Reyes came to the United States without any documentation, but he served in the army as a way to legalize his status. Service in the military is the highest form of loyalty and patriotism to the United States. Cisneros overemphasizes Inocencio's military service when the U.S. Immigration and Naturalization Service questions his documentation. The odd detail in this part of the narration is that Inocencio shows his papers confirming his service rather than another type of documentation to prove his residence or naturalized citizenship. Inocencio claims his right to live in the United States by showing his discharge papers from the U.S. Army. For many, there is no greater display of loyalty than to put one's life on the line.

Despite being an immigrant, Inocencio believes in military service to the United States and supports his son, Toto, when he enlists, despite his wife's contrary opinion.

The family goes through a transition that slowly tears it away from Mexico and anchors it in the United States, specifically Chicago. Soledad moves to Chicago to be close to her sons, and later she helps Inocencio buy a house in San Antonio. To make the purchase, she sells her house on Destiny Street in Mexico City, so the family no longer has a home there. After the grandmother's death, Inocencio decides to return to Chicago, where his brothers and sons live. The Reyes family is anchored to the city because several generations of Reyes men migrated and permanently settled there. Marriage outside of the ethnic group is one of the indicators that a group is assimilating. Uncle Baby and Toto both marry women from different immigrant groups in Chicago. Uncle Baby marries a woman of Italian descent, and Toto a Korean American. Although they assimilate, they maintain ties to immigrant Chicago.

Celaya learns during her last visit to Mexico City that her ties to Mexico are broken. She convinces Ernesto Calderón, her first boyfriend, to take her there to elope. She is only fifteen years old, but she wants to be in love. When Ernesto realizes that that they have made a mistake by going to Mexico City, he leaves Lala at the hotel. While Lala tries to figure out whom she is going to call, it becomes painfully obvious to her that she can no longer walk to Destiny Street to find her family. Her life and family are in Chicago, so there is a rupture with Mexico in two ways. First, the Reyeses have no reason to return to Mexico City after the grandmother dies. The migrant network that extends from the United States to Mexico is no longer necessary. The second way is more symbolic, because Lala has a second opportunity to break with the family's cycle of unplanned births, which limited the Reyes women's possibilities outside of the family. Lala says in the *Pilón*, "Then that red Rubicon. The never going back there. To that country I mean" (434). Lala does not have to go back physically to Mexico, because it is a country that she invented for herself within the United States. Her pride in her Mexican heritage allows her to pick and choose those values that are beneficial to her and discard those that are not. Although the novel does not explicitly discuss U.S. national identity, it is clear in the end

that the family has made its home in Chicago and assimilated into
the United States.

Mexican Americans Traveling South

Transnational communities are not just limited to migrants. Their
children and grandchildren often join their parents in their journeys
back to Mexico, and they transform their parents' national identity
into their own, albeit converted into an ethnic category. As Portes
and Rumbaut argue, the second-generation immigrants identify with
their parents when they feel discriminated against. In California,
such reactive formation was clear during the debates and passage of
Proposition 187. Many in the second generation and even the third
do more than just identify with their parents' country of origin; they
also travel to their hometowns, crossing back and forth between
Mexico and the United States. Many children and grandchildren
of migrants participate within migrant networks, depending on life
cycles and needs. Mexico in those cases is not a foreign country
or just their parents' home, but also their own. This contact with
Mexico, however, should not be taken in opposition to the process of assimilation. As Robert Courtney Smith notes of the *ticuanenses*, transnational life can facilitate assimilation, or incorporation
into U.S. society. Those of the second generation develop overlapping identities: they are *both* Mexican *and* American, using Penzenstadler's expression.

Rubén Martínez and Sandra Cisneros represent the migrant networks from the perspectives of those who were born in the United
States. Both narratives have an autobiographical element in which
the writers include their own accounts of crossing the border; their
styles of writing, however, diverge. Martínez offers us a view of how
the cheranense transnational community is transforming the hometown in Mexico and various towns in the U.S. Midwest. He does so
by exploring his relationship to the border, to Mexico, and to the
United States. Cisneros fuses stories that she heard from her family
with intertextual references to Mexican film and literature. Although
Cisneros was inspired by her father to write the novel, *Caramelo* is
a fictional account of the Reyes clan's drive between Chicago and

Mexico City. Martínez and Cisneros demonstrate that Mexican and U.S. national identities can coexist. Martínez sees how the second generation manages both cultures with ease. While the cheranenses are the main focus of his *crónica*, he tells his readers about his family and how he relates to the migrant networks. Although he never identifies himself as such, he is one of those New Americans whom he fondly describes. In *Caramelo*, Lala sees herself as a U.S.-born Mexican, and Chicago is her preferred city of residence.

The differences between the two narratives are connected to their literary genres, but one is not more accurate or more valid than the other. They do, however, have their limitations. Because Martínez was born in the United States to a middle-class family, there are moments when he cannot completely delve into the world of the migrants. He travels back and forth with much more ease than they do. Cisneros's intertextual references add a romanticized view of Mexican national identity that is characteristic of the cinema of the golden age. Both authors are aware of and self-reflexive about their limitations. Martínez understands the basic differences between him and the undocumented migrants, and his hope is that his writing will help to legalize his friends' statuses. Although Cisneros infuses *Caramelo* with intertextual references to Mexican film and literature that construct Mexican national identity, she also demonstrates that some traditions should be changed. The second and third immigrant generations are a node within these community networks and in Mexico, as a nation.

Conclusion

"I'm Mexican. Pull Me Over"

THE SUPPORT OUR LAW ENFORCEMENT and Safe Neighborhoods Act, also known as Senate Bill 1070, or simply S.B. 1070, was passed on April 23, 2010, in Arizona. The bill makes it a misdemeanor crime for immigrants to reside in the state without documentation, and it punishes anyone harboring an undocumented immigrant. It is being called the most stringent piece of legislation that ever passed in the United States. One particular section (2E) states that a police officer has the right to arrest any person with reasonable suspicion. The public quickly reacted to the possibility of racial profiling, so on April 30, 2010, Governor Jan Brewer passed House Bill 2162, stating that race, color, and national origin had to be excluded from any assessment of illegality. Right before the law went into effect, this provision was struck down. Protests of different types ensued and questioned the constitutionality of this legislation. In a fierce political climate that fosters a backlash toward immigrants, particularly those who are Mexican, the reaction by immigrants, second and third immigrant generations, and the larger Latino/a community is to shy away from a U.S. national identity. This type of legislation only thwarts the process of identification with the United States. Samuel Huntington argues that recent immigrants are less willing than their predecessors of primarily European descent to become Americans and accept what he considers to be mainstream American culture. Immigration opponents provoke the very reactions that they criticize, because this type of legislation serves to alienate the entire Latina/o community.

Many Latinas/os, particularly those of Mexican descent, believe that the attempt to reinforce immigration policies through racial profiling discriminates against all Latinas/os, not just immigrants. A variety of images of protest circulated on the Internet. One picture showed a car with "I'M MEXICAN PULL ME OVER" painted on the rear window.[1] Such a display of Mexicanness already shows the reactive formation of identity that Alejandro Portes and Rubén Rumbaut noted of the immigrant second generation in California following the passage of Proposition 187 in 1994. They argue that the children of immigrants during the 1990s in California understood that legislation as discriminatory, and as a result were more prone to identify with their parents' national identities. The passage of S.B. 1070 provoked the same type of reaction from the Latino/a community in the weeks following it.

On a personal level, I understand how it feels to perceive that an immigrant parent is being threatened in some way. When I was seventeen years old, my father made a terrible confession that would change our relationship for years to come. He admitted that when he was angry with my mother over visitation rights, he had wished that he could get her deported. My mother came to the United States more than a decade before she met my father, so she was a resident before my parents got married and a U.S. citizen (not through their marriage) when he made that comment. My father thought he was showing me affection by telling me that he had wanted to spend more time with me, and his comment was more an expression of anger than a real threat. What he did not realize was that he was rejecting a part of me, not just my mother. Much like Huntington's criticism of recent immigrants, my father always understood my pride in my Mexican identity as my opposition to him and to my American identity. He believes that I strive to segregate myself from mainstream society. I mention my father because he made me more Mexican. As I say that, I do not want to be misinterpreted. I am also American, but I do not identify with the United States as my father does. In many ways, I wrote this study in response to my father and to the number of people who think exactly like him. My Mexicanness and that of millions of people in the United States does not make us any less proud to be Americans.

Although I speak Spanish and identify with Mexico, these words you read are in English, and my American identity is alive and kicking.

While the atmosphere in the United States can be hostile toward immigrants, Mexico seems more willing to defend its people. The Sonoran state government ceased all official negotiations with Arizona, and President Felipe Calderón met with Barack Obama and addressed the Joint Session of Congress in May 2010 to discuss the United States' discriminatory practices toward Mexican migrants among other U.S.–Mexico border issues. The Mexican government's interest in protecting its citizens living in the exterior can be criticized on many levels, because the government has yet to provide a solution for its country's out-migration and its dependence on remittances. Despite the Mexican government's role in the process of migration, it is evident from Mexico's popular culture that there is a general consensus for a need to defend the Mexican compatriots living in the United States. Many of the bands that I discussed in chapter 3—including Maldita Vecindad and Molotov—organized a concert at the Zócalo in Mexico City to protest the legislation. They called it "Todos somos Arizona" (We Are All Arizona). Several Mexican organizations have mobilized through the Internet as a way to show their disapproval of S.B. 1070. México 2040, an organization in Mexico City that promotes social advancement, is listed on Facebook as the administrator of "1 millón de mexicanos contra la ley SB1070 Arizona." Ricardo Aguilar Castillo, the president for the Partido Revolucionario Institucional in the state of Mexico, is similarly listed as the administrator on Facebook for "Mexicanos contra la ley anti-inmigrante SB1070 de Arizona." Although the Facebook members of these two groups are harder to determine than the names of the administrators, these two groups probably include Mexicans on both sides of the border.

Even the most lighthearted commentaries over S.B. 1070 in Mexico condemn Arizona's recent legislation. *La familia del barrio* (Sergio Lebrija and Arturo Navarro, 2010), a series animation posted on YouTube.com and Mundobarrio.com, quickly released an episode about S.B. 1070 titled "Arizóname."[2] The animation is meant to be a feature-length film sometime in the near future, but the web series has already attracted a number of followers through YouTube,

Facebook, and Mundobarrio's blog. The episode features three of the characters from the series: el Noruego, Gaspar, and el Abuelo. El Noruego decides that he wants to migrate to Arizona, so he buys a kit called "Arizonize-Me," which helps its customers look less Mexican. The two-minute video gives the feel of an infomercial except that instead of selling the product, it pokes fun at this imaginary kit. El Noruego, who has curly, dark hair, uses the kit to show Gaspar and el Abuelo that it actually works. He returns with yellow hair and says, "I no speak Spanish," and "Fuck you, Mexican." Gaspar questions el Noruego's reasons for wanting to travel to Arizona and for believing that the kit will actually make him look less Mexican. He argues, "What they are doing in Arizona is wrong. They will be able to arrest someone only based on the way they look. That's racism, so leave your damn kit alone, and let's fight so they abolish that law." At the end of the clip, el Abuelo gives a message to S.B. 1070 to basically "suck his dick." (The animation is not meant for children and carries a disclaimer about the vulgarity contained in the video.) The display of Mexican masculinity is reminiscent of Santiago's machismo in *Babel*, which I discuss in chapter 5. In "Arizóname," the vulgar comment serves to challenge Arizona by reinforcing a masculinized notion of Mexican identity.

Transnational communities offer a sense of belonging that the United States as a country fails to provide. The Mexican imaginaries that I analyze in this book include those who live in Mexico and those who moved to the United States and have established permanent residence there. Each person forms a node within his or her community and nation, and contributes to how Mexico is imagined as a nation. Mexico is constructed as a nation in many ways, and each person's subject position, whether living in Mexico or in the United States, adds to the richness of these imaginaries. The Mexican migrants inevitably tie their hometowns to the United States, and their children learn about their parents' country of origin by traveling and making their own connections to those areas.

For the majority of this study, I opted for a dry tone, one that seemed more objective. I did not want my particular identity to limit my readings and analyses, so I used the social sciences as a tool to place the cultural production into context. Although this approach was useful, I found it harder and harder to use that dry tone, and in the last chapter I began using my own voice. My family's history of migration inevitably shaped how I read and understood the academic studies of migration. I am the daughter of a Mexican migrant and a white American, and I grew up in the U.S.–Mexico borderlands. My family on my mother's side, much like Rubén Martínez and Sandra Cisneros, connects me to Mexico, so I have used that insight to argue within this study that Mexico is imagined as a nation in transit.

Throughout the preceding chapters, I make repeated reference to the hometown associations and the transnational migrant circuits that Rouse, Smith, and others have analyzed within their sociological and anthropological studies. The theoretical base that these academics provide is fundamental for my articulation of how a community can extend from Mexico to the United States, but I see some limitations with these theories. My family has a history of migration that spans several generations. Unlike the migrants who return to their hometowns, most of my family members have kept moving to other areas. Multiple migrations have scattered my family in different directions. Each of my family members has a distinct regional identity and legal citizenship. Transnational communities function despite the differences between individuals, but the decentered nature of some transnational communities is hard to represent, and even harder to analyze.

My approach in organizing the chapters was to plot a line from Mexico to the United States, and then to plot another from the United States to Mexico. My thought in doing this was that I would be following the patterns of migration, south to north and north to south. The lines are segmented and form a spiraling pattern much like the chapters: residents in Mexico, migrants to the United States, and the immigrant second and third generations. The contexts of production were also a key point of organization for the layout of the book. Although this is an interdisciplinary study of migration, I organized each chapter so as to be able to place the representations in the specific context of their genres and, in many cases, a general location—Mexico City, northern Mexico, and the United States. The result, however, is not a circular study. The representations of migration from within Mexico that I analyze in the first two chapters are vastly different from those from the second and third immigrant generations, as analyzed in chapter 4. I am aware that I have focused my analysis on transnational community formation rather than highlighting some of the problems within these communities. While migrants work as intermediaries between the hometowns in Mexico and their families in the United States, the relationships between the U.S.-born children and the communities in Mexico can be ambivalent. Mexican Americans do not have a natural affinity to Mexicans residing in Mexico. More research needs to be done to explore the complex relationships between these groups.

The images on the Internet and the groups on Facebook that protest S.B. 1070 offer a point of comparison to the types of cultural production that I analyze in this book. I received the images that protest S.B. 1070, including the one of the car and a mug shot of Dora the Explorer, by e-mail. The context of the production of these pictures may be inferred by their contents, but it is difficult to find the people who took the pictures, painted them, or made them using graphic computer programs. Many times, the production of these images is less important than who is passing them along to their friends. They are small resistances to the legislation, but also to the mainstream media, which can be limited in its scope and point of view. The Internet brings a different reading from other types of commercially produced texts, because it provides articles, blogs, images, videos, and much more that function not just as representations, in this specific case of migration and national identity, but also as immediate forms of communication. The seeming invisibility of production is markedly different from the majority of the texts that I analyzed, because all the texts presented in the chapters were commercially produced. The context of production was a key point in providing a reading of the texts. I would read *De ida y vuelta*, for example, in a different way had it been made in the United States. The fact that it was produced with Mexican sources of funding and filmed completely in Mexico allowed me to read it as an autocriticism of Mexican national identity and an acceptance of migrant networks. Had it been made in the United States, it would have represented an outright rejection of Mexico.

Transnational studies are in vogue, and countless books have been published on the topic of Mexican migration to the United States. However, the vast majority of those studies are in the social sciences; few have ventured to tackle the topic within the humanities.

Mexico, Nation in Transit is unique because it taps into the social sciences and brings those discussions into the humanities. While the social sciences can play a significant role in policy making and implementation, the arts reflect our world and our beliefs. They can help us to understand how people construct their national and community imaginaries. Several collections of scholarly articles have brought together a number of disciplines, but this is the first to offer a comprehensive study of the transnational representations of Mexican migration to the United States in the past twenty years. I challenge other academics to explore the topic and dialogue with my ideas. Arizona's S.B. 1070 will be at the center of the debates, and it may prove to be the 2010 equivalent of Proposition 187 in California in 1994. Although Proposition 187 was blocked, it represented for many a legal attempt to discriminate against the Latina/o community. The same was true in 2010 with S.B. 1070. Considering the number of responses to S.B. 1070 on the Internet, it is likely that, within the next few years, the reaction through films, novels, music, and other types of cultural production will surge.

Notes

Introduction

1. The role of Mexican consulates in the United States cannot be denied. For more information, see Rose Mary Salum's interview with Mexican consul and diplomat Eduardo Ibarrola. Mexican consulates play an important role in connecting Mexican migrants to Mexico and, vice versa, connecting the Mexican government to migrants living in the United States.

2. For more information, see Jeffrey H. Cohen, *The Culture of Migration in Southern Mexico.*

3. Similarly, Jonathan Fox refers to "migrant civil society" to focus primarily on the migrants' political involvement.

4. John Carlos Rowe argues that transnationalism is commonly placed out of historical context, so he sees "that there is a tendency in these related approaches to alienate new global phenomena from their complex histories" (79).

5. Richard Alba and Victor Nee discuss this point at length in *Remaking the American Mainstream.*

Chapter 1. Romancing the Nation

1. The golden age refers to the period from the late 1930s to the early 1950s when there was a major development in Mexican film. For information on this period, see Eduardo de la Vega Alfaro, "Origins, Development and Crisis of the Sound Cinema (1929–1964)."

2. Maciel and García-Acevedo define auteur film as "a narrative film in which the director is acknowledged to conceive the idea and theme of the film, write or co-write the script, supervise each and every aspect of the filmmaking process, and participate actively in the post-production of the film—including frequently having a major say in the final cut of the film" (184).

3. Auteur cinema in Mexico dates to the 1930s, although it was in decline from the 1960s through the 1980s. Tomás Pérez Turrent in "Crises and Renovations" gives an overview of Mexican cinema from 1965 to 1991.

4. Michoacán is one of the traditional sending states of migration from Mexico to the United States. Bustamante et al. argue that "the west-central region (Michoacán, Guanajuato and Jalisco) traditionally has had the highest levels of out migration" (116).

5. Although Sommer focuses on nineteenth-century Latin American novels, her analysis hints that romance can be used in a distinct manner: "The great Boom novels rewrite, or un-write, foundational fiction as the failure of romance, the misguided political erotics that could never really bind national fathers to mothers, much less the *gente decente* to emerging middle and popular sectors" (27–28).

6. Jorge Martínez Zepeda reports in *Frontera*, a Tijuana newspaper, that there are two versions of the history of the city's name. The first is connected to an indigenous tribe by the name of Llantijuan (also spelled Llatijuan). The other comes from a ranch that carried the name Tía Juana.

7. Esperanza's visions as shown in the film are doubtful, and it is not clear whether she is really seeing a saint or hallucinating. These visions of San Judas Tadeo are not directly shown to the viewer, but rather recounted through Esperanza's confessions to the priest. It may also be misleading to say that her journey is led by saints, since Esperanza is the one doing anything possible to "see" San Judas Tadeo.

8. The femicides in Cd. Juárez have received international attention, but the cases continue unresolved. *Señorita Extraviada* (Lourdes Portillo, 2001), a documentary about the femicides, aired internationally.

9. José Manuel Valenzuela Arce recounts the history of Juan Soldado in *Nuestros piensos*. He was a soldier who was lynched by Tijuana natives in response to an accusation that he had raped a girl, although he was never tried or proved to have been involved in the rape. He is now revered and considered a local Tijuana saint.

Chapter 2. How to Cross the Border

1. The terms "push" and "pull" are commonly used in sociology to speak of the factors that cause people to migrate.

2. See Perucho's *Hijos de la patria perdida*.

3. For example, see Tabuenca Córdoba's "Apuntar el silencio" for information on the literary movements in Cd. Juárez.

4. For more information, see Bustamante et al., "Characteristics of Migrants."

5. Mummert argues that many women decided to migrate because the lack of men lowered their possibilities of getting married. Her study mainly focuses

on the attitudes and roles within the nuclear family and does not delve into other gender and sexual roles and attitudes.

6. A derogatory term meaning "half-breed": half Mexican, half American.

7. The debates about testimonial literature are represented in both *The Real Thing: Testimonial Discourse and Latin America*, edited by Georg M. Gugelberger, and *The Rigoberta Menchú Controversy*, edited by Arturo Arias.

8. Crosthwaite is said to be elusive and to avoid interviews with academics and critics. I sent him an e-mail asking for details about the collaboration, but I got no response.

Chapter 3. Rolas de migración

1. La Onda Chicana is not to be confused with the Chicano Movement. Although they share the same name, they were very different cultural movements that were not connected to each other.

2. By this time, the government had already repressed the protests at Tlatelolco on October 2, 1968, as a way to artificially maintain an appearance of national stability for the Olympics held in Mexico City that same year.

3. For more information on La Onda, see Zolov, *Refried Elvis*, and Monsiváis, "Dancing: El Hoyo Fonqui," in *Escenas de pudor y liviandad*.

4. Although Internet access may be limited for the lower classes, the availability of music over the Internet is still pertinent because Rojo and Ramírez are referring to the Tijuana middle-class youth. Rojo and Ramírez do not consider that many of Tijuana's youth do not have access to the United States, because the poor usually do not have the appropriate documentation to cross the border legally.

5. The airport in Orange County, California, is named after John Wayne. Orange County's political base is Republican.

6. See Zolov, *Refried Elvis*.

7. Rubén Hernández León, who observed several gangs from Monterrey, argues that the youth decide to travel to the United States for diversion instead of traveling with their families for work. The Monterrey youth have formed transnational networks that link Monterrey to Houston.

8. I use "patada" here because it is on the original track in *Indocumentado*. However, *Un cuarto de siglo* has a version of the song that uses "fregada."

9. Maná official website: http://mana.com.mx/historia.html (accessed October 29, 1999).

10. The comparison to the Police is so strong that a web page—http://holamun2.com/news/versus-mana-vs-the-police/—lists the attributes of both bands side by side.

11. Grupo Límite, an internationally known *norteña* band, is from Monterrey.

12. According to "Music of Mexico" on NationMaster.com, "The 1980s saw Colombian *cumbia* become even more popular in Mexico than its native

land, and it was by far the dominant genre throughout the decade, before banda overtook it in the 1990s."

13. The fusion of hip-hop and traditional music is not representative of all the rock music produced in Monterrey. The bands Jumbo and Zurdok do not mix traditional Mexican music with rock; instead, they use electronic equipment to create a new sound. Their lyrics are less polemical than those of Control Machete.

14. A few verses of "No sabemos amar" best describe this concern: "Our dreams are visions of a more commercial love, imprisoned hearts" (Nuestros sueños son visiones de un amor más comercial, corazones prisioneros).

15. It is often overlooked that illegal imports enter Mexico. These can include weapons that are not allowed in Mexico, makeup, and even toys. The *fayuca* is usually less expensive than legal imports.

16. Zacatecas is a sending state of migration, and Arizona is now one of the main places where migrants are crossing. For more information, see Bustamante et al., "Characteristics of Migrants."

Chapter 4. Diary of a Macuiltianguense

An earlier version of this chapter was originally published in *Aztlán: A Journal of Chicano Studies*, volume 34, number 1 (2009): 13–34. Reprinted with the permission of the UCLA Chicano Studies Research Center Press.

1. I acknowledge the influence of cultural norms. For many, migration is generational and is a way of life. For more information, see Kandel and Massey, "The Culture of Mexican Migration."

2. Relatively little information about Ramón Pérez exists beyond what he wrote in his diaries and the short biographical information on the cover of the books. I wrote the first formal biographical profile of Pérez for the *Greenwood Encyclopedia of Latino Literature*. To get more details, I contacted Dick J. Reavis to ask about his collaborations with Pérez, and I wrote to Pérez himself. The following discussion draws on our e-mail correspondence between April and June 2007.

3. It is probable that Ledesma's use of the term "undocumented immigrant" instead of *mojado* reflects his reading of the translated version of the diary. Based on the original Spanish text, I would suggest that the *mojado* identity, not the undocumented immigrant identity, is one that crosses national boundaries.

4. The word "indigenes" in this quote is probably a translation of *indígenas*, which is most likely the Spanish word that Pérez used. "Indigenous" would have been a better translation. As I argued in the preceding section, the translations of certain words used by Pérez change their connotations.

5. For example, Mixtecs from Oaxaca who migrate to Baja and Alta California are commonly referred to as "Oaxacalifornia," a term that combines several

regional identities into one. Gaspar Rivera-Salgado uses the term in the title of his article "Radiografía de Oaxacalifornia," which discusses the transnational political organizations that the Mixtec community has created.

6. Kandel and Massey divided their respondents into several categories according to their family history of migration: none, extended, nuclear, father 1–2 (one or two trips), and father 3+ (three or more trips). They conclude: "Whereas only 37 percent of respondents in families without migrant experience expressed a desire to work in the U.S., the percentage rises steadily through the extended, nuclear, and father 1–2 categories to read 62 percent among those in which the father had made at least three trips north of the border" (988).

7. For more information on migrant women's settlement patterns, see Pierrette Hondagneu-Sotelo, *Gendered Transitions*.

8. Migrant organizations based on hometown networks are common. Robert Courtney Smith's *Mexican New York* includes several chapters about the role of political organizations in a town he calls Ticuani, Puebla.

Chapter 5. Artistic Migrations

1. Perla Ciuk's *Diccionario de directores del cine mexicano* was fundamental in my research for this section. Unlike the research done by Norma Iglesias Prieto and David Maciel that I mention in chapter 1, Ciuk is not theorizing about Mexican film as a genre. I cite Ciuk's work, but the conclusions are mine.

2. Paul Julian Smith's monograph on *Amores perros* explores this point in more detail. Others writing about González Iñárritu and Cuarón's films include Jeff Menne, María Josefina Saldaña-Portillo, Hester Baer, and Ryan Long.

3. Anthony Quinn, for example, won two awards for best supporting actor in 1952 and 1957, for *Viva Zapata!* (Elia Kazan, 1952) and *Lust for Life* (Vincente Minnelli, 1956). Quinn portrayed "ethnic" roles but was not necessarily recognized as a Mexican actor.

4. For more information on *Pan's Labyrinth*, see Paul Julian Smith's *Film Quarterly* review.

5. In order for them to return to their country, many undocumented immigrants must hire *coyotes* (smugglers). Those with expired visas find it difficult to return home, because they might uncover their status.

6. Third cinema was a filmic movement of the 1970s in several Latin American countries as well as in other developing nations. The aesthetic imperfection of lower-budget films was used as a political tool to voice various concerns relating to developing countries. For more information on third and imperfect cinema, see Michael Martin, ed., *New Latin American Cinema*, vols. 1 and 2, and Charles Ramírez Berg, *Cinema of Solitude*.

7. Information from the Box Office Mojo website: http://www.box officemojo.com/movies/?id=childrenofmen.htm (accessed June 4, 2009).

Chapter 6. Beyond the First Generation

1. I mention this point in the introduction. Because my mother does not have a birth certificate, I was unable to petition for dual citizenship even though I technically qualify for it.

2. For more information, see Paredes, *Folklore and Culture on the Texas-Mexican Border*, and Ramón Saldívar, *The Borderlands of Culture: Américo Paredes and the Transnational Imaginary*.

3. I found a copy of *Lo que estará en mi corazón* in Tijuana. Later, I tried to order this text for a class, and it was impossible for the bookstore to find copies for my students. This is a common problem with Latin American literary texts published in smaller venues in Latin America.

4. In the past, U.S. Americans could cross without any type of documentation. All that was needed was to say "American citizen," and maybe answer a few questions. Since 9/11, those standards have changed. First, U.S. citizens were required to show some type of identification. From 2008, U.S. citizens have been required to show a passport when traveling by air and at least a birth certificate when traveling by ground.

5. Claudio Lomnitz-Adler in *Death and the Idea of Mexico* argues that the three great totems of Mexican national identity are Guadalupe, Juárez, and death. Cisneros uses two of the three totems, leaving Juárez out of her novel.

Conclusion

1. The image can be found at http://politicalhumor.about.com/od/funnypictures/ig/Funny-Protest-Signs/I-m-Mexican-Pull-Me-Over.htm (accessed January 24, 2011).

2. See http://www.youtube.com/watch?v=2bqoEU-l9ns (accessed January 24, 2011).

Bibliography

Acevedo-Muñoz, Ernesto R. "Sex, Class, and Mexico in Alfonso Cuarón's *Y tu mamá también.*" *Film and History: An Interdisciplinary Journal of Film and Television Studies* 34.1 (2004): 39–48.

Aceves, Fernando. *Ilusiones y destellos: Retratos del rock mexicano.* Barcelona: Plaza y Janés, 1999.

Alba, Richard, and Victor Nee. *Remaking the American Mainstream: Assimilation and Contemporary Immigration.* Cambridge, Mass.: Harvard University Press, 2005.

Alvaray, Luisela. "National, Regional, and Global: New Waves of Latin American Cinema." *Cinema Journal* 47.3 (2008): 48–65.

Anderman, Joan. "Flavorful Pop Songs Put Mana on Crossover Track." *Boston Globe*, September 7, 1999, D5.

Anderson, Benedict. *Imagined Communities: Reflections on the Origin and Spread of Nationalism.* New York: Verso, 1991.

Andreas, Peter. "The Escalation of U.S. Immigration Control in the Post-NAFTA Era." *Political Science Quarterly* 113.4 (1998/1999): 591–615.

Anzaldúa, Gloria. *Borderlands/La Frontera: The New Mestiza.* San Francisco: Spinsters, 1987.

Appadurai, Arjun. *Modernity at Large: Cultural Dimensions of Globalization.* Minneapolis: University of Minnesota Press, 1998.

Arias, Arturo, ed. *The Rigoberta Menchú Controversy.* Minneapolis: University of Minnesota Press, 2001.

Baer, Hester, and Ryan Long. "Transnational Cinema and the Mexican State in Alfonso Cuarón's *Y tu mamá también.*" *South Central Review* 21.3 (2004): 150–68.

Baez Hernández, Sonia, Anadeli Bencomo, and Marc Zimmerman, eds. *Ir y venir: Procesos transnacionales entre América Latina y el norte.* Santiago: Lacasa and Bravo y Allende Editores, 2007.

Barbano, Frank. "Tijuana No" (Interview). *Retila*, April/May 1995, 38–44.

Bartra, Roger. *La jaula de la melancolía: Identidad y metamorfosis del mexicano*. Mexico City: Editorial Grijalbo, 1996.

Beale, Lewis. "A New Kind of Mexican Revolution Hits the Screen." *New York Times*, November 4, 2001. Accessed November 5, 2001, http://nytimes .com/2001/11/04/movies/04BEAL.html.

Berg, Charles Ramírez. *Cinema of Solitude: A Critical Study of Mexican Film, 1967–1983*. Austin: University of Texas Press, 1992.

Berumen, Humberto Félix. *De cierto modo. La literatura de Baja California*. Tijuana: Universidad Autónoma de Baja California, 1998.

Beverley, John. "The Margin and the Center: On Testimonio (Testimonial Narrative)." In *The Real Thing: Testimonial Discourse and Latin America*, ed. Georg Gugelberger, 23–41. Durham, N.C.: Duke University Press, 1996.

Blanc, Enrique. "Monterrey, México: Mucho más que machacado, cerveza y cabrito." *La banda elástica* 8.36 (2000): 38–56.

Burgos-Debray, Elisabeth. *Me llamo Rigoberta Menchú y así me nació la conciencia*. Mexico: Siglo Veintiuno Editores, 1991.

Bustamante, Jorge, Guillermina Jasso, J. Edward Taylor, and Paz Trigueros Legarreta. "Characteristics of Migrants: Mexicans in the United States." In *Migration between Mexico and the United States* vol. 1, 91–162. Washington, D.C., and Mexico City: U.S. Commission on Immigration Reform and Mexican Ministry of Foreign Affairs, 1998.

Cabrera, Omar. "Persigue censura a Molotov." *Reforma.com*, January 23, 2003. Accessed March 12, 2003, http://www.reforma.com/espetaculos/ articulo/263254/.

Castillo, Debra A., and María Socorro Tabuenca Córdoba. *Border Women: Writing from la Frontera*. Minneapolis: University of Minnesota Press, 2002.

Cisneros, Sandra. *Caramelo, or, Puro Cuento*. New York: Knopf, 2002.

Ciuk, Perla. *Diccionario de directores del cine mexicano*. Mexico City: CONACULTA, 2000.

Cobo, Leila. "Latin Market Seeks Lift from Warner's Mana." *Billboard*, July 27, 2002, 1. LexisNexis, Tulane Howard Tilton Library. Accessed September 27, 2003, http://web.lexis-nexis.com.

Cohen, Jeffrey H. *The Culture of Migration in Southern Mexico*. Austin: University of Texas Press, 2004.

Crosthwaite, Luis Humberto. *Instrucciones para cruzar la frontera*. Mexico City: Joaquín Mortiz, 2002.

———. *Lo que estará en mi corazón (Ña'a ta'ka ani'mai)*. Mexico City: Edamex-INBA, 1994.

Cuarón, Alfonso, Guillermo del Toro, and Alejandro González Iñárritu. Interview by Charlie Rose. *Charlie Rose*, PBS, December 20, 2006.

de la Mora, Sergio. *Cinemachismo: Masculinities and Sexuality in Mexican Film*. Austin: University of Texas Press, 2006.

de la Vega Alfaro, Eduardo. "Origins, Development and Crisis of the Sound Cinema (1929–1964)." In *Mexican Cinema*, ed. Paulo Antonio Paranaguá, trans. Ana M. López, 94–115. London: British Film Institute, 1995.

Delgado, Fernando. "All Along the Border: Kid Frost and the Performance of Brown Masculinity." *Text and Performance Quarterly* 20.4 (2000): 388–401.

Fox, Claire F. *The Fence and the River: Culture and Politics at the U.S.–Mexico Border*. Minneapolis: University of Minnesota Press, 1999.

Fox, Jonathan. "Reframing Mexican Migration as a Multi-ethnic Process." *Latino Studies* 4.1/2 (2006): 39–61.

Fussell, Elizabeth. "La organización social de la migración en Tijuana." In *Migración internacional e identidades cambiantes*, ed. María Eugenia Anguiano Téllez and Miguel J. Hernández Madrid, 163–87. Zamora: El Colegio de Michoacán; Tijuana: El Colegio de la Frontera Norte, 2002.

Galarza, Ernesto. *Barrio Boy*. Notre Dame, Ind.: University of Notre Dame Press, 1971.

García, Rodrigo. "The Foundations of *Babel*: A Conversation between Rodrigo García and Alejandro González Iñárritu." In *Babel: A Film by Alejandro González Iñárritu*, ed. Maria Eladia Hagerman, 256–62. Los Angeles: Taschen, 2006.

García Canclini, Néstor. *La globalización imaginada*. Mexico City: Editorial Paidós, 1999.

García Hernández, Arturo. "En EU, la relación entre mexicanos y estadunidenses también es íntima." *La Jornada*, July 6, 2003. Accessed June 15, 2009, http://www.jornada.unam.mx/2003/07/06/04an1cul.php?origen=cultura.php&fly=1.

Glazer, Nathan. "Assimilation Today: Is One Identity Enough?" In *Reinventing the Melting Pot: The New Immigrants and What It Means to Be American*, ed. Tamar Jacoby, 61–73. New York: Basic Books, 2004.

González Iñárritu, Alejandro. Comments on photographs. In *Babel: A Film by Alejandro González Iñárritu*, ed. Maria Eladia Hagerman, 20–256. Los Angeles: Taschen, 2006.

Gugelberger, Georg M., ed. *The Real Thing: Testimonial Discourse and Latin America*. Durham, N.C.: Duke University Press, 1996.

Gutiérrez, David G. *Walls and Mirrors: Mexican Americans, Mexican Immigrants and the Politics of Ethnicity*. Berkeley: University of California Press, 1995.

Heredia, Juanita. "Voyages South and North: The Politics of Transnational Gender Identity in *Caramelo* and *American Chica*." *Latino Studies* 5.3 (2007): 340–57.

Hernández León, Rubén. "¡A la aventura! Jóvenes, pandillas y migración en la conexión Monterrey-Houston." In *Fronteras fragmentadas*, ed. Gail Mummert, 115–43. Zamora: El Colegio de Michoacán, 1999.

Herrera-Sobek, María. *Northward Bound: The Mexican Immigrant Experience in Ballad and Song*. Bloomington: Indiana University Press, 1993.

Hobsbawm, Eric J. *Nations and Nationalism since 1780: Programme, Myth, Reality.* Cambridge: Cambridge University Press, 1992.

Hondagneu-Sotelo, Pierrette. *Gendered Transitions: Mexican Experiences of Immigration.* Berkeley: University of California Press, 1994.

Huntington, Samuel. *Who Are We? The Challenge to America's National Identity.* New York: Simon and Schuster, 2004.

Iglesias Prieto, Norma. "El desarrollo del cine fronterizo: Análisis de los últimos tres sexenios." In *Frontera Norte: Chicanos, pachucos y cholos,* ed. Luis Hernández Palacio and Juan Manuel Sandoval, 501–24. Mexico City: Ancien Régime, 1989.

Irizarry, Guillermo. "La traducción imposible o la inoperabilidad de la gran familia humana: A propósito de The House on the Lagoon, de Rosario Ferré, y Raining Backwards, de Roberto Fernández." *Chasqui: Revista de Literatura Latinoamericana* 32 (2003): 17–34.

Irwin, Robert McKee. "Toward a Border Gnosis of the Borderlands: Joaquín Murrieta and Nineteenth-Century U.S.–Mexico Border Culture." *Nepantla: Views from South* 2.3 (2001): 509–37.

Jacoby, Tamar. "The New Immigrants: A Progress Report." In *Reinventing the Melting Pot: The New Immigrants and What It Means to Be American,* ed. Tamar Jacoby, 17–29. New York: Basic Books, 2004.

Kandel, William, and Douglas S. Massey. "The Culture of Mexican Migration: A Theoretical and Empirical Analysis." *Social Forces* 80.3 (2002): 981–1004.

Kanellos, Nicolás. "Introducción." In *Las aventuras de don Chipote, o Cuando los pericos mamen,* Daniel Venegas, 1–10. Houston: Arte Público, 1999.

Kun, Josh. *Audiotopia: Music, Race, and America.* Berkeley: University of California Press, 2005.

———. "The Sun Never Sets on MTV." In *Latino/a Popular Culture,* ed. Michelle Habell-Pallán and Mary Romero, 102–16. New York: New York University Press, 2002.

Ledesma, Alberto. "Undocumented Crossings: Narratives of Mexican Immigration to the United States." In *Culture Across Borders: Mexican Immigration and Popular Culture,* ed. David R. Maciel and María Herrera-Sobek, 67–98. Tucson: University of Arizona Press, 1998.

Limón, José E. *American Encounters: Greater Mexico, the United States, and the Erotics of Culture.* Boston: Beacon, 1998.

Lomnitz-Adler, Claudio. "Concepts for the Study of Regional Culture." In *Mexico's Regions: Comparative History and Development,* ed. Eric Van Young, 59–89. San Diego: Center for U.S.–Mexican Studies, University of California, San Diego, 1992.

———. *Death and the Idea of Mexico.* New York: Zone Books, 2005.

López, Ana M. "Tears and Desire: Women and Melodrama in the 'Old' Mexican Cinema." In *Mediating Two Worlds: Cinematic Encounters in the Americas,* ed. John King, Ana M. López, and Manuel Alvarado, 147–63. London: British Film Institute, 1993.

López, Jaime. "El rockenrondero." In *Mitos mexicanos*, ed. Enrique Flores-cano, 393–400. Mexico City: Taurus, 2001.

Maciel, David R. *El Norte: The U.S.–Mexican Border in Contemporary Cinema*. San Diego: San Diego State University, 1990.

Maciel, David R., and María Rosa García-Acevedo. "The Celluloid Immigrant: The Narrative Films of Mexican Immigration." In *Culture Across Borders: Mexican Immigration and Popular Culture*, ed. David R. Maciel and María Herrera-Sobek, 149–203. Tucson: University of Arizona Press, 1998.

Maciel, David R., and María Herrera-Sobek, eds. *Culture Across Borders: Mexican Immigration and Popular Culture*. Tucson: University of Arizona Press, 1998.

Martin, Michael, ed. *New Latin American Cinema*. 2 vols. Detroit: Wayne State University Press, 1997.

Martínez, Rubén. *Crossing Over: A Mexican Family on the Migrant Trail*. New York: Metropolitan Books, 2001.

———. *The Other Side: Notes from the New L.A., Mexico City and Beyond*. New York: Vintage, 1993.

Martínez Zepeda, Jorge. "Llantijuan o Tía Juana." *Frontera*, July 11, 2001, Suplemento Especial, 7.

Menne, Jeff. "A Mexican *Nouvelle Vague*: The Logic of New Waves under Globalization." *Cinema Journal* 47.1 (2007): 70–92.

Monsiváis, Carlos. *Escenas de pudor y liviandad*. Mexico City: Grijalbo, 1992.

———. *Imágenes de la tradición viva*. Mexico City: Landucci, Universidad Nacional Autónoma de México, Fondo de Cultura Economica, 2006.

———. "México en su sitio: México en Chicago, Tucson, Los Angeles, Dallas, San Antonio, Nueva York, y la lista se amplía." In *Ir y venir: Procesos transnacionales entre América Latina y el norte*, ed. Sonia Baez Hernández, Anadeli Bencomo, and Marc Zimmerman, 329–43. Santiago: Lacasa and Bravo y Allende Editores, 2007.

Morales, Ed. *Living in Spanglish: The Search for Latino Identity in America*. New York: St. Martin's, 2002.

Mummert, Gail, ed. *Fronteras fragmentadas*. Zamora: El Colegio de Michoacán, 1999.

———. "Juntos o desaparecidos: La fundación del hogar." In *Fronteras fragmentadas*, ed. Gail Mummert, 451–73. Zamora: El Colegio de Michoacán, 1999.

Muñoz, Germán. "Identidades culturales e imaginarios colectivos: Las culturas juveniles urbanas vistas desde la cultura *rock*." In *Cultura, medios y sociedad*, ed. Jesús Martín Barbero and Fabio López de la Roche, 263–73. Bogotá: Universidad Nacional de Colombia, 1998.

"Music of Mexico." NationMaster.com. Accessed April 30, 2004, http://www.nationmaster.com/encyclopedia/Music-of-Mexico.

Negrón-Muntaner, Frances. "Feeling Pretty: *West Side Story* and Puerto Rican Identity Discourses." *Social Text* 18.2 (2000): 83–106.

Oliver-Rotger, Maria Antònia. "Ethnographies of Transnational Migration in Rubén Martínez's *Crossing Over.*" *MELUS* 31.2 (2006): 181–205.

Pacini Hernández, Deborah, Héctor Fernández L'Hoeste, and Eric Zolov. "Mapping Rock Music Cultures Across the Americas." In *Rockin' Las Américas: The Global Politics of Rock in Latin/o America*, ed. Deborah Pacini Hernández, Héctor Fernández L'Hoeste, and Eric Zolov, 1–21. Pittsburgh: University of Pittsburgh Press, 2004.

Paredes, Américo. *Folklore and Culture on the Texas-Mexican Border.* Austin: University of Texas Press, 1993.

Parra, Eduardo Antonio. *Los límites de la noche.* Mexico City: Ediciones Era, 2001.

———. *No Man's Land.* Trans. Christopher Winks. San Francisco: City Lights, 2004.

———. *Tierra de nadie.* Mexico City: Ediciones Era, 2001.

Paz, Octavio. *El laberinto de la soledad, Postdata y Vuelta a El laberinto de la soledad.* Mexico City: Fondo de Cultura Económica, 2002. Orig. pub. 1950.

Penzenstadler, Joan. "La frontera, Aztlán, el barrio: Frontiers in Chicano Literature." In *The Frontier Experience and the American Dream: Essays on American Literature*, ed. David Mogen, Mark Busby, and Paul Bryant, 159–79. College Station: Texas A&M University Press, 1989.

Pérez, Ramón "Tianguis." *Diario de un mojado.* Houston: Arte Público, 2003.

———. *Diary of a Guerrilla.* Trans. Dick J. Reavis. Houston: Arte Público, 1999.

———. *Diary of an Undocumented Immigrant.* Trans. Dick J. Reavis. Houston: Arte Público, 1991.

Pérez Turrent, Tomás. "Crises and Renovations (1965–1991)." In *Mexican Cinema*, ed. Paulo Antonio Paranaguá, trans. Ana M. López, 94–115. London: British Film Institute, 1995.

Perucho, Javier. *Hijos de la patria perdida.* Mexico City: CONACULTA and Instituto Nacional de Bellas Artes, 2001.

———. "Un espejo cercano: Eduardo Antonio Parra." *Página de literatura fronteriza mexicana* de Scott Bennet. Accessed April 10, 2004, http://www.uweb.ucsb.edu/~sbenne00/Unespejocercano.html.

Poblete, Juan. "Literatura, heterogeneidad y migrancia transnacional." *Nueva Sociedad* 201 (February 2006): 90–105.

Portes, Alejandro, and Rubén G. Rumbaut. *Legacies: The Story of the Immigrant Second Generation.* Berkeley: University of California Press, 2001.

"Principal Raises Mexican Flag, Faces Discipline." *Washington Times*, March 30, 2006. Accessed November 7, 2008, http://www.washingtontimes.com/news/2006/mar/30/20060330-111616-2046r/.

Reavis, Dick J. Translator's foreword. *Diary of a Guerrilla*, Ramón "Tianguis" Pérez, v–vii. Houston: Arte Público, 1999.

Rivera-Salgado, Gaspar. "Radiografía de Oaxacalifornia." *La Jornada*, August 9, 1998. Accessed February 1, 2004, http://www.jornada.unam.mx/1998/ago98/980809/mas-rivera.html.

Rojo, Luis, and Cynthia Ramírez. "El rock de Tijuana en los noventa. Lo alternativo, las nuevas corrientes. Expresiones de una generación." In *Oye como va: Recuentro del rock tijuanense*, ed. José Manuel Valenzuela Arce and Gloria González, 163–85. Mexico City: Centro Cultural de Tijuana; Instituto Mexicano de la Juventud, 1999.

Romero, César G. "Reflexiones ante un espejo divisorio: Una entrevista con María Novaro." *Nexos* (October 1995): 84–87.

Rosaldo, Renato. "Cultural Citizenship and Educational Democracy." *Cultural Anthropology* 9.3 (1994): 402–11.

Rouse, Roger. "Mexican Migration and the Social Space of Postmodernism." In *Between Two Worlds: Mexican Immigrants in the United States*, ed. David G. Gutiérrez, 247–63. Wilmington, Del.: Scholarly Resources, 1996.

Rowe, John Carlos. "Nineteenth-Century United States Literary Culture and Transnationality." *PMLA* 118.1 (2003): 78–89.

Ruiz, Olivia Teresa. "El ir y venir: La relación transfronteriza." In *Reflexiones sobre la identidad de los pueblos*, ed. Ramón Eduardo Ruiz and Olivia Teresa Ruiz, 56–64. Tijuana: Colegio de la Frontera Norte, 1996.

Rulfo, Juan. *Pedro Páramo*. Mexico City: Fondo de Cultural Económica, 1981. Orig. pub. 1955.

Saldaña-Portillo, María Josefina. "In the Shadow of NAFTA: *Y tu mamá también* Revisits the National Allegory of Mexican Sovereignty." *American Quarterly* 57.3 (2005): 751–77.

Saldívar, José David. *Border Matters: Remapping American Cultural Studies*. Berkeley: University of California Press, 1997.

Saldívar, Ramón. *The Borderlands of Culture: Américo Paredes and the Transnational Imaginary*. Durham, N.C.: Duke University Press, 2006.

Salum, Rose Mary. "Interview with Mexican Consul and Diplomat Eduardo Ibarrola." Trans. Brad Davis. *The Hispanic Experience*, Houston Institute for Culture, Special Feature. Accessed June 3, 2007, http://www.houston culture.org/hispanic/ibarrola_eng.html.

Sanmiguel, Rosario. *El callejón sucre y otros relatos*. Chihuahua: Ediciones del Azar, 1994.

———. *Under the Bridge: Stories from the Border / Bajo el puente: Relatos desde la frontera*. Trans. John Pluecker. Houston: Arte Público, 2008.

Sassen, Saskia. "Spatialities and Temporalities of the Global: Elements for Theorization." In *Globalization*, ed. Arjun Appadurai, 260–78. Durham, N.C.: Duke University Press, 2001.

Segura, Denise A., and Patricia Zavella, eds. *Women and Migration in the U.S.–Mexico Borderlands: A Reader*. Durham, N.C.: Duke University Press, 2007.

Simonett, Helena. *Banda: Mexican Musical Life Across Borders*. Middletown: Wesleyan University Press, 2001.

Sisk, Christina L. "Ramón 'Tianguis' Pérez." In *The Greenwood Encyclopedia of Latino Literature*, vol. 2, ed. Nicolás Kanellos, 869–70. Westport, Conn.: Greenwood Press, 2008.

———. "*Revista Generación*: Mexican Regionalism and Migration in Tijuana and Chicago." *Latino Studies* 5.4 (2007): 439–54.

———. "Toward a Transnational Reading of Ramón 'Tianguis' Pérez's *Diario de un mojado*." *Aztlán* 34.1 (2009): 13–34.

Sklodowska, Elzbieta. "Spanish American Testimonial Novel: Some Afterthoughts." In *The Real Thing: Testimonial Discourse and Latin America*, ed. Georg M. Gugelberger, 84–100. Durham, N.C.: Duke University Press, 1996.

Smith, Paul Julian. *Amores perros*. London: British Film Institute, 2003.

———. "Pan's Labyrinth (El laberinto del fauno)." *Film Quarterly* 60.4 (2007): 4–9.

Smith, Robert Courtney. *Mexican New York: The Transnational Life of Migrants*. Berkeley: University of California Press, 2005.

Sommer, Doris. *Foundational Fictions: The National Romances of Latin America*. Berkeley: University of California Press, 1991.

Suárez, Ray. "Conversation: Cisneros." PBS.org, October 15, 2002. Accessed January 17, 2011, http://www.pbs.org/newshour/conversation/july-dec02/cisneros_10-15.html.

Tabuenca Córdoba, María Socorro. "Apuntar el silencio: La literatura de la frontera norte, sus escritoras y los espacios para su expresión." *Puentelibre: Revista de Cultura* 2 (1994): 25–31.

———. *Mujeres y fronteras. Una perspectiva de género*. Chihuahua: Instituto Chihuahuense de la Cultura, 1998.

———. "The Rearticulation of the Border Territory in the Stories of Rosario Sanmiguel." In *Ethnography at the Border*, ed. Pablo Vila, 279–305. Minneapolis: University of Minnesota Press, 2003.

———. "Reflexiones sobre la literatura de la frontera." *Puentelibre* 4 (1995): 8–12.

Tierney, Dolores. *Emilio Fernández: Pictures in the Margins*. Manchester: Manchester University Press, 2007.

Urrea, Luis Alberto. *Across the Wire*. New York: Doubleday, 1993.

———. *The Devil's Highway: A True Story*. New York: Little, Brown, 2004.

Valenzuela Arce, José Manuel. "Identidades culturales: Comunidades imaginarias y contigentes." In *Decadencia y auge de las identidades: Cultural nacional, identidad cultural y modernización*, ed. José Manuel Valenzuela Arce, 97–120. Tijuana: El Colegio de la Frontera Norte, 2000.

———. "Luis Güereña: Transgresores de la ley." In *Oye como va: Recuento del rock tijuanense*, ed. José Manuel Valenzuela Arce and Gloria González, 125–33. Mexico City: Centro Cultural de Tijuana; Instituto Mexicano de la Juventud, 1999.

———. *Nuestros piensos: Culturas populares en la frontera México-Estados Unidos*. Mexico City: CONACULTA, 1998.

———. "Roco: Los territorios simbólicos del rock." In *Oye como va: Recuento del rock tijuanense*, ed. José Manuel Valenzuela Arce and Gloria González, 196–204. Mexico City: Centro Cultural de Tijuana; Instituto Mexicano de la Juventud, 1999.

Vasconcelos, José. *La raza cósmica, la misión de la raza iberoamericana*. Mexico City: Porrua, 2001. Orig. pub. 1925.

Venegas, Daniel. *Las aventuras de don Chipote, o, Cuando los pericos mamen*. Houston: Arte Público, 1999. Orig. pub. 1928.

———. *The Adventures of Don Chipote, or, When Parrots Breast Feed*. Trans. Ethriam Cash Brammer. Houston: Arte Público, 2000.

Vila, Pablo. "Conclusions: The Limits of American Border Theory." In *Ethnography at the Border*, ed. Pablo Vila, 306–41. Minneapolis: University of Minnesota Press, 2003.

———. *Crossing Borders, Reinforcing Borders: Social Categories, Metaphors, and Narrative Identities on the U.S.–Mexico Frontier*. Austin: University of Texas Press, 2000.

Vilanova, Núria. "El espacio textual de la frontera norte de México." *Cuadernos de literatura* 30 (2000): 5–24.

Waldinger, Roger. "Between Here and There: How Attached Are Latino Immigrants to Their Native Country?" Pew Hispanic Center, October 25, 2007. Accessed November 9, 2008, http://pewhispanic.org/reports/report.php?ReportID=80.

Waxer, Lise. "Colombia III: Popular Music." *Grove Music Online*. Ed. L. Macy. Accessed April 30, 2004, http://www.grovemusic.com.

Zizek, Slavoj. Commentary. *Children of Men*. DVD. Universal City, Calif.: Universal Studios Home Entertainment, 2007.

Zolov, Eric. *Refried Elvis: The Rise of the Mexican Counterculture*. Berkeley: University of California Press, 1999.

Music

Control Machete. *Artillería pesada*. Polygram Records, 1999.

———. *Mucho barato*. Polygram Records, 1997.

El Gran Silencio. *Chúntaros Radio Poder*. EMI Music Mexico, 2000.

———. *Libres y locos*. EMI Music Mexico, 1998.

———. *¡Súper riddim internacional!* EMI Music Mexico, 2003.

Maldita Vecindad y los Hijos del Quinto Patio. *El circo*. BMG International, 1991.

———. *Maldita Vecindad y los Hijos del Quinto Patio*. BMG Music, 1989.

Maná. *¿Dónde jugarán los niños?* Warner Music Mexico, 1992.

———. *Revolución de amor*. Wea International, 2002.

Molotov. *Dance and Dense Denso.* Universal Latino, 2003.

———. *¿Dónde jugarán las niñas?* Universal Music Latino, 1997.

Tijuana No. *Contra-Revolución Avenue.* BMG Music, 1998.

———. *Transgresores de la ley.* BMG Music, 1994.

El Tri. *Indocumentado.* Warner Music Mexico, 1992.

———. *Un cuarto de siglo.* Wea International, 1995.

Index

Malinche, la, 46, 156
Maná, 14, 88, 89, 113; music, 102–5
Mandoki, Luis, 140
marginalization, 17, 52
María Candelaria, 139, 145, 195–96
marriages, 58; interracial, 23, 189–90
Martínez, Rubén, 179, 200, 206; *Crossing Over,* 15, 178, 180–90
media, 8, 88; on migrants, 71–72, 73
Medrano Mederos, Florencio, 114, 123
Menudo, 86
mestizaje, 46, 127, 135, 181; Chicanas and, 176, 177–78; identity and, 193, 197–98; indigenous peoples and, 122–23
Metropolitan Books, 178, 184
Mexican Americans, 79; identity, 12, 25–26, 28–29, 107, 203–4; in literature, 51–52; and Mexicans, 197–98; and migrants, 126–27; second- and third-generation, 171–72, 182–83, 203; ties to Mexico, 169–74, 178, 182–84; transnationalism, 15, 174–75
Mexican-American War, 95–96, 102, 176
mexicanidad, 49, 71, 104, 156–57; in *Babel,* 151–54; in *Da ida y vuelta,* 45–48; in *El jardín del Edén,* 27–30, 34–35; recreating, 194–98; rock music and, 88, 105; stereotypes of, 20–21
Mexicanness, 8, 173, 203
Mexican Revolution, 119, 170
Mexico, 54, 72, 193, 209n1: border stereotypes in, 36–38; film industry in, 17–18; Mexican American ties to, 169–74, 178, 182–84; nationalism, 5–7, 51; regional and national identity in, 14, 48, 127; regional tensions in, 13, 89–90; rock music in, 85–87; as romantic, 148–50
Mexico, state of, 3, 55, 204
Mexico City, 3, 14, 55, 84, 176, 204; film industry in, 17, 18; film portrayal of, 19, 20, 45l; history of, 190–91; rock music in, 89, 90, 96–100
México 2040, 204
Michoacán, 21, 41–42, 48, 66; cultural change in, 180–81; migrants from, 2, 128–29; as sending state, 55, 210n4

migrant networks, 22, 49, 115, 191–92, 200–201
migrants, 16, 22; from Cherán, 181–82; cultural production, 4, 7; deaths of, 99–100; as film theme, 24–26, 35–36, 38–39; identity of, 7–8, 26–27, 46–47, 119, 127–28; mistreatment of, 123–24; Mixtec, 73–76; narratives, 117–18; stereotypes of, 101–2; types of, 69–70; in United States, 124–29
militarization, 163; of border, 92, 94, 111, 159–60, 168
military service, 198–99
Mixtecs, 24, 212–13n5; migration testimonial of, 73–82
mobilization: through rock music, 86
"Mojado," 97, 99–100
Mojado Power, 20
mojados: experience as, 120–21
Molotov, 88, 89, 100–102, 113, 204
Monterrey, 63, 211n7; rock music in, 90, 14, 84, 105–12, 212n13
Morales, Ed, 105–6
Moreno, Antonio, 138, 139
Mortiz, Joaquín, 56–57
motherhood: as theme, 32–33, 146–48
Mucho barato, 106
"Muerte y esperanza en la frontera norte," 70, 71–73
Mujeres insumisas, 19
multinational corporations, 116–17
Mummert, Gail, 57–58, 65–66
Murieron a mitad del río. 51
music, 211n4, 105–6, 211–12nn11–13. *See also* rock music
myths, 17, 20, 28, 182. *See also* American Dream

national consciousness, 22–24
nationalism, 143; Mexican, 5, 6–7, 21, 48–49, 51, 102; as theme, 159–60, 161–65
nation-state, 4, 134–35; and globalization, 116–17
Navarro, Arturo, 204–5
Navarro, Guillermo, 142
New York University (NYU), 139, 140

About the Author

Christina L. Sisk is an assistant professor in the Department of Hispanic Studies at the University of Houston. She received her PhD (2004), MA (1999), and BA (1996) from Tulane University. Her areas of interest are U.S. Latina/o Studies, U.S.–Mexico Border Studies, Mexican Literary and Cultural Studies, and Latin American Cinema. She is particularly interested in bridging the gaps between Latin American and U.S. Latina/o Studies. She has published articles in *Latinos Studies* and *Aztlán*. Her current research projects include the representations of the criminal immigrant within the U.S. media and state funding of contemporary Mexican cinema.